PETERLOO
VOICES, SABRES AND SILENCE

PETERLOO
VOICES, SABRES AND SILENCE

GRAHAM PHYTHIAN

The History Press

First published 2018

The History Press
The Mill, Brimscombe Port
Stroud, Gloucestershire, GL5 2QG
www.thehistorypress.co.uk

British Library Cataloguing in Publication Data.
A catalogue record for this book is available from the British Library.

ISBN 978 0 7509 6749 5

Typesetting and origination by The History Press
Printed in Great Britain TJ International Ltd, Padstow, Cornwall

Contents

You will meet on Monday next my friends, and by your *steady, firm and temperate* deportment, you will convince all your enemies, you feel that you have an *important* and an *imperious public duty* to perform, and that you will not suffer any private consideration on earth, to deter you from exerting every nerve, to carry your praiseworthy and patriotic intentions into effect.[1]

From Henry Hunt's message to the people of Manchester,
the week before Peterloo

The people shouted, and then the soldiers shouted, waving their swords. Then they rode amongst the people, and there was a great outcry, and a moment after, a man passed without a hat, and wiping the blood off his head with his hand, and it ran down his arm in a great stream. The meeting was all in a tumult; there were dreadful cries; the soldiers kept riding amongst the people, and striking with their swords.[2]

Jemima Bamford, eyewitness at Peterloo

This can be for no good purpose; it is a mere wanton attack from first to last, the motive of which [is] … to agitate the feeble mind, and keep alive animosities at a time when it is advisable that every thing connected with the late events should be buried in oblivion, and all effervescence subside.[3]

Mr Ashworth, barrister, in response to evidence given about the Yeomanry's cutting at
the people with sabres (at the Coroner's inquest on John Lees, September 1819)

The soldiers were not attacked…some little resistance, too faint indeed and ineffectual, was made after the slaughter began.

…the Yeomanry attacked the people without warning, without provocation. I will take this opportunity to observe that the abettors of this outrage (for so I must call it) have not replied to this charge.[4]

John Cam Hobhouse, speech in House of Commons,
15 May 1821

The site of St Peter's Fields where on 16 August 1819 Henry Hunt radical orator addressed an assembly of about 60,000 people. Their subsequent dispersal by the military is remembered as 'PETERLOO'.

The first Manchester plaque commemorating Peterloo, until replaced
with a less equivocal version in 2007

Preface

The story has been told dozens of times already, from many different standpoints. So why another book about Peterloo?

Firstly, the bicentenary in 2019 will see the pinnacle of the steadily growing wave of interest in the events of St Peter's Field on 16 August 1819, and Mike Leigh's eagerly awaited film will no doubt reinforce this. Students of the incident and its Regency context will be familiar with most (but possibly not all) of the details narrated herein; however, it was more for those with only a sketchy idea of what the day entailed that this book was conceived.

'But everybody knows about Peterloo!' you might say. I beg to differ: some A-Level nineteenth-century history courses scarcely mention the episode – an inexcusable gloss – and I won't dwell on the library locum who responded to my enquiry with 'Peter who? I've not heard of him.'

At the risk of preaching to the choir, then, this book aims to look again at the background, explosion of violence, and far-reaching consequences of the episode, sticking as closely as possible to primary sources and eyewitness reports. I have no particular political axe to grind, so material that is too obviously swayed by ideology or self-interest will be taken with a pinch of salt (or in some cases, a large tin of Saxa).

I would imagine many people's first port of call in discovering Peterloo will be Wikipedia, which, as often, supplies a sound enough launchpad for those interested in the topic. The Wiki entry, though – at least at the time of writing – is over-reliant on the standard secondary sources, apparently without checking with the contemporary evidence. Obviously, primary sources have to be sifted too, because of political and personal bias, but a comparative study of this material ultimately renders a richer and more convincing narrative than by simply quoting from the late twentieth-century works of, say, Walmsley, Marlow and Read, as significant as these undoubtedly are. Mostly, I have used these and other secondary sources only as a link to the original newspaper reports, letters, and official documents. More recent scholarly work, for example by Michael Bush, Robert Poole and Katrina Navickas, has given the previously received wisdom a thorough overhaul, and has been instrumental in the recent rekindling of interest in Peterloo.

No current book on the topic should be without a mention of the annual memorial organised by the indefatigable Paul Fitzgerald (aka Polyp the political cartoonist) and his equally dedicated team. There is a well-supported Facebook page which is constantly updated, and if the reader is within 100 miles of Manchester on any 16 August (or the nearest Sunday) they should make a point of getting to the area around the northern side of Manchester Central and the Midland Hotel. The 2019 event promises to be something special, and the plans for the memorial monument are well under way (see Appendix 17).

Acknowledgements

I owe a debt of thanks to the following: Robert Poole, for advice and access to invaluable material; Stewart and Elizabeth Bailey of the Friends' Meeting House on Mount Street, who have supplied me with documents, and useful and fascinating information; Debbie Rose, for the story of her ancestor, Mary Ward; Clare Hamer of the Greater Manchester Police, for information on equine training; Fergus Wilkie, for access to Chetham's Library documents; Geoff Higginbottom, Bob Ashworth and Martin Gittins – The Free Radicals – for 'Soldiers on the Rampage'; Mikaela Sitford-Howarth, for her review of Maxine Peake's recital of *The Masque of Anarchy*; Rosie Gnatiuk of the Platt Hall Gallery of Costume, for access to the original J. Slack calico handkerchief print; Paul Fitzgerald, for access to visuals; Ed Glinert, for his instructive 'Peterloo Walk'; Trevor Fisher, for his lecture on the Blanketeers; Oliver Lomax, for permission to quote from his poem 'Peterloo'; Sean Hannan, for loan of Steeleye Span's *Peterloo the Day*; John Howarth of the Oldham Tinkers, for permission to quote from Harvey Kershaw's lyrics to 'Peterloo'; Dorothy Topping, for information on the Ashton contingent; Kevin Parslow, great-great-great-great-grandson of James Moorhouse, for information on the Moorhouse family; Colin Smith, for his Living History performance of 'Peterloo'; Neil Wishart, for information on the 15th Hussars, and allowing me the opportunity to handle a Regency regimental sabre; James Hobson, for pointing out some newspaper sources; Phil Blinston and Rob Hall, for art work and calligraphy.

The staff of the following libraries and collections: The National Archives, Kew; Manchester Central Archives+; John Rylands, Manchester; Chetham's School, Manchester; Working Class Movement Library, Salford; People's History Museum, Spinningfields, Manchester; Trafford Archives; Tameside Local History and Archives; Stockport Local Heritage; Oldham Local Studies and Archives; Middleton Local History Resources;

Greater Manchester Police Museum; Saddleworth Museum; Rochdale Touchstones Local History; Failsworth Local History; Sheffield Archives; Lancaster Local Studies; Leeds Local and Family History; Liverpool Record Office; The Portico, Manchester; Cheshire Archives and Local Studies.

Introduction

From the outset, before we get side-tracked into questions of semantics, ideology, apologetics, cover-ups, or whether or not stones were thrown, we should hold fast to one unassailable truth: St Peter's Field Manchester on the early afternoon of Monday, 16 August 1819 was a killing field. Directly or indirectly due to the uneven conflict, there were at least fifteen mostly well-documented fatalities:

John Ashton: sabred and trampled by crowd
John Ashworth (Special Constable): sabred and trampled
Thomas Buckley (died 1 November): sabred and stabbed by bayonet
James Crompton: trampled on by the cavalry
Edmund Dawson (died 31 August): sabre wounds
William Dawson: sabred and crushed
Margaret Downes: sabred
William Evans (Special Constable): trampled by cavalry
William Fildes (aged 2): knocked to the ground by cavalry
Mary Heys (died 17 December): injuries sustained at Peterloo resulted in premature birth of her child, and her subsequent death
Sarah Jones: beaten on head by Constable's truncheon
John Lees (died 7 September): sabred and truncheoned. The subsequent inquest was halted without a verdict being reached
Arthur Neil/O'Neil: internal injuries caused by beating
Martha Partington: forced or thrown into cellar
John Rhodes (died 18 November): sabre wound to the head. The coroner's verdict was that he had died of natural causes[5]

Sometimes included among the deaths is John Hulme of the Manchester and Salford Yeomanry, who, according to some accounts, was struck by a stone and then fell or was pulled from his horse, being trampled by his own cavalry and suffering a fractured skull. William Bradshaw of Whitefield was shot and killed by the militia during the New Cross riots on the evening of Peterloo, as was 17-year-old Joshua Whitworth of Hyde. Special Constable Robert Campbell of Millers Lane was beaten to death by a vengeful mob near his house two days later. This would bring the total of Peterloo-related fatalities to an admittedly disputable nineteen.

A list of those known to be wounded or killed is first given in Wroe's pamphlets of December 1819,[5] and in his 2005 book *Casualties of Peterloo* Michael Bush cross-checks his added details from several contemporary sources, so we may assume that the above record, which is based on the information from *Casualties*, is a fair reflection of what happened on that day.

Other details are harder to pin down. There has been some difference of opinion as to the size of the crowd, but I have my own twopennorth to add to that one, if I may. James Wroe[6] estimated 150,000, but I think he bases his calculations on two erroneous assumptions. Firstly, he uses 'nine people per square yard' as a starting point. As an experiment, I measured out a square yard on the floor of the playing room of Chorlton Chess Club and asked nine svelte members of the club to occupy the space. It was just possible, but with an uncomfortably tight squeeze, and most of the guinea pigs agreed that six or seven per square yard would seem a more feasible number. However, as one participant pointed out, close to the stage at a rock concert fans would be jam-packed, so shoe-horning nine people into the space, especially close to the hustings, might have been a reasonable supposition. But we now come to Wroe's second basis for calculation, easier to disprove: the 150,000 assumes that pretty much the whole space of St Peter's Field (around 20,000 square yards – the size of four full-size football pitches) was covered with such a uniform crowd density. But the multitude would no doubt have thinned out towards the edges, and the Reverend Stanley, watching from an upstairs room overlooking the field, describes a comparatively sparsely populated space at the periphery of the field, crossed by stragglers and the odd latecomer.[7] It was into a part of this space that the squadron of Manchester and Salford Yeomanry rode into view, by the corner of the garden wall of Cooper's Cottage. All things considered, then, I would concur with the figure currently given: 50,000–60,000 were on the field that day.

There are many other details on which to some extent the jury is still out. What was the real purpose of the military-style drilling on the moors?

Was the 16 August meeting illegal? Was the Riot Act read and, if so, when and by whom? Why were the hustings carts moved? Had the Manchester Yeomanry been drinking before they arrived on the field? Were Hulton's two messages to the cavalry detachments deliberately vague and provocative? Why didn't Assistant Chief Constable Nadin make his arrests before the militia arrived? Was there a defensive circle around the hustings, made up of men with arms linked? Why was there such a high proportion of women amongst the casualties? Were gunshots fired at any time during the dispersal, and if so, from where, by whom, and at whom? Were stones thrown by the crowd at the military, and were any members of the crowd armed in any way? Were the people's 'heavy cudgels' really just walking sticks? Was the whole affair a deliberately laid trap? Is 'massacre' a justifiable description of Peterloo?

Subsequent literature and lampoons have in many cases only added to the confusion. At one extreme are the loyalist accounts which minimised the number and gravity of the casualties, whilst seeking to badmouth Hunt and the 'rebelly crew' by harping on – or inventing – their personal shortcomings, and insisting that the crowd were the first to resort to premeditated violence; at the other the well-known satirical cartoons and the garish, nightmare carnival of Shelley's *The Masque of Anarchy*: justifiable caricature or unfair distortions?

It doesn't take a lot of study to realise that Peterloo is still a *cause célèbre*. Echoes reverberate until this day, and no doubt the arguments, trailed by their attendant issues, will volley back and forth for a long time yet. At the very least, I'm hoping that this narrative of the 'tragedy', 'massacre', 'incident' – the reader is at liberty to choose their own caption – will furnish a comprehensive and accessible re-examination of the events and questions of that day of two centuries ago. No history is a fossilised phenomenon, and this one is alive and kicking.

Graham Phythian, 2018

PART ONE

Forewarnings

1

The Janus Country

Viewed from certain angles, Regency Britain was a glorious era, and a cause for national pride.

It was a cultural high-water mark: Jane Austen was reinventing the novel and fine-tuning the English language; Keats, Byron, Blake, Shelley and the Lake Poets were pushing back the boundaries of verse; Sir Walter Scott breathed new life into the historical yarn, and Mary Shelley hit a nerve with *Frankenstein*. Edmund Kean was enthralling theatre audiences with his Shakespearean roles. In the visual arts, Constable, Turner and Sir David Wilkie were at their most prolific. John Nash's London and Brighton architecture and the innovative and neo-Gothic designs of Sir John Soane and James Wyatt shouted the nation's confidence to the world.

The glow of military glory had been assured after Trafalgar and Waterloo. The taming of the Corsican anti-Christ, the quelling of the extreme experiment of republicanism in France, and the restoration to the throne of the Bourbon dynasty with Louis XVIII (who had spent his years of exile in England) had re-established political stability in a near neighbour, thus, it was hoped, greatly reducing the threat of insurrection on home soil.

In technology, the power of steam was transforming travel and commerce. The first steamship crossing of the Atlantic took place, and the new age of the train had been ushered in with Trevithick's 'Puffing Billy' prototype. Innovative steam-powered machines increased textiles output phenomenally. Humphry Davy added the introduction of the miners' safety lamp to his list of scientific achievements. Davy's understudy, Michael Faraday, was on the verge of constructing the first electric motor. Gas street lamps were erected in Piccadilly, London, and John Macadam's new road surface heralded the end of the bone-shaker stagecoach journeys.

And financing the military and technological triumphs was the greatest trading Empire the world had ever seen.

Beneath this dazzling armada of achievements, however, there ran a dark and toxic undertow.

There occurred a number of conspicuous symptoms of the unease and discontent. The 1812 assassination of Prime Minister Spencer Perceval – in the lobby of the House of Commons, no less – had sent shock waves around the world. Britain was nominally ruled by a mad Hanoverian king, and in practice by his obese and profligate son the Prince Regent, whose general unpopularity was expressed by the missile thrown at him through the window of the royal coach in the Mall. A telling detail points to the underlying feeling of insecurity in the weeks immediately following Waterloo: when HMS *Bellerophon* dropped anchor in Plymouth Sound in late July 1815 one of its passengers was Napoleon, en route to his exile on St Helena. After being relieved of 4,000 gold coins, the ex-Emperor was transferred to the HMS *Northumberland* for the long voyage to the South Atlantic. He had remained seven days on the water in Plymouth Sound, the docksides and estuary heaving with sightseers, but was prevented from setting foot on English soil, such was the Establishment's fear of the people being seduced by a dangerously charismatic demagogue.[1]

Some of the Regency success stories had brought with them a severe downside. The end of the Napoleonic Wars meant the return to civilian life of thousands of working-class soldiers, thus swelling the agricultural and urban labour markets which were already suffering major problems. Irish immigrant workers, and the introduction of low-waged child labour, increased the number of unemployed. The new machines that were bringing such profits to the textiles mill-owners were the source of much of the deprivation. Among the most cruelly hit were the weavers.[2]

Samuel Bamford, the radical weaver-poet who would march to Peterloo at the head of the Middleton contingent, paints a vivid, if slightly idealised, picture of the skilled handloom weaver's existence in pre-industrial times. It is easy to over-gild the 'golden age' of the cottage industry, when it seemed that every village artisan had a market garden to supplement his income in times of recession, and the country or semi-rural life was beneficial to body and soul. Even allowing for the rose-tinted spectacles, there was still much to recommend the Old Way. The sought-after skills of the small-scale craftsman attracted a degree of respect, and the largely self-sufficient village community benefited in turn.

Bamford's father Daniel – a muslin weaver by trade – was no stranger to the odd season of poverty, but the many traditions and observances recorded by Samuel reflect a vibrant and fairly affluent society. There was the custom of dealing out work to the younger apprentices, which had to be completed before Christmas treats – 'spiced bread, ale, or some good old cheese' – could be enjoyed. There was the Shrove Tuesday race to finish eating a pancake before the second serving, with the forfeit of a dump in the midden for slowcoaches. Easter was an extended holiday, involving peace-egging, gallons of mulled ale, and various forms of dressing up. The major summer festival was based on the August tradition of rush-bearing, with the Morris dancers, musicians, and procession of extravagantly decorated and garlanded rush-carts. This announced the beginning of the Wakes, when all work stopped for a week or so, and the holiday was celebrated with much feasting and consumption of ale. For these traditions to be properly observed there had to be at least an adequate supply of work, and a plenty of basic foodstuffs supplemented by the occasional more exotic addition. Sadly, with the coming of the factory machinery and the population shift to the towns, the rural version of these customs was virtually to disappear within a generation.[3]

The new textiles machines could produce the high quality finished article far faster, and in much greater quantities, than could the solo worker. Cotton exports from the north-west of England in the twenty years before Peterloo multiplied by seventy-five,[4] which led to a five-fold increase in Manchester's population, as former villagers and a fair number of Irish immigrants flooded into town to work the machines. Within the same period the upland settlements of Oldham, Middleton, Bolton, Ashton and Rochdale grew apace. With the overcrowding, and the economy still jittery nationally following the war years, came widespread poverty.

The Corn Law of 1815 (or as Henry Hunt termed it, 'that infamous starvation law'),[5] which banned the importation of cheap corn from abroad, was obviously unjust, favouring the rich man's profits over the poor family's basic needs. But the wildly fluctuating price of corn (which the Corn Law was an unsuccessful attempt to remedy), and the resultant periodic difficulty in affording a loaf of bread, was not the major ongoing cause of distress. For one thing, the Irish influx in the early years of the century had helped to popularise the potato as a cheap and nutritious alternative staple, at least for those town dwellers who could grow or obtain them.[6] The most ruinous long-term effect on workers' living standards was caused not so much by the Corn Law, as pernicious as this undoubtedly was, as by the creeping reduction in wages.

Once more, the weavers were hardest hit. A typical daily average wage in 1805 was 2s 4½d (12p), which had dwindled by January 1808 to 10½d (4½p).[7] An attempt to create a legal minimum wage was defeated in the House of Commons in April of that year, and as a result on two successive days at the end of May there took place, on St George's Field, Manchester, a demonstration by some 15,000 weavers. In some ways it was a grim rehearsal for Peterloo, since although the demonstrators were 'patient and passive, and their hands unaided by any thing like a weapon of hostility',[8] the Riot Act was read, the military was called in, and the dispersal resulted in one weaver killed and several injured. Manchester manufacturer Colonel Joseph Hanson was imprisoned for supporting the demonstration with 'malicious and inflammatory words'.[9] One detail mentioned by the *Gazette's* leader column would have surprising and far-reaching repercussions in later years: the 'woe-worn and altogether wretched appearance' of the weavers.

When the deputation of the Committee for the Relief of the Peterloo wounded and bereaved travelled to Manchester and the surrounding towns in January 1820, the shock felt by the Londoners when discovering the families' living conditions fairly leaps off the page in the Report. The people they visited were found to be,

> …almost generally clothed in rags, and the hovels and cellars which they inhabit nearly stripped of every article of furniture, which have been sold to satisfy the cravings of hunger of themselves and children.[10]

As James Cooper, an Oldham man and veteran of Peterloo, was to reminisce many years later: 'There was a universal state of starvation; children crying for bread, and their parents unable to give it to them'.[11]

The prime motive of the vast majority of mill and factory owners being profit, justifications were sought for reducing wages and implementing other methods of cutting corners on expenses. Not only sought, but openly expressed, as according to the employers wage reductions and induced poverty in the working class was beneficial not only for the economics of business, but also for the labourers' soul: 'It is a fact well known…that scarcity…promotes industry.'[12] It was a belief generally held amongst the better-off classes (and that included the clergy) that weavers especially, not so long before, had enjoyed such prosperity that they could work just three or four days a week and still afford lashings of ale and the weekly bottle of rum.[13] Clearly, the threat of poverty and starvation kept the workers on the straight and narrow.

Justification for child labour, which of course helped to keep wages down, was forthcoming via a dose of eyewash on the front page of a Manchester newspaper. The claim that including a child in a household's factory workforce actually strengthened family ties was the gist of the following, supposedly written by a weaver:

> To 'Fellow Weavers' –
> Spinners and weavers, are ye injured [by Machinery]? Least of all persons are ye entitled to complain. For four times your number are employed since the invention of machinery: and why? Because your little children, by the help of machinery, can earn their own livelihood, and it is easier to rear a family.[14]

The timing of publication is important: this item appeared the week after the Luddite attack on Burton's mill and house at Middleton, and the destruction of the Westhoughton mill, both described below. E. P. Thompson delivers the merited raspberry in response to the views expressed in the *Gazette* article: 'The family was roughly torn apart each morning by the factory bell.'[15]

Robert Southey, Lake Poet, historian and critic – and, incidentally, the first one to christen Henry Hunt with the sobriquet 'Orator' – assumed the persona of a visiting Spanish nobleman in delivering a scathing view of child labour in a Manchester cotton mill:

> [We were conducted] to one of the great cotton manufactories [and shown] the number of children who were at work there, and [the guide] dwelt with delight on the infinite good which resulted from employing them at so early an age. I listened without contradicting him…
>
> [The guide] remarked… 'You see these children, Sir… they get their bread almost as soon as they can run about, and by the time they are seven or eight years old they bring in money. There is no idleness among us: they come at

five in the morning; we allow them half an hour for breakfast, and an hour for dinner; they leave work at six, and another set relieves them for the night; the wheels never stand still.'

...I thought that if Dante had peopled one of his hells with children, here was a scene worthy to have supplied him with new images of torment.[16]

The 1808 literary disguise of Don Manuel Alvarez Espriella was no doubt Southey's means of avoiding any accusation of his sowing seeds of insurrection. Some ten years later the left-wing publication *Black Dwarf* would hammer home the details about the working conditions in the mills and factories:

The workmen...are trained to work from six years old, from five in a morning to eight and nine at night...

...the squalid appearance of the little infants and their parents taken from their beds at so early an hour in all kinds of weather...the miserable pittance of food, chiefly composed of water gruel and oatcake broken into it, a little salt, and sometimes coloured with a little milk, together with a few potatoes, and a bit of bacon or fat for dinner...

There they are (and if late a few minutes, a quarter of a day is stopped in wages) locked up until night...and allowed no time, except three-quarters of an hour at dinner in the whole day.[17]

A typical cotton mill – this one is in Ancoats, east Manchester. (McConnell and Co.)

Children, with their frailer constitutions and more malleable bones, were especially susceptible to industrial injuries. A typical example was Robert Blincoe, who worked for fourteen years as a child and young man in a cotton mill, as he testified later in life: 'I got deformed there; my knees began to bend in when I was fifteen...I have not the strength of those who are straight.' He mentioned the heat, the dust, the cruelly long hours, the possibility of losing a finger in the works, and related the horrendous tale of a 10-year-old girl who was caught up and crushed to death in a drawing frame machine.[18]

Poor harvests and the near-collapse of the agrarian economy accelerated the mass migration to the towns, further increasing the problems of overcrowding in the poorer areas. It was the living conditions of Manchester's factory workers that came under Engels's appalled scrutiny:

> I may mention just here that the mills almost all adjoin the rivers or the different canals that ramify throughout the city, before I proceed at once to describe the labouring quarters. First of all, there is the Old Town of Manchester... Here the streets...are narrow and winding, like Todd Street, Long Millgate, Withy Grove, and Shude Hill, the houses dirty, old, and tumble-down, and the construction of the side streets utterly horrible. Right and left a multitude of covered passages lead from the main street into numerous courts...which contain unqualifiedly the most horrible dwellings which I have yet beheld. In one of these courts there stands directly at the entrance...a privy without a door, so dirty that the inhabitants can pass into and out of the court only by passing through foul pools of stagnant urine and excrement.[19]

This was written some twenty years after Peterloo, but the depiction of extreme deprivation is of course still relevant. Also significant is Engels's list of Manchester's satellite towns, which 'vary little from the central city': Bolton, Wigan, Bury, Rochdale, Middleton, Oldham, Ashton, and Stockport. These towns are among those generically described as 'badly and irregularly built with foul courts, lanes, and back alleys, reeking of coal smoke, and especially dingy from the originally bright red brick, turned black with time'.[20] He also mentions Salford's 'filth and wretchedness'.[21] Unsurprisingly, Engels's list tallies almost exactly with that of the towns which sent marchers to St Peter's Field.

In such appalling living conditions, disease was rife. Writing in 1832, Dr Kay noted the prevalence of diarrhoea, typhus and cholera.[22] Child mortality

View of the Collegiate
Church from the
poorer dwellings
along the River Irk.
(Stockport Local
Heritage)

rate was shockingly high. Where figures exist for Manchester workers, the
news is invariably bad. In 1833 almost one half of the children born to a
mill's spinners had died at birth or in early infancy.[23] Nine years later the
following figures emerged regarding average age at death in Manchester:

Gentry	38
Tradesmen	20
Labourers	17[24]

The physical stresses of the labour, poor diet, overcrowding and woefully
inadequate sanitation were responsible not only for malnutrition and chronic
disease but also, as we have seen, occupational deformities.[25]

To add to the financial burden, a succession of taxes was imposed on the populace. A Failsworth man and veteran of Peterloo would bitterly recall some sixty-five years later: 'Everything you touched was taxed. They could scarcely stir without being taxed. If they washed their faces the soap was taxed. When they went to the looking-glass that was taxed, too. If they even put a clean collar on the very starch that had stiffened it was taxed.'[26] The most hated of these taxes, understandably, was the bread tax (closely followed by the malt tax, which added to the price of beer.) At the same time it was no longer thought necessary, by 1816, to continue to burden the wealthy with the Property Tax which had helped finance the wars.

Moreover, the vast majority of the population, male as well as female, had no right to vote, nor had they any established way of getting their voices heard by the powers in the land. The rallying cry 'TAXATION WITHOUT REPRESENTATION IS UNJUST AND TYRANNICAL' was displayed on one of the Saddleworth banners at Peterloo, echoing the 1776 American Colonies' slogan: 'No Taxation without Representation'. One of the initial purposes of the St Peter's Field meeting was to examine ways of legally putting forward a House of Commons representative who could speak for the great numbers of citizens – 98 per cent of the population, most of whom were working class – who were unable to vote. Prentice expressed 'the grossly defective state of the representation' in the clearest of terms:

> They saw Manchester, Salford, Bolton, Blackburn, Rochdale, Bury, Ashton-under Lyne, Oldham, and Stockport without [Parliamentary] members, whilst Old Sarum – a mound of earth without inhabitants – and a host of villages, decayed and rotten, each sent two.[27]

The small number of voters in this 'host of villages' (popularly dubbed 'rotten boroughs') meant that it was relatively easy, if one had the wherewithal, to bribe one's way into House of Commons membership. Bribery was a proven fact in the politics of the village of Ilchester in Somerset, and it was widely believed that the Ilchester MP Sir William Manners (later Lord Huntingtower) was guilty of demolishing the houses of his rivals, since one had to have property to be able to vote.[28] The Peterloo banner 'NO BOROUGH-MONGERING' – the practice of buying and selling of constituency seats – was a protest against the corrupt, venal network that typified much of the country's approach to Parliamentary representation.

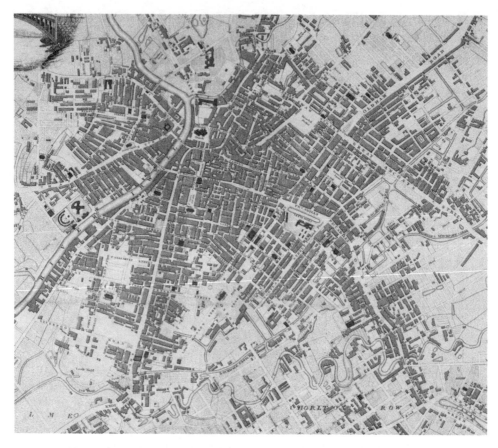

Detail from an 1819 map of the town of Manchester. (Manchester Central Library Archives+ (historical map collection))

This, then, was Regency England: the Janus country with the split personality, in which, despite the surface glories, injustice and gross inequality were legitimised and perpetuated by the powers in the land. The legal, civil and military machinery formed a daunting united front, whose sole object was to maintain the status quo, to the lasting benefit of the privileged few.

2

Law and Order

Everyday policing of Manchester and Salford in the early nineteenth century had a threadbare look. With a more than six-fold increase in the population between 1770 and 1830, the basic forces of law and order had not fully developed to keep pace with the numbers. In August 1819 the higher echelons of the Manchester and Salford policing system comprised:

> Boroughreeve Edward Clayton, by trade a calico printer: the position of Boroughreeve was somewhere between Lord Mayor and Chief of Police, the first citizen and principal municipal officer of a town; two Chief Constables, each elected for twelve months by the Court Leet: Jonathan Andrew from Harpurhey, and John Moore from Sale Moor; around 60 magistrates, all well-off men of property, a powerful oligarchy described by Chief Constable Moore as 'persons of the first consequence and character',[1] and whose word, quite literally, was law; assorted beadles who had minor peacekeeping functions, and the Deputy Chief Constable, the notorious Joseph Nadin, the enforcer: 'a famous local character of sombre repute.'[2]

> *With Henry Hunt we'll go, we'll go,*
> *With Henry Hunt we'll go,*
> *We'll raise the cap of liberty,*
> *In spite of Nadin Joe.*[3]

A jobsworth with a warrant, a truncheon and (sometimes) a blunderbuss, Joseph Nadin, a former cotton spinner, was Deputy Chief Constable of Manchester for nearly twenty years (1803–1821). Nadin will bulk large – in more ways than one – in our story. Samuel Bamford, who was to have several run-ins with the official over the years, described him thus:

Joseph Nadin was about 6 feet 1 inch in height, with an uncommon breadth and solidity of frame. His head was full sized, his complexion sallow, his hair dark and slightly grey; his features were broad and non-intellectual, his voice loud, his language coarse and illiterate, and his manner rude and overbearing to equals or inferiors.[4]

Although Manchester's two Chief Constables worked on a voluntary basis, their Deputy received a wage of £350 a year, which was supplemented by a 'payment by results' system. Successful charges were rewarded with a £2 bonus, plus a valuable Tyburn ticket. This ticket was a much sought-after document which exempted the possessor from police or legal duties and changed hands on the black market for anything up to £20.[5] This lucrative arrangement would give rise to the very strong suspicion that Nadin was engineering arrests, either by setting up a situation that could be interpreted as seditious or criminal, or by having one or more of his spies infiltrate a radicals' meeting. According to E.P. Thompson, 'Nadin...would stop short at

Deputy Chief Constable Joseph Nadin, 'a man of more bluster than courage'. (Stockport Local Heritage)

no violence or trick to secure a conviction.'The Habeas Corpus Suspension Act in February 1817 virtually gave him a free hand. A letter from 'A Constant Reader' in the *Manchester Observer* in April 1818 accused Nadin of arranging for an accomplice to plant some stolen material in a milliner's on Market Street.The Deputy Constable promptly arrived and arrested the shopkeeper.[6]

Nadin certainly showed a sadistic tendency. He appeared to relish his position of power over the arrested man: one of his quips was to promise the prisoner an increase in height before he got back home, as a result of his being hanged.When Bamford and his fellow radicals were apprehended in March 1817, Nadin, after chaining the detainees together by the feet, gave the order that neck irons be fitted too. This was overruled by the accompanying King's Messengers, however.[7] After the arrest of one John Royle, during which Nadin broke the detainee's nose with a truncheon blow, the prisoner protested his innocence so persistently that the Deputy Constable gagged him by buckling a bridle – a medieval instrument used to silence nagging wives – into his mouth![8] Prentice, in his *Historical Sketches*, described Nadin as 'a man of more bluster than courage'.[9]

It was in Nadin's interest to keep the Establishment's apprehension about the Reform movement simmering; not that it would have taken much effort on his part. On 26 March 1814 he wrote to the Home Office, essentially to claim some expenses, as hiring spies did not come cheap, but the letter also contained the following:

> I think it my duty to apprise you that all Trades in the Manufactory of this neighbourhood again meet in different Societys [*sic*]. But I believe they are forming Combinations against their Masters to raise their wages, the weavers met about 500 last Tuesday evening at Shaw Brow near this town.[10]

One revealing detail about Nadin, which at this distance in time has attained the tone of low farce, emerged from his cross-examination at the John Lees inquest in October 1819. Perhaps it was the unseasonably hot day, or the cramped and uncomfortable conditions in the makeshift courtroom in the Star Inn on Deansgate, Manchester; or it could have been due to Nadin's feeling that he had lost face during the questioning (one of his more unconvincing responses had provoked scornful laughter in the public gallery).Whatever the reason, as the red-faced Deputy Constable left the room, he gave vent to the bruiser streak which he often displayed when dealing with those he felt were his inferior:

[Here the witness retired, and in quitting the court, with the assistance of his constables, he forced many auditors from the further end of the room, with the most brutal violence.]

Mr. Harmer: Mr. Nadin, you ought not to use such violence; and I do not know what business you have to turn anyone out who is not misbehaving.[11]

In making his arrests it was Nadin's style to display excessive force: brandishing truncheon or blunderbuss, he would swoop, backed up by a considerable armed military or police presence. At the Prince Regent's Arms reform meeting in June 1812, he was accompanied by around thirty of the Royal Scots Greys Regiment, all of whom were carrying muskets with fixed bayonets.[12] When he arrested Bamford (not for the last time) and charged him with high treason in Middleton in March 1817, he had his blunderbuss again, and six armed officers were supporting him.[13]

From these incidents (and there were many more similar) it will be seen that any threat of unrest could be held in check by a formidable concatenation of civil and military power. The government could call on troops of regular soldiers, which resource was of course more readily available once the Napoleonic Wars were over.

Besides the professional soldiery (cavalry and field cannon as well as infantry), the authorities could call upon help from the civil ranks. Special Constables from the mercantile and property-owning classes could be sworn in at a few hours' notice. From the same social strata came the volunteer Yeomanry.

The Cheshire Yeomanry – who were to play a peripheral role at Peterloo – were formed in 1797, in response to fears that England was about to be invaded by the French: so in conception a sort of Dad's Army on horseback, albeit with potentially much greater capacity for damage. In 1817 they were instrumental in dispersing the Blanketeers' March (see pp. 46–8). Not to be outdone by their generally more affluent neighbours, the shopkeepers, inn landlords and small businessmen of Manchester and Salford decided to form their own mounted militia later that year. They would receive a government grant for uniform and sabre, but had to supply that most visible of status symbols: their own horse. (Since the cost of a horse at the time was between £200 and £270, this was an excellent way of keeping out undesirables.) No svelte Arabian racing steeds these, but more akin to lumbering half-ton English shire horses, but still capable of a fearsome turn of speed, the combat descendants of the Norman and Plantagenet kings' warhorses. The

Yeomanry's chargers were a formidable asset when under proper control, but potentially devastating to both sides if that control should be impaired. Despite their lack of experience and proper military training, the Manchester and Salford troop at least cut a dash in their uniform: bright blue clothing with white facing, and a black shako hat the shape of a truncated cone sporting a red plume. This differed from the uniform of the Hussars in that the professional soldiers wore blue with yellow facings. The general character and specific shortcomings of the volunteer cavalry will be looked at in more detail in Part Two.

The ultimate wielders of power in Manchester and the surrounding towns were the magistrates, a networking oligarchy comprising men of the cloth, landowners, and mill and factory managers. Born into, and steeped in, privilege, they were for the most part intransigently reactionary, jealously guarding their wealth and sweeping control with all the available civic and military resources. A brief biographical introduction to a few of the major incumbents will suffice.

William Hulton, chairman of
the magistrates at Peterloo.
(Touchstones Rochdale)

William Hulton, High Sheriff of Lancashire, Constable of Lancaster Castle, and chairman of the Manchester and Salford magistrates at Peterloo, was a member of a prosperous landowning family. The riches came principally from the coal deposits underneath their Hulton Park estate, 3 miles south-west of Bolton.

The Reverend William Hay could boast an impressive ancestry: his father had been Governor of Barbados, and his grandfather Archbishop of York. Born near Lisbon in 1761, he gained an Oxford law degree before becoming ordained as an Anglican priest. Chairman of the Salford Quarter Sessions and Steward of the Manor Court of Manchester, he had a reputation for his severity in dealing with radical dissenters.[14]

Despite being an Anglican minister, Hay seems not to have been above the odd excursion into fiction if it suited his purpose. At the height of the Luddite activity in Lancashire in 1812, he sent a report to the Home Office in which he told of three Luddites from Nottingham who had ridden to Manchester 'on piebald horses' to give orders, before immediately riding off again. No details were supplied as to who or what this involved, nor when, where or why this highly implausible episode took place.[15] This would appear to be another example of the scaremongering strategy used at the time, although, as shown elsewhere, more usually by government spies and *agents provocateurs*. It may be worth our while to remember this communication of Hay's when we consider his contributions to the narrative later.

Hay's close associate the Reverend Charles Ethelston was also an Anglican minister, a Fellow of the Collegiate Church, and member of the mutual benevolence society based at the Portico[16] on Mosley Street. He was to claim to have read the Riot Act before the Yeomanry's attack at Peterloo, a claim backed up by Hay. He had been the author of some poems of dubious rectitude earlier in his career, a biographical snippet which would be gleefully seized upon by radical opponents.

Colonel John Silvester (or Sylvester), originally from Chorley, had gained his title from the formation of 'Silvester's Volunteers'. This paramilitary corps had been consecrated in 1802 in the Collegiate Church by the Reverend Ethelston, the chaplain of the regiment. Other such civilian troops were raised in Manchester and Salford at about the same time, and many of the members were soon to join together under the banner of the Yeomanry.[17]

James Norris was a lawyer, and of all the magistrates present at Peterloo he was the only one who was at the time a resident of Manchester. Since assuming the role of magistrate in March 1818, he had been assiduously

communicating with the Home Office, reporting activity which he had construed as organised unrest and insurrection.[18] Norris's name appears regularly on the official documents relevant to Peterloo, and he maintains a constant presence: he gave the order for the reading of the Riot Act at New Cross, and was Chairman of the Bench at Hunt's New Bailey hearing.

Another magistrate in constant communication with the Home Office was Bolton's Colonel Ralph Fletcher. From a family whose affluence was based on the Atherton coal mines, Fletcher was a Justice of the Peace, Colonel in the Bolton Volunteers, member of the local 'Church and

King' club, and bearer of the imposing title Deputy Grand Master of the Grand Orange Lodge of England.[19] A powerful loyalist supporter, he ran a widespread network of spies, and was granted Home Office permission to open suspicious-looking mail at the Post Office. He would be in charge of the military who suppressed the riot at the Westhoughton mill.[20] He was one of the magistrates who signed the arrest warrant for Hunt, and was seen by one witness to strike people with his staff at Peterloo.[21]

Also in a position of power, although answerable to Hulton's magistrates, was the cotton mill owner and former Boroughreeve Hugh Hornby Birley, or Captain Birley of the Manchester and Salford Yeomanry, as he had styled himself. He was known to rule his workers with a rod of iron and was to dismiss three of his employees once he discovered that their father, William Marsh, had been one of the wounded demonstrators at Peterloo.[22]

Amongst his peers, however, Birley was well respected. In the House of Commons his character was declared to be one of 'mildness and humanity', and personal friend Lord Stanley repeated the assertion that at Peterloo, 'Capt. Birley had never taken his sabre from his shoulder except once, when he was near the hustings and this was done for the purpose of directing a passage to be made for two women who wished to escape.'[23] The glittering career of Birley post-Peterloo is summarised in Part Three.

A more remote, but militarily significant and influential, figure was General Sir John Byng, the supreme Commanding Officer of the military of Northern District of England. Although absent from St Peter's Field – he was at York races on 16 August – the communications between him and the Home Office on the subject of military intervention at reformers' assemblies make interesting reading.[24]

Besides the more overt displays of repression, the government also employed a widespread and secret network of spies and informers. They were generally unsavoury characters, in it blatantly for the money, or lapsed radicals who were trying to save their own skin. Many of them were recruited from word of mouth contacts in debtors' prison.[25] For a while it had been relatively easy to infiltrate the reformers' groups: one of their number, with the rumly cognate name of John Bent, was instrumental in Nadin's arrest of the thirty-seven supposed conspirators at the meeting at the Prince Regent's Arms on Ancoats Lane in June 1812 (which is described in more detail in the next chapter). He had been elected the group's treasurer. Spies also had a crucial role to play in the planned attack on the mill at Westhoughton (see pp. 35–6).

One of the more notorious of this execrated breed was one Oliver (real name William Richards), immortalised in the pages of Bamford, Prentice, and Hansard. Frank Peel described him as 'the most wicked, unscrupulous, and infamous of the whole vile troop'.[26] A plausible-looking fellow, he was involved in the organisation (and, clandestinely, in the swift termination) of the Blanketeers' March in the spring of 1817. The following year he was described in the House of Commons as 'guilty of frauds upon his employers for a great number of years...wholly destitute of truth and principle'. One of his misdemeanours had been to urge his daughter to commit perjury.[27] By then his true role had been exposed by Edward Baines Snr of the *Leeds Mercury*, who described him as 'a prototype of Lucifer'.[28]

The role of the informer or *agent provocateur*, besides keeping the Home Office up to speed about local radical developments, was to keep the pot of unease boiling. This helped justify the government's repressive measures, and often the bigger the scare – whether fabricated or real – the more money changed hands. It was to some extent another 'payment by results' scam, such as the one allegedly used by Nadin. It was also a ploy to persuade the dissidents to show their hand, as is explained in the next chapter.

By 1819, with more open public rallies now very much in vogue, the spy system had mostly had its day. The main target of the informer network had been the Luddites and similar factions with their secret oaths, passwords and hand signals. Now with the more transparent approach favoured by the moderate reformers, spies had become largely redundant.

Nevertheless, the few but violent years of Luddism were a signal stage on the road to Peterloo.

3

Of Machines and Mammon

On Monday, 20 April 1812 an angry crowd of over 2,000 gathered outside the steam-powered cotton mill of Daniel Burton & Sons in Middleton. At a given signal several fusillades of stones were unleashed, smashing many windows. The mill owners had been tipped off about the demonstration, so had placed armed men inside the building. A warning shot was fired from a musket,[1] but this was ignored, whereupon the defenders opened fire on the crowd, killing three and wounding ten.

About noon the next day the mob was back, fewer in number[2] but armed with guns and pickaxes. By now the mill was defended by the military, and the attackers were easily beaten off. So they decided to turn their anger onto the house of Emanuel Burton, Daniel's son, half a mile distant, which they broke into and set on fire. The Burton family had gone away the night before, and the man they had left as caretaker quit the house when he saw the mob arrive. The soldiers in the mill were informed about the riot and came quickly on the scene, shooting dead five on the spot. Another two demonstrators, severely wounded, escaped into the fields where they later died from their injuries.[3]

The *Leeds Mercury* in describing the march of the crowd on the second day added the detail: 'At the head of this armed banditti a *Man of Straw* was carried, representing the *renowned* General Ludd whose standard-bearer waved a sort of red flag.'[4]

The Middleton riot, with ten dead and an estimated £3,000 damage, was the worst of the Luddite protests of those years. Inspired by the mythical General Ludd, insurgent groups around the country had taken it upon themselves to destroy these infernal machines – the steam-powered looms – which, despite creating a phenomenal rise in output and therefore profit for the owners, were seen to be robbing the weavers of their jobs, income, employability and dignity.[5] In a year of soaring wheat, oatmeal and potato prices, plus the increase in weavers' unemployment, families had been reduced to starvation level, and there had been food riots across the south Lancashire area at about the same time.

The very same week as the Middleton incident, there was more to come.

On the Friday another power-loom mill, Wray and Duncrough's at Westhoughton, just 12 miles due west of Middleton and an hour's horse ride from Bolton, was the object of an attack. The details here, however, reveal a more convoluted tale than at Middleton, since it involves prior bluffs from Colonel Fletcher's regiment of spies and *agents provocateurs*. It was Fletcher's strategy to plant a large number of these agents into Luddite meetings, where they would be instrumental in encouraging acts of mob violence. The Westhoughton mill had been a putative target for some while, and it was one of Fletcher's plants, a man named John Stones, who had been one of the principal agitators. The point of this had been to flush the most active Luddites out into the open, where an example and a deterrent, such as imprisonment, transportation or execution, could be implemented.[6] It was claimed that '10 or 11 spies…*armed*, and disguised with *blackened faces*' had infiltrated the Dean Moor gathering on the Sunday before the Westhoughton incident.[7] On 6 April Fletcher had written to the Home Office outlining his strategy of allowing the 'traitors' enough scope to proceed as far as possible 'without *actual mischief*', so as to arrest more people and find out more about the 'first movers'.[8]

Jonathan Edward Taylor was even more outspoken on the policy of entrapment:

> The spies were amongst the poor, spreading devilish snares to entrap them… to encourage and stimulate to the adoption of their infernal schemes. Every means were tried, every attempt made, to induce individuals to commit themselves…the casual and whispered invitation to join in crime…[9]

On the fateful Friday, however, the slyly contrived insurrection gained a violent momentum of its own.

The Westhoughton mill was not itself defended, although following recent riots in the town a dozen muskets had been placed in the building, and the soldiers stationed in Bolton were on standby. In the morning a sense of alarm brought a troop of Scots Greys from the town, but as all seemed quiet on their arrival around midday it was decided that the call to arms had been a hoax, so the military returned to base.

However, by around 4 p.m. the mill owner witnessed the approach of a large crowd, some of them armed with pitchforks, billhooks and scythes. Fearing for his own safety, he saddled his horse and rode off, followed by the angry shouts of the mob. By the time he reached Bolton and could inform the Scots Greys that this time it was for real, the destruction of the mill had already begun.

After the initial bout of window smashing – in which activity two teenage girls were among the most enthusiastic – the doors were broken open and a fire was started inside. By the time the Scots Greys arrived the mill had burned to the ground, with an estimated damage of £6,000.

The death penalty for frame- and loom-breaking had been introduced in February of that year. It would be commuted to transportation in 1814, before the capital offence definition was reinstated three years later. After the trial of the Westhoughton rioters, the four deemed to be the ringleaders were condemned to death, even though one of them was aged just 16. The presiding magistrate who ordered the executions was the 24-year-old High Sheriff of Lancashire, William Hulton.[10]

The spring of 1812 had seen two further episodes of unrest: in March there was an attack on a power weaving firm's warehouse in Stockport, and a matter of days before the Middleton and Westhoughton incidents there was the occupation of the Exchange building in the heart of Manchester.

The original intention had been for Manchester loyalists to hold a congress in the Exchange dining room, at which an expression of support for the Prince Regent was to be toasted, recorded, and sent to London. The list of signatories supporting the assembly includes the names of several people who would feature in the Peterloo drama: the Reverend Charles Ethelston, Colonel John Silvester, Francis Philips the cotton manufacturer, and the Headmaster of the Grammar School, Jeremiah Smith.[11]

Given the degree of poverty suffered by the majority of workers at the time, and therefore the potentially volatile situation, calling such a meeting was a red rag to a bull. Once word got round that Wednesday, 8 April was to be a gathering of 'Church and King' members who in effect were to express satisfaction with the status quo, the idea of a counter-demonstration took hold. Besides local workers, there would be protestors – mostly weavers – from Stockport, Ashton, Oldham, Bolton, and other outlying cotton centres.

Suspecting that the loyalist assembly would be too provocative for public quiescence, late on the Tuesday the organisers circulated handbills announcing its cancellation. The official reason given was an unstable interior staircase, which would not support the weight of the expected numbers. Too late: by 8 a.m. the following day a crowd had begun to gather in Market Place and St Ann's Square. By 9.30 the numbers were considerable, and an outer door of the Exchange building was forced open. Hugh Hornby Birley was passing and tried to remonstrate with the crowd, but feelings were already running high, and the former Boroughreeve was 'pursued with blows, and taunting, hooting, and the grossest insults'. He managed to escape into a nearby shop 'with the loss of part of his coat'.[12]

Inside the building, horseplay amongst the younger infiltrators shifted via an accidental breakage of a window into a general impulse to wreck and smash. Windows, chandeliers and oil lamps were broken, maps and pictures were defaced, and furniture was heaped into a potential bonfire in the centre of the room. By now, however, magistrates John Silvester and Richard Wright had read the Riot Act, and a troop of Scots Greys accompanied by the Cumberland Militia arrived on the scene. The crowd was dispersed, but not before an estimated £1,000 worth of damage had been caused. The pubs were cleared, a curfew was imposed, and the military presence patrolled the streets throughout the night. *Wheeler's Chronicle* offered a reward of £100 for information leading to the conviction of any of the 'depredators, or their abettors'.[13]

Manchester Cotton Exchange in Regency times. Market Place and Old Millgate lead down to the Collegiate Church. (Stockport Local Heritage)

Some left-wing factions claimed a victory of sorts. Prentice quotes from eyewitness Thomas Kershaw: 'But we had no Church-and-King mobs after that!'[14] Perhaps not, but the forces at play on the day of the Exchange building occupation brought Peterloo that much closer.

By then, the vandalism of that day was the exception rather than the rule. Factories and mills had been attacked before, but in April 1812 the day of the Luddite was all but over. The occupation and wrecking of the Exchange was one of the last occasions when workers' energies were not politically focussed, but had simply gained expression in an indiscriminate attack on the perceived temple of Mammon. Jonathan Edward Taylor, writing in 1820, spotted the innate worth and political potential of the workers, 'the mass of the manufacturing population which surrounds Manchester'. He noted their 'sobriety, good conduct, shrewdness, industry, and intelligence'.[15] It was a refreshingly positive view, and in marked contrast to the one of expendable factory fodder and mere means of profit.

The shift away from the violent protest to the meeting and the considered petition found an early example in the Prince Regent's Arms affair in June of that year. The pub on Ancoats Lane, Manchester, was the venue for a gathering of reformers, chaired by Oldham weaver John Knight, who would be on the hustings at Peterloo. Since one of Nadin's spies was among the assembly, it was an easy matter for the blunderbuss-wielding Deputy Constable to locate and gatecrash the gathering, aided by a troop of Scots Greys carrying muskets with fixed bayonets. John Knight tried to show the list of non-violent resolutions to Nadin, but the official would have none of it, and arrested thirty-seven (later thirty-eight), who were immediately sent to the New Bailey prison to await trial for 'holding an unlawful meeting, combining for seditious purposes, tending to overthrow the government'. The arrested included ten weavers and six spinners, but also small manufacturers such as hatters. The areas of origin of those present, besides Manchester itself, ranged as far afield as Salford, Oldham, Hyde, Failsworth, Hadfield, Ashton and Stalybridge.

At Lancaster Assizes in August, all the accused were found not guilty of the charges, the evidence being considered too vague and contradictory to convict.[16]

Nadin would have to wait another seven years before he could successfully arrest John Knight.

4

Voices of Dissent

If we look upon the group of post-Luddite reformers as an extended and active family, then Major John Cartwright (1740–1824) from Boston, Lincolnshire, was their patriarch. He was invited to attend Peterloo, but the near-octogenarian was unable to make the journey. Cartwright based his democratic ideas on a partly idealised version of the Anglo-Saxon system of tythings and frankpledge, in which the common people directly contributed to legal decisions.[1] He was a major participant in the movement to abolish slavery, and was a prolific author of radical texts. Disliking the extreme measures of the Luddites, he advocated moderate reform, his watchword being 'hold fast by the laws'.[2] Once established in London, he founded the first Hampden Club, in which reformers met to debate, share ideas, and read the left-wing press. The major goals of these societies were to persuade the government to establish universal adult male suffrage and annual parliaments, and to repeal the Corn Laws. Cartwright was present at the launch of the Middleton Hampden Club in 1817, at which Bamford composed this thumbnail sketch of the 'venerable patriot':

> …rather above the common stature, straight for his age; thin, pale, and with an expression of countenance in which firmness and benignity were most predominant. I saw him walking up the room, in his long brown surtout and plain brown wig, and seating himself placidly in the head seat. A mild smile played on his features, as a simultaneous cheer burst from the meeting.[3]

Within a few months Hampden Clubs had mushroomed around the area, in many cases founded by local radicals who would be present on the St Peter's Field hustings: Joseph Healey in Oldham, and John Knight and Joseph Johnson in Manchester. The Clubs were also formed in Royton, Rochdale, Ashton-under-Lyne, and Stockport. The left-wing newspapers disseminated at the meetings were *Black Dwarf, Manchester Observer,* and Richard Carlile's *Sherwin's Political Register.* The Manchester Club evolved into the Patriotic Union Society, from which sprang the idea of the Peterloo rally.

In Cartwright's absence at Peterloo, the real celebrity of the day – *pace* Bamford, Knight and Carlile – was the charismatic and wildly popular Henry Hunt. The eldest son of a wealthy Wiltshire farmer – at his trial he presented himself as 'Lord of the Manor of Glastonbury, in Somerset'[4] – the tall, handsome and well-built Hunt was one of the iconic radical figures of the time. With his trademark white top hat, booming public speaking voice and his penchant for razzamatazz, he enjoyed rock star status for many a year. When his carriage travelled from Lancaster jail to Manchester when he was released on bail after his arrest, it was pulled part of the way by teams of his supporters.[5] At the Smithfield rally a month or so earlier, a heckler who was unwise enough to call out: 'Hunt, how much a year does Castlereagh give you for spouting?' was escorted away by members of the audience and 'gently ducked in the channel for his pains'.[6]

Hunt had spent a lively, headstrong youth. He ran away from school because of bullying, was married at age 23, and eloped six years later with a friend's wife. A one-time member of the Wiltshire Yeomanry, he challenged his Colonel to a duel, and was then imprisoned when he refused to apologise.[7]

On the downside, his vanity and ego, observed by others on several occasions, were the least appealing of his personality traits, although he was ahead of his time in realising, and exploiting, the power of image in politics and public speaking.[8] Nevertheless, he could deliver the steak as well as the sizzle: he was an articulate debater and capable orator, able to hold the attention of large audiences. He possessed a quick and knowing wit: when it was pointed out to him that Parliament kept him perpetually in hot water, he replied that he found that no problem as his opponents acted as steam engines, and so kept him raised on high.[9] While passing through Stockport accompanied by a band of supporters on his way to Manchester, he was harangued from a first-floor window by an officer of the local regiment. Seeking to discomfit the visiting reformer by drawing attention to his recent divorce, the officer shouted: 'Who does not live with his wife?' Hunt's response was quick, apt and stentorian: 'The Prince Regent'.[10]

It was during his trial for trespass in 1799 that he had been influenced by his left-wing lawyer and came to embrace the new radical ideas. In 1819 he was living with his mistress Catherine Vince and his two sons in Andover,

'Orator' Hunt on the hustings. (Stockport Local Heritage)

Hampshire. He had stood for Member of Parliament three times – twice in Bristol in 1812 and then in Westminster in 1818 – but had failed to make any great waves at these polls.

Again it is Bamford who has left us a memorable description of Hunt, although it betrays his later disillusion with the 'Orator':

> He was gentlemanly in his manner and attire; six feet and better in height, and extremely well formed… He wore his own hair; it was in moderate quantity, and a little grey. His features were regular, and there was a kind of youthful blandness about them which, in amicable discussion, gave his face a most agreeable expression. His lips were delicately thin, and receding… His eyes were blue or light grey – not very clear, nor quick, but rather heavy; except as I afterwards had opportunities for observing, when he was excited in speaking; at which times they seemed to distend and protrude; and if he worked himself furious, as he sometimes would, they became blood-streaked, and almost started from their sockets. Then it was that the expression of his lip was to be observed – the kind smile was exchanged for the curl of scorn, or the curse of indignation. His voice was bellowing; his face swollen and flushed; his griped hand beat as if it were to pulverize; and his whole manner gave token of a painful energy, struggling for utterance.[11]

He was also something of a businessman. When he pledged to abstain from tea, coffee and alcohol whilst fighting for the radical cause, he was not so much avoiding the unnatural stimuli as advocating by example the boycotting of payment of tax.[12] It was also an opportunity to market his own brand of coffee substitute or 'Breakfast Powder', an untaxed chicory roast concoction that by some accounts tasted vile and was the subject of much right-wing satire. It has to be said, though, that his supporters were ready with a counter-barb. After the Excise Officers had seized Hunt's supply of the stuff in March 1820, an entertaining letter appeared in the *Manchester Observer*, singing the praises of the health-giving properties of the beverage, as opposed to the allegedly additive-infested alternatives of tea and alcoholic drinks.[13]

Another nationally renowned reformer present at Peterloo was Richard Carlile. The son of a Devon shoemaker, and a tinsmith by trade, Carlile was an ex-pupil of Ashburton Grammar School. He moved to London where he became a publisher. One of the works he sold – in a series of pamphlets so the poorer people could afford it – was *The Rights of Man*, the supposedly inflammatory and blasphemous work by the demonised freethinker Tom Paine. He also published *The Republican*, a left-wing newspaper which contained, besides political tracts, poems by Shelley and Lord Byron, ardent liberals both. Carlile was to escape arrest at Peterloo, but the reprieve was temporary.

Fifty-seven-year-old John Knight – 'the Cartwright of the North' – a handloom weaver from Saddleworth, was also on the St Peter's Field hustings. As already narrated, he had been one of the thirty-seven arrested in June 1812 at the Prince Regent's Arms, so, like Bamford, was no stranger to Nadin and his cohorts. He had abandoned his small textiles business to throw himself into political activism soon after his brother William died, apparently as a result of a prison sentence for seditious activities. John himself had spent two years in prison because of his political beliefs, and even continued to make his radical speeches when out on bail. Along with Joseph Johnson, John Thacker Saxton and James Wroe, he was owner of the *Manchester Observer*, a radical newspaper with a weekly circulation of around 4,000.[14]

Richard Carlile.
(Working Class
Movement Library)

Also based in Oldham was 'Doctor' Joseph Healey. Although nearly illiterate (and a believer in the existence of witches on the moors) he was an energetic member of the Reform movement, and a good friend to Bamford. He was unqualified as a doctor, and the hilarious tale of the tooth extraction without anaesthetic in a Holcombe Valley pub is well worth a read.[15] He was wounded on St Peter's Field, but like Bamford, Carlile and John Knight he evaded arrest on the day, only to be apprehended at his house in Lees on the following Saturday.

Part owner of the *Manchester Observer* and a brush manufacturer by trade was Joseph Johnson, at whose house in Harpurhey Hunt stayed the week before Peterloo. At his and Hunt's trial he was to cooperate too easily with the prosecution,[16] which went a long way to severing amicable relations between the two men. In January 1819, Wroe, Knight and Johnson formed the Patriotic Union Society, the aim of which was Parliamentary reform.

Mary Fildes, the immediately noticeable woman in white in the pictures of the Peterloo hustings, was born Mary Pritchard in Cork in 1789. At the time she was the mother of seven children, two of whom she had had named after radical writer Thomas Paine and Henry Hunt. An eighth child, born in 1821, would be christened John Cartwright Fildes. She formed the Manchester Female Reform Society a month or so before Peterloo, and later supported the campaign for birth control, which brought some scathing remarks in the press.[17]

George Swift, a shoemaker originally from Doncaster, was just 19 on the day of Peterloo. He gave a short speech from the platform before Hunt's arrival, and was sitting 'betwixt Saxton and Baines'[18] when the short-lived proceedings began. Whilst under arrest in the New Bailey prison later that day, he wrote an impassioned letter to his brother relating the incident.

William Fitton, a surgeon from Royton, was a frequent and noticeable participant in radical meetings throughout south Lancashire in those years, often being elected chairman. Although not present at Peterloo, having been indicted for participating in a seditious assembly at Blackburn, he was an author of some allegedly inflammatory letters, and would be a victim of the subsequent witch hunt.[19]

Other figures in our *dramatis personae* would include John Tyas, the reporter for *The Times*; the more moderate reformer John Edward Taylor, who was to be instrumental in the launch of the *Manchester Guardian* two years later; and James Moorhouse, the owner of a Stockport coach business – at whose house Hunt stayed on 8 August before the final leg of his journey into

Manchester. Moorhouse was a keen bible reader, and had eleven children, six of them by his current wife, who was pregnant again on the day of Peterloo, which she attended.[20]

Archibald Prentice, a warehouse clerk originally from Lanarkshire, was witness to the arrivals of the crowds at Peterloo from a friend's house on Mosley Street, then to the trek back home of the Salford wounded several hours later. He was to write an article about the incident which appeared in a London newspaper within forty-eight hours – one of the first accounts to reach national attention. Another narrative, also sent by night mail coach within hours of the incident, was written by John Edward Taylor, Prentice's colleague on the *Gazette*.

The reformers' friends in high places included Sir Francis Burdett, that rare bird, a Regency radical in Parliament. Although there was a marked difference of opinion between the Hunt and Burdett factions around mid-decade, Burdett would campaign vehemently for an independent inquiry into Peterloo. The government would try, unsuccessfully, to quell his outspokenness with a prison sentence for the frequently cited 'seditious libel'.

Sir Charles Wolseley, a wealthy radical baronet from Staffordshire, would supply bail for many of the Peterloo prisoners. Aged just 20, he had been present at the 1789 storming of the Bastille, and along with Cartwright, was one of the founding members of the original Hampden Club. He would be imprisoned in April 1820 for a speech made as chairman of the open-air rally at Sandy Brow, Stockport, on 28 June 1819.

The year 1816 had seen a further shift in the reformers' approach: the year that had started with uncoordinated bread riots ended with the proliferation of Hampden Clubs and the first of the orderly mass meetings. However, it was this very order, visible in the painstaking and systematic preparation, which was a cause for concern to loyalists in the Spa Fields riots of December of that year.

Henry Hunt had been invited to speak at Spa Fields, thus ensuring a good crowd. But within the reformer wrapping there was a hidden revolutionary agenda: a hard core of extremists had planned to use the rally as a pretext for attacks on the Bank of England, the Tower, Newgate Prison, and the Royal Exchange. Gunsmiths' shops were to be raided, and the ultimate aim was to create a Committee of Public Safety in imitation of Paris of 1793, and thereby take over control of London.

In the event, the revolutionary aims proved to be far too ambitious for the insurgents, and after a series of pitched battles with soldiers in the streets around Fleet Market, Snow Hill and the Minories, the armed mob was dispersed. One of the ringleaders would be hanged for raiding a gunsmith's shop, whilst the others would be found not guilty of High Treason – to the exasperation of the Home Secretary, Lord Sidmouth.[21]

Nevertheless, an article published in *The Times* the next day highlighted the authorities' fears:

> Wild and desperate as such a scheme must have been, yet a scheme the rioters certainly had: they marched under their own banners; they armed themselves… Their forces were divided into separate bands…the whole proceeding was arranged long beforehand.[22]

It was these very fears – of an organised and capable working-class radical force – which were to resurface so vividly at Peterloo.

Public dissatisfaction with the Prince Regent gained expression in the missile which smashed the window of his coach as he was returning from opening Parliament the following month. The Prince was unharmed, and there was some difference of opinion as to the nature of the missile, depending on one's position in the political spectrum. It was suggested in the House of Commons that a bullet from an air gun or pistol (there having been no gunpowder flash observed) had done the damage. Then it was concluded that the projectile had been a stone thrown 'from a height', since no bullets had been found in the coach.[23] According to Hunt the window had been broken by 'some gravel or a potatoe [sic]'.[24]

Following closely on the heels of this incident, the Habeas Corpus Act was suspended in February. This meant that – until the following January, when the Act was restored – people could be imprisoned without the legal obligation of bringing them to trial. Several times through the year the suspension contributed to bringing the labour strife to a head, often violently. Besides the incidents mentioned below, the armed Pentrich uprising, during which a house servant was shot dead by one of the insurgents, took place in Derbyshire in June. The insurrection had been partially instigated by the notorious government plant, Oliver the Spy, who had circulated the bogus news of a revolutionary army marching to join them from the north. The movement collapsed when the demonstrators were scattered by the soldiers. The three ringleaders, found guilty of treasonable acts, were hanged and beheaded.

On 10 March 1817 radicals Samuel Drummond, John Johnston and the 18-year-old John Bagguley chaired an assembly of 'four or five thousand' (according to Bamford) on St Peter's Field. The intention was to march *en masse* to London, to present a petition for reform to the Prince Regent. The hope was that those who started out would gather support on the way; Johnston predicted 100,000 supporters by the time the marchers reached Birmingham. Bamford had been dismissive of the whole enterprise, and despite the lack of foresight as regards food and accommodation on the way, and the immediate arrest of many of the crowd including the three chairmen, several hundred set off in the 'gentle but chilling rain' down the road to Stockport.[25]

The logistical naivety of the marchers was apparent by their carrying of blankets in their knapsacks, the intention being to sleep by the side of the road if accommodation could not be found – hence the monicker 'Blanketeers'. The numbers were to dwindle dramatically: 300 reached the Mersey Bridge at Stockport, where the Cheshire Yeomanry dispersed the column and made a few more arrests. Several of the marchers received sabre wounds, and one local resident was accidentally shot dead.

The deputation reassembled and around 180 made it to Macclesfield by nightfall, where some of them stayed at houses of radical sympathisers, while others slept on the ground. Beyond there, another unforeseen hazard awaited: the Blanketeers had to pass through rotten boroughs, the inhabitants of which, obviously, would not have been sympathetic to their cause. Fifty of the Blanketeers got as far as Leek, and by Ashbourne the numbers had dwindled to twenty. Eventually one Abel Couldwell from Stalybridge is said to have arrived in London, where he presented the petition to Lord Sidmouth. True to form, the government gave no reply.[26]

Beset on all sides by reactionary forces and riddled with government spies (including the ubiquitous Oliver), the poorly planned Blanketeers' march was doomed from the start. However, one aspect of the endeavour was to leave a lasting legacy: the working class had shown that it was capable of mass organisation in the face of military intervention. The authorities' fears now spawned the Manchester and Salford Yeomanry, and one more piece of the Peterloo machinery was in place.

Manchester Mercury's view of the Blanketeers:

Yesterday morning, according to the expectations entertained, crowds of people flocked into town from all directions, as early as eight o'clock, and at about nine, the instigators appeared, on their temporary stage in a cart, and continued to harangue the multitude till their vast increasing numbers suggested the expediency of putting into practice the well-formed arrangements of the civil and military powers. Accordingly, a party of the first Regiment of Dragoons, under Colonel Teesdale, accompanied by the Magistrates of the District, appeared among them, and with an adroitness and decision almost electrical, surrounded the erection, and immediately conveyed the entire group upon it to New Bayley Prison; their attention was then directed to the concourse of auditors, who were forthwith dispersed, without the infliction of any severity. A considerable number of people set out on their mission to London, taking the route of Stockport, but about forty of them were re-conducted back to Manchester, and added to their other unfortunate companions; others were furnished with secure accommodation in Stockport. Most of them were provided with knapsacks, &c., containing blankets and other articles. Upon the examination of some of these travelling equipages, two unusually large knives were discovered.[27]

We see the right-wing press style of the time: the superior, patronising tone, the disregard or trivialisation of the reformers' purpose, the praise for the intervention of the military, and the emphasis on the marchers' weapons (and yet the omission of mention of their injuries).

In a similar sardonic tenor, the *Mercury* was also renowned for the *ad hominem* approach to criticising the reformers:

Of Hunt, we shall say nothing, for the best reason, that there is nothing to say. Who would descant upon a fool's cap, and a rattle of bells, to prove the wearer worthy of the honours with which he has decked himself?[28]

Although it could be argued that the egotistical Hunt had to some extent brought the acid of this depiction upon himself, the same could not be said about the *Mercury*'s vindictive dismissal of Cartwright as 'a weak man with the usual share of the confidence of folly'.[29] And, following the monster gathering at Newhall Hill, Birmingham, in July 1819 the radical Sir Charles Wolseley was treated to the following pen-picture: 'Sir Charles is about forty-five years of age, nearly five feet nine inches high, long pale features, and (as may be guessed) a remarkably wild look, &c.'[30]

A couple of weeks after the Blanketeers started their walk down the Stockport Road, there was an even more fruitless reformers' assembly in a house at Ardwick Bridge, Manchester. A couple of spies had infiltrated the group, so it was a simple matter for Nadin to turn up with the usual reinforcements and arrest twelve people. For good measure, the next day he travelled to Middleton and arrested Bamford and Healey as well, even though they had nothing to do with the Ardwick Bridge assembly. Bamford gives a detailed – and surprisingly good-humoured – account of his arrest and his journey with the accused down to London, where all were acquitted of the charge of High Treason, and eventually released without trial.[31]

This was despite the Reverend Hay's attempt to make a volcano out of a molehill: he accused the Ardwick Bridge group of 'purposes of the blackest enormity', even though the professed intentions of the meeting were well within the parameters of moderate reform.[32] This seems typical of Hay's gadfly persona of the time: his letter to Lord Sidmouth of 30 March contained the report of the theft of a large leaden cistern from a farm at Woodhouses (between Failsworth and Ashton). The purpose of the theft, according to Hay, was to melt the cistern down and make bullets from the lead![33]

The government's reaction to the Blanketeers was to pass the Seditious Meetings Act, which forbade the gathering of more than fifty people without the magistrates' prior knowledge and permission. The mass open-air rallies continued all the same, each major industrial centre having its favourite venue: for example, Sandy Brow in Stockport, Newhall Hill in Birmingham, and St Peter's Field in Manchester.

An artist's impression of St Peter's Church in 1819. (Author's Collection/Phil Blinston)

St Peter's Field was on the southern edge of the town, close to the junction of Oxford Street and Mosley Street. The church of St Peter's, situated immediately to the north-east on the site of the present-day Metrolink station, was not at the time in use, but was still a notable landmark and rendezvous point with its clock tower and its portico entrance affording shelter in bad weather.[34] The field, an unmaintained, rubble-strewn expanse of about 20,000 square yards was roughly the shape of a truncated right-angled triangle: its hypotenuse was Windmill Street, and its eastern base line was formed by the new houses on Mount Street and part of the high wall surrounding the garden of Cooper's Cottage. Its uneven third northern edge took in the Quakers' Meeting House and school building, and a large enclave further west, before ending by the New Jerusalem Church and the junctions of Windmill Street, Watson Street, Lad Lane, and the beginnings of the newly developed Peter Street. Windmill Street had lost its windmill several years before, but the extensive knoll where it had stood remained, and a pub of the same name, situated around halfway along the row of terraced, cellared houses, was a popular watering hole.

The field had already been used several times as a venue for radicals' meetings. Apart from the Blanketeers' assembly, the most significant ones were: 4 November 1816, (5,000 present) chaired by William Fitton, 'to take into consideration the present state of the country'; 9 March 1818, chaired by James Wroe, 'petitioning for Parliament reform', more specifically in protest at the recent suspension of Habeas Corpus; and the largest one to date, 18 January 1819, chaired by Henry Hunt during his first visit to Manchester, drew an estimated crowd of 8,000.

The 18 January gathering was almost a dry run for the following August – at least, until the shenanigans at the theatre later in the week. Aspects that would be echoed at Peterloo were: some of the radicals on the hustings (Wroe, Saxton and Knight), the circuitous route taken by Hunt's carriage and supporters to the field (from Stockport, through Ardwick Green, Piccadilly, Market Street, St Mary's Gate, and after that, as on 16 August), and the cap of liberty and banners on display. Prominent were the slogans NO CORN LAWS, UNIVERSAL SUFFRAGE, RIGHTS OF MAN, and, in gold letters on a red background, HUNT AND LIBERTY.

The meeting itself passed without incident, apart from the platform collapsing at one point. Unperturbed, the radicals tried to declaim from an upper window of the Windmill pub, but when this was stopped by the landlord, they rebuilt the hustings and carried on.[35] The military were on standby but were not ordered into action. All quiet on the St Peter's Field front; but then on the following Friday the reformers, Hunt included, occupied the front row of a box at the Theatre Royal. Some sympathisers in the audience recognised Hunt, whereupon cheers and cries of 'Hunt and Liberty!' went up. Unfortunately, in the predominantly middle-class audience there were plenty of those with anti-reform views, and the cheers were quickly followed by hoots and hisses.

Hunt and renowned reformers parading themselves large as life at the theatre was construed as an affront by many of those present, and one George Torr, a Special Constable, helped by a posse of officers from the 7th Light Dragoons, swords drawn, managed to eject Hunt forcibly from the building. Hunt brought legal proceedings against Torr, accusing the Constable of assault and an attempt to steal his watch, but the case was thrown out of court the following Monday by the magistrates.[36]

By now word of the altercation had spread, and Hunt had sent a note to Bamford, asking him to bring some tough Middleton lads armed with cudgels and iron-rimmed clogs to the Fountain Street entrance of the Theatre Royal that same Monday evening, where their services might be required. The theatre manager, hearing rumours of possible trouble, had closed the theatre for the night, while a crowd, which contained Nadin and some of his troops and the magistrate Colonel John Silvester, gathered outside. Eventually Hunt arrived in a coach. He gave a brief and fervent speech in the street and suggested everyone go peaceably home, which most of them did. Unfortunately, a group of loyalists followed the Orator to his lodgings at the Spread Eagle Inn on Hanging Ditch, where some of them actually entered his room, either to insist he was an unwelcome presence in Manchester, or to offer him out for a fight. Nothing came of it, though, and Bamford's lads, who had repaired to the Robin Hood pub, were not called upon.[37]

When Hunt left for Hampshire on the midnight coach on the Wednesday of that week, the Manchester authorities breathed a sigh of relief. He was not expected to return in the foreseeable future.

Inexorably, matters were coming to the boil. The month after the Theatre Royal incident William Fitton chaired a reform rally of several thousand at Sandy Brow. Fitton took the place of Bagguley, Drummond and Johnston, the three Stockport radicals who had been imprisoned following the Blanketeers' incident of two years previously.

A cap of liberty had been brought in from Manchester, and despite efforts by Chief Constable John Lloyd and his men to intercept it at the Mersey bridge, the talismanic emblem had been smuggled into the meeting. Mounted Special Constables and militia tried to ride through the crowd intending to seize the cap that was provocatively on display on the speakers' platform. They were unsuccessful, driven off by showers of stones and mud thrown by the crowd.[38]

Once again, Bamford made a literary contribution, celebrating the temporary victory by penning the dialect poem 'The Fray of Stockport', in which he mentions William Birch the Chief Constable of Stockport, and the inescapable Joseph Nadin:

> *Then amblin' up the 'Gemmen' came,*
> *Towards the front o'th' hustin';*
> *But soon their folly they did blame,*
> *The 'rabblement' for trustin';*
> *For sticks were up and stones they flew,*
> *Their gentle bodies bruisin',*
> *An' in a hurry they withdrew*
> *Fro' such unmanner'd usin'.*[39]

'Gemmen' is a dialect contraction for 'gentlemen', and in contrasting them and the 'rabblement' Bamford is quite clearly highlighting the class divisions implicit in the confrontation. The crowing tone of the whole poem must have rankled with the forces of law and order present.

Throughout the midsummer weeks of 1819 the south Lancashire area saw a spate of reformers' rallies, the main topic of which was fair Parliamentary representation. Prentice gives the list of participants as: 'Manchester... Oldham, Bolton, Royton, Bury, Heywood, Stockport, Ashton-under-Lyne, Failsworth, Gee Cross, Lees, Middleton, Rochdale, Todmorden...and other towns, all unrepresented in Parliament'.[40] The Manchester assembly, held peaceably on St Peter's Field on 21 June, also recommended a boycott of non-essential taxable items such as beer and tea. The carefully worded major purpose of the meeting was to '[take] into consideration the propriety of petitioning the House of Commons either to devise some means of meliorating our present starving condition at home, or sending us to any of the northern States of America where we can exist'.[41] Clearly desperate times called for desperate measures.

On 1 July, five Manchester magistrates wrote to Lord Sidmouth at the Home Office:

> We cannot have a doubt that some *alarming insurrection* is *in contemplation...* We cannot but applaud the hitherto *peaceable demeanour* of many of the labouring classes, yet we do not calculate upon their remaining unmoved. *Urged on by the harangues of a few desperate demagogues, we anticipate* at no distant period a GENERAL RISING, *and possessing no power to prevent the meetings which are weekly held,* we as magistrates are at a loss how to stem the influence of the dangerous and seditious doctrines which are continually disseminated.
>
> ...We are most anxious to do everything in our power to preserve the *peace* of the Country, but upon this most important point we are UNARMED.
> J. SILVESTER
> R. WRIGHT
> W. MARRIOT
> C. W. ETHELSTON
> J. NORRIS[42]

Here we see – and not for the first or last time – the real source of the Establishment's fears. You could stop a Luddite wrecker with a sword or a musket ball; you could disperse a mob with a posse of truncheon-wielding constables or a cavalry charge; you could arrest and imprison (and *in extremis,* have transported or executed) the obvious ringleaders; but how did you put an end to an idea?

On 12 July the 50,000-strong assembly at Newhall Hill, Birmingham – the reform power base of the Midlands – took matters to another level. The banners included:

THE SOVEREIGNTY OF THE PEOPLE
MAJOR CARTWRIGHT AND THE BILL OF RIGHTS AND
   LIBERTIES
SIR CHARLES WOLSELEY AND NO CORN LAWS
THOMAS JONATHAN WOOLER AND THE LIBERTY OF THE
   PRESS

Wooler was the editor of the ultra-left-wing *Black Dwarf.* The meeting's announced purpose was to 'obtain the Representation of the People of Birmingham in Parliament, and also the Representation of all the unrepresented inhabitants of the Empire'.[43] Sir Charles Wolseley – not present because of a recent bereavement – was unanimously (although illegally) elected by the assembly to the role of 'Legislatorial Attorney and Representative of the inhabitants of Birmingham', tantamount to being MP for the area. This was seen as the first step towards serious and lasting reform.

The very next day, however, a warrant was issued for Wolseley's arrest, purportedly for seditious opinions expressed at a Stockport meeting in June. His principal crime was supposedly to 'invite and stir up the people to hatred and contempt of the government and constitution'.[44] Whether a deliberate ploy by the government or not, the warrant and subsequent court hearing robbed the Birmingham resolution of its thunder, and the huge rally came to nothing.

The comments on the Birmingham meeting in *Wheeler's Manchester Chronicle* cast an ominous shadow:

> Surely this kind of proceeding has been endured long enough: it is time for the apostate sons of John Bull to be restored to common-sense notions, and for their minds to be adjusted to sober and innoxious pursuits. Sedition is too bold, and must receive that salutary check which the present arrangements here and elsewhere are about to apply to her audacity.[45]

This appeared in print just over four weeks before Peterloo, when the recommended 'salutary check' was to become bloody reality.

5

'Make Way for the Female Reformers!'

Throughout the summer of 1819, as a parallel, yet often intertwining, strand of radicalism, there appeared many Female Reform Unions and Societies in the south Lancashire area. The members of these societies often had another battle to fight: that of the engrained attitude of the male.

One of the many illuminating, but less well known, exchanges that took place during one of the post-Peterloo litigations was between the Reverend William Hay and prosecuting counsel Mr Evans. Hay was being questioned about Elizabeth Gaunt, a badly injured woman who had been brought in to Buxton's house (via Hunt's carriage) out of the way of the mayhem on St Peter's Field:

> Mr. Evans: Did you look at her accurately?
>
> Revd Hay: Upon my word, there seemed to be no great temptation.
>
> Mr. Evans: Did you see any blood flowing from her? It may be very laughable to you, but that day is not so laughable to other people.[1]

Despite being an Anglican minister, the Reverend Hay could not resist an unforgivably insensitive (and oafishly sexist) attempt at humour. But the mindset was not unusual: Elizabeth Gaunt was a woman as well as being a member of a lower social class, therefore to Hay doubly open to his facetious remark.

The identities of women, at least in men's eyes, were restricted to a few well-defined types, such as the iconic, the domestic nurturer, the decorative, and the morally suspect. To many who saw her pass on Hunt's barouche, the white-clad Mary Fildes was the embodiment of 'The Goddess of Reason' or 'Liberty'.[2] Carlile compared her to Joan of Arc.[3] Both views sought to idealise the person and co-opt her into the male-specified politics of the day. The patronising notion of women as politically of no consequence, and little more than ornamental accessories to the proceedings, was expressed in the loyalist broadsheet which appeared on the Manchester streets the morning after Peterloo:

> Upon the box was display [*sic*] an amiable specimen of the jem le [*sic*] branch of these philanthropists, who was very busy buffering the air as she went along with a white handkerchief...[4]

When a delegation from the Blackburn Female Reform Union visited Manchester in July, the right-wing *Wheeler's Manchester Chronicle* gave a depressing display of reductionism: 'Amazons harangued the audience on the usual topics, and at considerable length... Might not *Women* be better employed?'[5]

A loyalist lyric, 'The Answer to Peterloo!', which was doing the rounds a couple of months later, pushed the insults further. A woman accompanying Hunt on the hustings (no name is given, but it was probably intended to be Mary Fildes) is described as 'Hunt's concubine'. This foisted identity no doubt made the writer feel that he was justified in penning the gloating couplet:

> *[Hunt's] mistress sent to the hospital her face for to renew,*
> *For she got it closely shaven on the plains of Peterloo.*[6]

Aston's Exchange Herald, one of the town's entrenched reactionary newspapers, would join in with its so-called 'Metrical History of Manchester' some years after Peterloo. The depiction of Mary Fildes, who was in Hunt's barouche as it made its way to St Peter's Field, needs no further commentary:

> *On the box of the carriage, disgracing her sex,*
> *Sat a woman, doll'd out, with a countenance brazen,*
> *Who acted the part of the Goddess of Reason –*
> *'Twas worthy the party – 'twas worthy the wench –*
> *It was just what was done by the worst of the French.*[7]

The right-wing *Manchester Courier* pulled out all the stops in its defamation of females who espoused the cause of reform:

The 'petticoat reformers' of Manchester were described in the *Courier* as 'degraded females', guilty of the 'worst prostitution of the sex, the prostitution of the heart,' 'deserting their station' and putting off the 'sacred characters' of wife and mother 'for turbulent vices of sedition and impiety'.[8]

Another courtroom exchange, this time from the John Lees inquest, between witness John Shuttleworth, a cotton dealer, and coroner Thomas Ferrand, is instructive:

Coroner: You said that the women behaved properly. Do you call it proper for women to carry flags?

Shuttleworth: When I said they behaved properly, I meant that they were peaceable and tranquil; as to their carrying flags, that is another question.[9]

The presence of women bearing flags as a revolutionary emblem at the rally in Leigh marketplace the week before Peterloo provoked reactions of puzzled reproof from the authorities. Colonel Fletcher had written to Lord Sidmouth the day before: 'The female reformers are to act a conspicuous part, by addressing the assemblage from the hustings, and furnishing a cap of liberty.'[10]

A government informant present at the meeting observed with mild astonishment:

…a parade of the female reformers took place, headed by a committee of twelve young women. The members of the female committee were honoured with places in the carts. They were dressed in white, with black sashes; and what was more novel, these women planted a standard with an inscription 'No Corn Laws, Annual Parliaments, and Universal Suffrage'; as well as another standard, surmounted with the cap of liberty, on the platform. Both the flag and the cap were presents from the *Ladies' Union!!*[11]

The male's disapproval of women's political movements did not end with Peterloo. The one-off right-wing satirical organ the *Manchester Comet* of October 1822 contained a supposed illustration of a female reform assembly at the Union Rooms. The crowd of gossiping and gin-swilling women is being harangued by a woman on the table-top. The text indicates she is Peg Files (no doubt a play on Mary Fildes). Also visible in the picture are a

Satire on a female reform meeting, from the *Manchester Comet* (1822). (Chetham's Library)

couple sneaking a kiss and a cuddle in the open doorway, and – a sly dig at Hunt – a parcel of breakfast powder, addressed to 'J. T. Saxton'. Other women who were supposed to be present were Moll Flanders, and recently executed murderesses Mother Brownrigg and Mary Bateman. Beneath the table is the reporter taking notes. According to the text, this fellow when discovered was sent flying down the stairs, propelled by a kick up the backside. The humour is as heavy-handed throughout.[12]

In the post-Napoleonic warrior culture of late Regency Britain, overt masculinity was seen as a vital – if in reality fragile and jealously guarded – attribute. One of the most biting public insults was to question the virility of a male opponent, since according to the inbuilt assumptions of the day this implied so many imperfections. Hunt's jibe of 'Polly Hulton'[13] was echoed by the sobriquet bestowed by Fairburn on 'that egregious coxcomb…Miss Hulton'.[14] Any behaviour deemed craven, duplicitous or unworthy of a gentleman was termed 'unmanly'. The word was used, along with 'degraded, unteachable, unamiable, querulous', by a reviewer to vilify the poet Shelley.[15] Hunt referred to the upper-class scaremongers of Manchester as 'old women in breeches'.[16] William Fitton, in a letter to the *Manchester Observer*, referred to Lord Sidmouth as 'old Mother' and 'old Lady', before dismissing the moneyed class of Manchester as 'our pigtail gentry'.[17]

Since the idea of the dominant and forceful male cannot exist without a well-sequestered notion of the female to help define it, it was felt by many that there was something unnatural and threatening about women who demanded change and marched around in rank and file like the men, brandishing banners and caps of liberty. All this goes a long way to explain the venom shown towards the women at Peterloo, expressed in the comparatively large number of truncheon and sabre attacks on them. This idea will be further explored in Part Two.

Far from being passive extras, the women activists provided a vital contribution to the radical movement in 1819. Of the south Lancashire groups, the Blackburn Female Reformers were the first to achieve wider recognition: firstly because of their address in the *Manchester Observer* in July, in which they advocated annual parliaments, universal suffrage and election by ballot, and secondly from George Cruikshank's cruel 'Belle Alliance' cartoon satirising their involvement in the Reform movement. The women are represented as grotesque caricatures, ugly, bloated and clad in shabby ill-fitting trousers. The one handing over the scarlet silk cap of liberty to a gaggle of leering males is giving a speech full of crude double entendres. The caption – 'The presentation of the Cap of Liberty was accompanied by a short emphatic speech delivered by Mrs. Kitchen!!!' – says it all. The woman's name was actually Alice Kitchin, but no doubt Cruikshank was delighted with the opportunity for a play on words.

Actually, Cruikshank's gross exaggerations were unwarranted, and the satirical swipe was way off target. The main speech was read out by Chairman of the meeting the venerable John Knight, and was 'frequently interrupted by repeated cheers'. His offer to read out the Female Reform Society's address had been greeted with shouts of 'Read! Read! The women forever!' Typical of the speech's emotive power was the following:

> But above all, behold our innocent wretched children! Sweet emblems of our mutual love! How appalling are their cries for bread! We are daily cut to the heart to see them greedily devour the coarse food that some would scarcely give to their swine. – Come then to our dwellings, ye inhabitants of the den of corruption, behold our misery, and see our rags![18]

A letter of support from 'A Female Reformer of Ashton' appeared in the following week's *Observer*; then Stockport, which prided itself in being in the forefront in such matters, acknowledged and praised Blackburn's lead in a letter written to the same newspaper by Mary Hallam, the Secretary of the Stockport Female Reform Society. The objectives of the Society were clearly stated:

> WE WILL instil into the minds of our children…principles which will safely carry them through the maze of political ignorance which now pervades the circle of the HIGHER ORDER.[19]

Around 300 members of the Society of Female Reformers attended the Rochdale meeting on 26 July. They presented a cap of liberty to chairman William Fitton.[20]

Despite appearing in the wake of Mary Wollstonecraft's startlingly progressive views on female emancipation,[21] the manifest stance of these societies was one of auxiliary support for the men, the main concern appearing to be the worsening of quality of life on the domestic front. The Blackburn correspondent bemoans the fact that 'we cannot boast of much female courage', and the theme of home and family recurs in the women's addresses and writings of the time. The idea of votes for women was rarely even considered. However, if words were weapons, the women packed an arsenal. The incendiary letter signed by Susannah Saxton, John Thacker's wife, published in the *Observer* of 31 July, had a view and purpose way beyond the domestic. Susannah was Secretary of the Manchester Female Reformers, whose President was Mary Fildes. The letter predicts that, thanks to an ever more pronounced economic and social divide, the day was fast approaching when Britain would have 'luxury, idleness, dissipation and tyranny on the one hand; and abject poverty, slavery, wretchedness, misery and death, on the other'.

The fulminating statement also presents a near-treasonable deconstruction of the recent wars:

> …the simple story is this, that all this dreadful slaughter was in cool blood, committed for the purpose of Placing upon the Throne of France, contrary to the people's interest and inclination, the present contemptible Louis, a man who has been living for years in this country in idleness, and wandering from

one corner of the island to the other in cowardly and vagabond slothfulness and contempt.

...this war, to re-instate this man...has tended to load our beloved country with such an insurmountable burden of taxation...[22]

Since Susannah must have known the degree of risk when she put her name to it, the letter demonstrates courage indeed.

And sixteen days after publication, Female Reformers in their hundreds from Lancashire towns and villages would march with pride, banners held high, to St Peter's Field.

6

Manoeuvres

On 4 August, Henry Hobhouse, Home Secretary Lord Sidmouth's undersecretary and spokesman, wrote to the magistrate James Norris:

> It will be the wisest course to abstain from any endeavour to disperse the Mob, unless they proceed to acts of Felony or Riot. We have the strongest Reason to believe that Hunt means to preside & to deprecate disorder.[1]

This has often been quoted as proof of the government's recommendation of restraint at the coming meeting. However, it is unrepresentative of the noises issuing from on high. Throughout that year, Hobhouse's communications had shown another side to the Home Office stance:

> (2 March): …your country will not be tranquillized, until Blood shall have been shed either by the Law or the Sword. Lord Sidmouth will not fail to be prepared for either alternative, and is confident that he will be adequately supported by the Magistracy of Lancashire.[2]

> (16 June): If it [the Cap of Liberty] shall be displayed again with Impunity, it will be a deep subject of Regret. And if the Magistrates shall see an opportunity of acting with Vigour, they will recollect that there is no situation in which their Energy can be so easily backed by Military aid as at Manchester, where the Troops are at hand, and may be kept on the alert, if the Civil Power should appear likely to stand in need of their assistance.[3]

> (15 July): …avail yourself of all the [military] Force conceded to you…because confidence will be given to the Civil Authorities from the Knowledge that a considerable armed Force is at their Backs.[4]

Unsettled by the proliferation of mass platform rallies in 1819, the government, via the unequivocal advice (or fuzzy and inclusive innuendoes) delivered by Hobhouse's passing on of Lord Sidmouth's thoughts, appeared to give free rein to the use of military force at these assemblies. Or they at least contributed to the torrid and uncertain atmosphere of the gathering storm, which was to burst with such violence on 16 August.

Norris, writing in July, saw the planned St Peter's Field meeting in terms of an inevitable confrontation: 'it will surely prove a trial of strength and there must be a conflict'.[5]

The radical *Manchester Observer* turned up the heat towards the end of the month with a flamboyant, italicised leader column strewn with capital letters and exclamation marks:

> *No; not with the rack and the scaffold, in our face, will we ever be intimidated from suppressing the TRUTH... Our Cause is the Cause of Our Country...and to our most inveterate Foe, we declare, before God and our Native Land, that we stand upon a Rock, which cannot be removed by hired Magistrates, Parliaments, or Kings!!!*
>
> *...A whole host of SPIES and INFORMERS we are aware has been set upon us – the civil and the military power have in their turns been placed in array against us...*[6]

Just over a week later, the right-wing Manchester newspaper *British Volunteer* stated with ominous clarity what it perceived to be the authorities' stance:

> The Cheshire Magistrates have come to a determination to act with decision, and *suppress all Seditious Meetings immediately as they assemble*, and if the civil power be not sufficient then to read the Riot Act and call in the aid of the military – This is as it should be.[7]

Invited by Joseph Johnson on behalf of the Manchester Patriotic Union Society to preside at an open-air mass meeting on Monday, 9 August, Hunt arrived in Stockport the day before. Hunt was the reformers' man of the moment, having eloquently chaired a peaceable 40,000-plus strong rally in London's Smithfield Market on 21 July. The intention had been to make a triumphal entrance into Manchester on the Monday, but the deputation which met him at Bullock Smithy (Hazel Grove) informed him that the scheduled meeting had been postponed to the following week. This surprised and angered Hunt, whose immediate reaction was to turn

New Bailey Court-House,

SATURDAY, 31st JULY, 1819.

WHEREAS

It appears by an Advertisement in the

"Manchester Observer" Paper.

OF THIS DAY, THAT A PUBLIC AND

Illegal

MEETING,

IS CONVENED

FOR MONDAY,

THE 9th DAY OF AUGUST NEXT,

TO BE HELD ON THE AREA,

Near St. PETER'S CHURCH, in Manchester,

WE, the undersigned *Magistrates* acting for the Counties Palatine of Lancaster and Chester, do hereby Caution all Persons to abstain,

At their Peril

FROM ATTENDING SUCH

ILLEGAL MEETING.

William Hulton,	*J. Holme,*
James Norris,	*R. Marsh,*
John Entwisle,	*Trafford Trafford,*
William Marriott,	*Ralph Fletcher.*
Thomas William Tatton,	

J. and J. HARROP, PRINTERS, MARKET-PLACE, MANCHESTER

Magistrates' notice declaring the 9 August meeting illegal. No such prior ban was placed on the assembly of 16 August. (Chetham's Library) around and head back to Hampshire. It was 'quite in opposition to my own judgement'[8] that he ultimately agreed to stay on the extra week.

The reason for the postponement was that the original aims had been declared illegal by the magistrates:

> To take into consideration the most speedy and effective mode of obtaining Parliamentary Reform in the Commons House of Parliament; and to consider the propriety of the unrepresented inhabitants of Manchester electing a person to represent them in Parliament.

Hunt dismissed this wording as 'a foolish proposition',[9] especially since the resolutions of the Birmingham meeting of a few weeks before, which had 'elected' Sir Charles Wolseley as the people's representative, had also been designated illegal. Saxton had taken expert advice and had been informed that the St Peter's Field aims expressed in this way could easily be interpreted as seditious. So the reformers amended their intention thus:

> To consider the propriety of adopting the most legal and effectual means of obtaining a Reform in the House of Commons.

Hunt spent the night of 8 August at James Moorhouse's Stockport house, and after Herculean persuasion from brush-maker Joseph Johnson, he finally agreed to travel on to Smedley Cottage, Johnson's home situated north of Manchester in Harpurhey.

The location of the cottage was pleasant enough, on the banks of the sylvan river Irk and next door to St Michael's Church, but Hunt seems to have passed the week impatient to be elsewhere. He was later to declare his time at Smedley Cottage 'the most disagreeable seven days that I ever passed in my life, not excepting the period of my solitary imprisonment in the Manchester New Bailey and Ilchester Bastille'. This extreme comment is hard to believe, although it no doubt stemmed from his burgeoning dislike of Johnson, whom he came to see as 'a composition of vanity, emptiness, and conceit'.[10]

Hunt spent the first couple of days at the cottage drafting out a notice, which appeared in the Manchester streets on Wednesday, 11 August. Despite his private misgivings about the rearranged meeting, none of these doubts show in the handbill. It is a stirring appeal to the best qualities of the working classes:

INHABITANTS
OF
Manchester
And Neighbourhood.

FELLOW COUNTRYMEN,

Our enemies are exulting at the victory they profess to have obtained over us, in consequence of the postponement, *for a week,* of the PUBLIC MEETING intended to have been held on Monday last.

The Editor of the London Courier, (although he admits that we are only *checked,* not *subdued*) appears to be as much rejoiced as if he, and his *coadjutors,* had for a time escaped unhurt from the effects of an Earthquake or some other great National Calamity; his *blood-thirsty imitators* of the local press of Manchester, cannot disguise the fears of their employers, although I am informed that they attempt to do it, by resorting to the most vulgar and impotent abuse. To reply to any of their malignant and contemptible efforts, would only tend to drag them forth, for a moment, from their natural insignificance and obscurity; therefore you will bestow on their petty exertions the most perfect indifference; for as they are beneath your anger, so you will not even suffer them to attract your notice.

You will meet on Monday next my friends, and by your *steady, firm, and temperate* deportment, you will convince all your enemies, you feel that you have an *important* and an *imperious public duty* to perform, and that you will not suffer any private consideration on earth, to deter you from exerting every nerve, to carry your praiseworthy and patriotic intentions into effect.

The eyes of all England, nay, of all Europe, are fixed upon you; and every friend of real Reform and of rational Liberty, is tremblingly alive to the result of your Meeting on Monday next.

OUR ENEMIES will seek every opportunity by the means of their sanguinary agents to excite a RIOT, that they may have a pretence for SPILLING OUR BLOOD, reckless of the awful and certain retaliation that would ultimately fall on their heads.

EVERY FRIEND OF REAL AND EFFECTUAL REFORM is offering up to Heaven a devout prayer, that you may follow the example of your brethren of the Metropolis; and by your *steady, patient, persevering,* and *peaceable* conduct on that day, frustrate their HELLISH AND BLOODY PURPOSE.

Come, then, my friends, to the Meeting on Monday, armed with NO OTHER WEAPON but that of a self-approving conscience; determined not to suffer yourselves to be irritated or excited, by any means whatsoever, to commit any breach of the Public Peace.

Our opponents have not attempted to show that our reasoning is fallacious, or that our conclusions are incorrect, by any other argument but the *threat of Violence,* and to put us down by the force of the *Sword, Bayonet,* and the *Cannon.* They assert that your leaders do nothing but mislead and deceive you, although they well know, that the eternal principles of *truth* and *justice* are too deeply engraven on your hearts; and that you are at length become (fortunately for them) too well acquainted with your own rights, ever again to suffer any man, or any faction, to mislead you.

We hereby invite the Boroughreeve, or any of the *Nine wise Magistrates,* who signed the Proclamation declaring the meeting to have been held on Monday last, *Illegal,* and threatening at the *same time* all those who *abstained from going* to the said Meeting; we invite them to come amongst us on Monday next. If we are *wrong* it is their duty, as *Men,* as *Magistrates,* and as *Christians,* to endeavour to set us right by argument, by reason, and by the mild and *irresistible precepts of persuasive truth;* we promise them an attentive hearing, and to abide by the result of *conviction alone.* But once for all we repeat, that we despise their THREATS, and abhor and detest those, who would direct or controul the mind of man by VIOLENCE or FORCE.

I am, my Fellow Countrymen,

Your sincere and faithful Friend,

Henry Hunt.

Smedley Cottage, Wednesday, August 11, 1819.

J. WROE, PRINTER, OBSERVER OFFICE, MARKET-STREET, MANCHESTER.

Hunt's handbill, posted in the Manchester streets five days before Peterloo.
(John Rylands Library)

You will meet on Monday next my friends, and by your *steady, firm, and temperate* deportment, you will convince all your enemies, you feel that you have an *important* and an *imperious public duty* to perform, and that you will not suffer any private consideration on earth, to deter you from exerting every nerve, to carry your praiseworthy and patriotic intentions into effect.

The non-violent approach is very clearly exhorted. Hunt calls for '*steady, patient, persevering,* and *peaceable* conduct' at the gathering, and insists that the demonstrators attend '*armed* with NO OTHER WEAPON but that of a self-approving conscience'.[11]

Bamford paid Hunt a visit on the Friday, while the Orator was having the finishing touches put to his portrait. Hunt repeated his insistence on there being no weapons brought to the meeting, but Bamford declared himself less than happy with the ban. The Middleton man foresaw the possibility of trouble and was of the opinion that during the 'King's Peace' it was justifiable – and legal – to retaliate if you were attacked whilst engaged in a lawful activity. Perhaps remembering the Theatre Royal incident, Bamford suggested 'a score or two of cudgels, just to keep the specials at a respectful distance'. But Hunt was adamant. With what appears in hindsight to be a naive optimism, he was convinced that a peaceful and legal assembly would not be attacked, and that the magistrates and constables would be an effective peace-keeping presence.[12] Eventually Bamford agreed, and was to communicate the weapons ban to the Middleton and Rochdale contingents.

Later that day Hunt was visited by two gentlemen from Bury, who told him that they had heard he was to be arrested on some pretext during the Monday's gathering, and offering bail should this be the case. Intent on covering every base, and not wishing the authorities to have an excuse to disrupt the meeting, Hunt drove to the New Bailey courthouse the next day to get more information on the matter. He first asked the magistrate Richard Wright if there was any charge against him: if so, he was willing to surrender himself there and then. Wright appeared surprised at the question and called for Nadin, who also insisted there was no charge against Hunt. Even though he was 'not wholly satisfied with the sincerity of their language' Hunt returned to Smedley Cottage.[13]

Adding to the generally taut feeling, on early Sunday morning there was an incident on the White Moss moors which was to have serious and long-lasting repercussions.

It was a result of a session of 'drilling' or infantry-style marching and wheeling, an activity which had become very popular with the workers, especially from the upland settlements of Bury, Middleton and Bolton.

Bamford, having noted that newspaper reports of workers' rallies had hitherto taunted the participants on their 'ragged, dirty appearance', saw the rationale of marching practice (and the wearing of smart clothing) as creating 'a display of cleanliness, sobriety and decorum...an expertness and order while moving in bodies'.[14] This was why large groups of men – often accompanied by the womenfolk[15] – would repair to the moors to engage in drilling sessions, practising marching in file and halting to orders. The response to the command to fire was simulated by a clap of the hands.

Elsewhere, Bamford presents the sessions in an Arcadian, nay, Wordsworthian light:

> When dusk came, and we could no longer see to work, we jumped from our looms, and rushed to the sweet cool air of the fields, or the waste lands, or the green lane sides. We mustered, we fell into rank, we faced, marched, halted, faced about, counter-marched, halted again, dressed, and wheeled, in quick succession, and without confusion; or, in the grey of a fine Sunday morning, we would saunter through the mists, fragrant with the night odour of flowers, and of new hay, and ascending the Tandle Hills, salute the broad sun as he climbed from the high moors of Saddleworth. Maidens would sometimes come with their milk-cans from the farms of Hoolswood or Gerrard-hey, or the fold near us; and we would sit and take delicious draughts...whilst a favoured youth or so might be permitted to add a tender word or a salute – when, blushing and laughing, away would the nymphs run...[16]

All this might have been more persuasive had it not been for a violent confrontation on the White Moss moors the day before Peterloo. Early in the morning James Murray the confectioner – 'Gingerbread Jack' – who had been involved in the hounding of Hunt after the Theatre Royal episode the previous January, went onto the moors with police clerk John Shawcross to get a closer look at what appeared to be military-style manoeuvres. Before long Murray was asked to fall in to the ranks, to which he replied 'soon'. The delay made him – and presumably Shawcross too – only the more noticeable, and the word 'spy' ran through the ranks. Murray claimed he heard, 'They are constables...d—n them, murder them', so both men thought it prudent to make themselves scarce. As they ran off they were pursued by 'eighty or ninety men' throwing clods of earth. Shawcross was overtaken first, and the crowd 'beat him, and knocked him in the ditch'. By the time the swifter Murray was reached, the pack had dwindled to 'twenty or thirty men', who, according to the quarry, 'began to beat me with sticks and kick me most violently with their clogs'. After issuing a death threat and forcing their victim to get down on his knees and renounce his role of constable and allegiance to the King, the mob allowed Murray to stumble away. It was early the next day that he returned home to Withy Grove, where he was confined to bed.[17] The *Manchester Observer* could not resist the waspish comment: 'After his arrival at home, he was visited by no less than four surgeons, who declared that his brain was not affected; the skull, it seems, was proof even to *clogs*. He is now convalescent.'[18]

Nevertheless, right-wing fears seemed to be vindicated: a local farmer James Heap, of Thornham Fold between Middleton and Rochdale, had been witness to a gathering of a 'great number' of drillers on the Tandle Hills on Sunday, 1 August. He claimed to have felt so threatened by the numbers involved that henceforward he kept two pitchforks and a gun at the top of his bed.[19] Magistrate Norris wrote to Lord Sidmouth on 5 August, expressing the fear that 'drilling…promises to become a most formidable engine of rebellion'.[20]

Despite Hunt's and Bamford's insistence on a peaceable approach to the St Peter's Field meeting, and the fact that the overwhelming majority of participants never had any intention of using violence, in the loyalists' eyes the attack on Murray and Shawcross was surely proof that the radicals were up to no good, and that they had planned militant insurrection all along. It also bestowed a more sinister colour upon the 'drillings', and did nothing to lessen the Establishment's fears for the morrow. During the subsequent and prolonged litigations, 'Gingerbread Jack' would become a star witness for the authorities, for whom the White Moss incident was like manna from heaven. Murray's tale, however, may have grown in the telling. He accused one Thomas Ryder of being one of his attackers, but when it was later proved in court that Ryder had an alibi, Murray withdrew his accusation.[21]

Hunt, who generally disapproved of this 'playing at soldiers', had been invited to go and review the Sunday drilling, but suspecting that the invitation had come from a spy and, smelling some sort of trap, he had declined.[22]

It was not only the authorities who felt apprehensive. The young radical George Swift related that on Sunday morning he was walking down Market

Street with John Thacker Saxton, when the newspaperman suggested they go to the Union Rooms (where the Female Reform Committee met) and tell the women not to go to the next day's gathering on St Peter's Field, 'for it will be a bloody day every Yeoman's sword is ground on purpose'. Swift commented that he felt that 'Mr. Saxton knew more than he dare tell me'. Also, Hunt confesses in his *Memoirs* that he felt 'a degree of anxiety' throughout the day.[23]

The magistrates had had daily consultations to decide on a course of action, and on the day before Peterloo they 'gave notice to Lt.-Col L'Estrange…of our wish to have the assistance of the Military on the 16th'.[24]

At 11 p.m. on that Sunday evening magistrate James Norris penned a note addressed to Lord Sidmouth at the Home Office, stating that it was 'scarcely possible' to expect peace, and that the town was in 'a state of painful uncertainty'.[25]

Beset by such a climate of attrition and mistrust, so dawned Monday, 16 August – the ghastlier morrow.

PART TWO

Flashpoint

(16 August 1819)

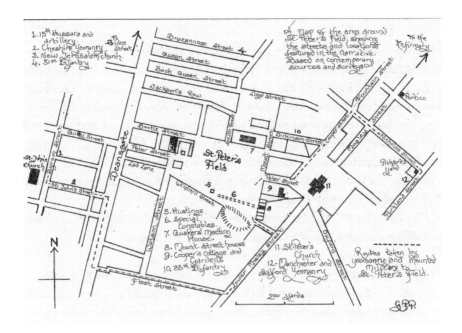

(Author's collection/Rob Hall)

On the Roads to Manchester

(7 a.m.–1 p.m.)

Monday morning dawned bright and sunny, and would remain so, warm and cloudless with a slight breeze. The day's business was soon set in motion.

From 7 a.m., following the instructions of the Boroughreeve, a team of workers under Thomas Worrell the Assistant Surveyor of Paving set about clearing the as-yet deserted St Peter's Field of stones, brickbats, and anything else that could conceivably improvise as a weapon. As there had recently been building sites close to the croft, this must have taken a while, and 'about a quarter of a [wagon] load' of stones and fragments of brick was removed.[1] This seemingly routine chore was to assume great significance later.

From around 8 a.m. a blizzard of large printed placards appeared on walls throughout central Manchester and Salford. The text read:

> The Boroughreeves and Constables of Manchester and Salford most earnestly recommend the peaceable and well disposed inhabitants of those towns as much as possible to remain in their own houses during the whole of this day Monday Aug. 16th inst. and to keep their children and servants within doors.
>
> Edward Clayton   Boroughreeve of Manchester
> John Moore Jnr.   Constables
> Jonathan Andrew
> John Greenwood   Boroughreeve of Salford
> James Cooke   Constables
> Josiah Collier[2]

That word 'servants' is the giveaway: it is clear which segment of Manchester society this notice was aimed at.

By 8.30 a.m. the military presence was already mobilising in Manchester. Six troops of the 15th Hussars, a cavalry regiment under the command of Lt-Col Dalrymple, were making their way from the barracks in the area that was to become St George's Park, Hulme (renamed Barracks Park in 1994) to their position on Byrom Street, a block to the west of Deansgate. They were accompanied by two field cannon and a troop of horse artillery with a Major Dyneley in charge. It was a Lt-Col L'Estrange who was in overall command of these troops. A squadron of the Cheshire Yeomanry, having mustered on Sale Moor close to Chief Constable John Moore's house, would soon join them, nearby on St John's Street. During the morning the volunteer Manchester and Salford Yeomanry – with their freshly sharpened sabres – were gathering in Pickford's Yard on Portland Street. A few policemen on horseback rode out onto the main thoroughfares into Manchester, so as to monitor the progress of the marchers.

People had started to assemble on St Peter's Field soon after 9 a.m.[3] Out in the satellite towns, preparations for the day had begun early too.

In many cases village bands accompanied the walkers. Usually performing at social functions or local processions, the musicians typically played flutes or fifes, slide trumpets, keyed bugles, French horns, bassoons, clarinets and snare drums.[4] Perhaps predictably, the Mancunian reactionary set heard the fifes and drums, and immediately made a military connection. Indeed, after twenty years of almost constant warfare, the piercing sound of fifes backed by the rhythmic thunder of drums had gone a long way towards conditioning people to link this music with the battleground. The instruments were also associated with the American and French revolutionary armies. It was another piece of supposed evidence, reinforced by reports of the drilling on the moors, leapt on by those wishing to claim that the marchers had insurrectionist aims.

The authorities would point to two other salient aspects of the march, both paraded on tall poles for all to see: the Phrygian bonnets or red 'caps of liberty', and the banners.

The bonnet, of course, had been a famous emblem of the revolutionaries in France. It would remain as symbolic headgear of *la Marseillaise*, the iconic figure ever to be associated with the *Liberté, Egalité, Fraternité* motto. For the forces of law and order, this was further proof that the marchers had revolution in mind. The words on some of the banners pushed their fears a stage further, reminiscent of recent insurrectionary watchwords in the American colonies and France:

LIBERTY AND FRATERNITY
UNITY AND STRENGTH
NO BOROUGH-MONGERING – UNITE AND BE FREE
LIBERTY IS THE BIRTHRIGHT OF MAN
TAXATION WITHOUT REPRESENTATION IS UNJUST AND
   TYRANNICAL
THE PEOPLE THE SOURCE OF ALL JUST GOVERNMENT
HENRY HUNT, THE UNDAUNTED FRIEND OF LIBERTY
NO CORN LAWS
THE PEOPLE ARE THE LEGITIMATE REPRESENTATIVES OF
   SOVEREIGNTY
SUFFRAGE UNIVERSAL
PARLIAMENTS ANNUAL
SUCCESS TO THE FEMALE REFORMERS OF STOCKPORT
BREAD OR BLOOD
LET US DIE LIKE MEN AND NOT BE SOLD LIKE SLAVES
ELECTION BY BALLOT
EQUAL REPRESENTATION OR DEATH[5]

The vast majority of these attractively embroidered banners were works of art, sending out a clear signal: the marchers were no makeshift gang, but were the manifestation of serious purpose and forethought.

Nevertheless, the sinister impression made by the last-mentioned banner – 'the black flag' – borne before the Saddleworth and Lees Union contingent by Joseph 'Doc' Healey, would be made much of by the authorities. Even Bamford described it as 'one of the most sepulchral looking objects that could be contrived'.[6] Attorney Edward Owen would declare that many people were of the opinion: 'That black flag scared me.'[7] One of the standard-bearers, John Ashton of Cowhill near Oldham, would not survive the day, sabred by the Yeomanry and trampled on by the fleeing crowd. Also prominent in the Saddleworth procession were Edmund and William Dawson, who between them carried a cap of liberty on a tall pole. William would be sabred and crushed to death on St Peter's Field, and Edmund would die in the Infirmary of sword wounds to his head.[8]

By late afternoon nearly all of the banners and caps of liberty would have been taken or destroyed. At Hunt's initial hearing at the New Bailey, magistrate James Norris, Chairman of the Bench, summed up the establishment's fears, albeit with a highly selective – and therefore distorted – gloss:

Replicas of the Saddleworth banner. (Author's Collection/Saddleworth Museum)

[They came] with such insignia and in such a manner, with the *black flag*, the *bloody dagger*, with 'Equal Representation or Death'.

...They came in a threatening manner – they came under the banner of death, thereby showing they meant to overthrow the Government.[9]

'Overthrowing the Government' would have been laughingly denied by the vast majority of the demonstrators. Despite the underlying seriousness of the issues to be aired in Manchester, there was more of a celebratory atmosphere to the processions. Many of the participants had packed picnic lunches, typically plain fare of bread and cheese; and of course, they would have the option of visiting hostelries en route. With the music, the flags, the women and children in the ranks, and the prospect of an extra day's holiday, sinister intentions were furthest from most people's minds.

Hunt, watching the passage of some of the walkers from his bedroom window at Smedley Cottage, noted their happy yet intent demeanour:

...men, women and children, accompanied by flags and bands of music, cheerfully passing along towards the place of meeting. Their appearance and manner altogether indicated that they were going to perform an important, a sacred duty to themselves and their country, by offering up a joint and sincere prayer to the Legislature to relieve the poor and needy, by rescuing them from the hands of the agents of the rich and powerful, who had oppressed and persecuted them.[10]

The whole community of Middleton had been alive to the event from around 8 a.m., either as participants on the march, or to watch the procession gather and leave from Barrowfields. A fine musical band accompanied the walkers. Sprigs of laurel were worn on hats as a symbol of peace. There was a red velvet cap of liberty atop a pole, and two smart silk flags: blue with gold lettering declaring UNITY AND STRENGTH, and on the opposite side LIBERTY AND FRATERNITY; then another with gold lettering on a green background: PARLIAMENTS ANNUAL, with SUFFRAGE UNIVERSAL on the reverse. Both flags would have a story to tell: the green and gold one, carried by journeyman hatter Thomas Redford of Wood Street, would be hacked out of his hands by the Yeomanry; and the blue banner would be the only one to survive the day in the hands of the demonstrators.[11]

Bamford stood on a chair to address the gathering before moving off. He exhorted them not to break ranks, but to 'walk comfortably and agreeably together'. They were to offer no insult or resistance to anyone they met, and to leave all sticks and similar weapons behind.[12] Dressed in their Sunday best (or close enough as to make no difference), marching in ranks of five abreast, and with the handsomest youths – both male and female – strategically placed at the front of the procession, the walkers were keen to impress upon onlookers that they were anything but the 'mob-like rabble' that certain press reports had hitherto presented them as.

Bamford's wife Jemima left their daughter with a responsible neighbour, and 'joined some other married females at the head of the procession... neatly dressed as the wives of working men'. Husband and wife would be separated by the crowds and the events of the day, and Jemima was later to claim that she had felt a premonition of disaster the closer they got to Manchester.[13]

Once joined by the 3,000-strong Rochdale contingent, the column numbered around 6,000.[14] The Rochdale group had gathered its supporters, again predominantly weavers, from the mills of the town itself, as well as from outlying hamlets such as Lower Place. They had assembled in the Market Place and took the new (1808) toll road to Manchester. Among their

Replica of one of the Middleton banners. (Author's Collection/ Middleton Local History Resources)

Samuel Bamford, some years after Peterloo. (Middleton Local History Resources)

number was 43-year-old weaver William Kershaw, who within a few hours would be ridden down by a cavalry horse, sustaining serious injuries in his chest and head, his 'flesh stripped from his legs'.[15]

Rochdale had a reputation for militancy, as had been evident from the burning down of the town prison in 1808. Local people had been imprisoned in 1814 for collecting signatures to one of Cartwright's petitions.[16] There had been a reformers' meeting on Cronkeyshaw Moor in 1817, shortly after the Blanketeers' incident. One of the standards had displayed the highly provocative DESTRUCTION TO ALL LEGITIMATE GOVERNMENTS, and among the estimated 30,000 crowd there were a claimed 5,000 female reformers.[17]

Those taking exception to the popular cause were occasionally treated to the reprisal known as 'Old Betty', which meant having their windows smashed. Within the next decade or so there would be several worker-management disputes, sometimes ending in violence or even deaths.[18] Eventually, of course, a less confrontational version of the town's radical stance would have a permanent and internationally significant result, as twenty-five years after Peterloo, Rochdale would be the birthplace of the Cooperative movement.

By the time the halfway point at Blackley was reached, the Rochdale-Middleton procession had collected even more support, and a halt was called in order to partake of some 'Sam Ogden's ale' at the Red Lion in Harpurhey. Mid-morning, a bricklayer by the name of John Whittaker was working at the side of the road when he saw 'very large crowds of people going to the meeting…marching in military order with flags and caps of liberty and bands of music'. His banter with them included the ominous prediction that 'you will not come back as merry as you go'.[19]

Bamford was half-expecting the procession to be blocked at the toll bar where the road split at Collyhurst. But no; apart from a couple of policemen on horseback who merely observed the marchers, there was no sign of their being prevented from entering Manchester.

Hunt had left Smedley Cottage around noon in his open-top carriage drawn by two horses. Riding with him were Richard Carlile, John Knight, and co-owner of the *Observer*, Joseph Johnson.[20] He was accompanied by a large crowd of supporters whose numbers were to grow as they made their way south along the road to Manchester. The procession was soon met by Mary Fildes with her Committee of Female Reformers, all dressed in white. Hunt thought it a good idea to allow Mary, 'a remarkably good figure',[21] to join him in the carriage, which again shows his eye for image – and an attractive woman. She took her position alongside the driver and rode into town waving a white handkerchief.[22] The Female Reformers, who followed the barouche on foot, held aloft a large flag depicting a woman in the style of Britannia holding the scales of justice and, in an oblique biblical reference, stamping on a symbolic serpent. This banner will have a substantial part to play in our story.

It was a message from Hunt that caused the Middleton and Rochdale contingent to return to the Collyhurst junction and take the alternative route to St Peter's Field, via Oldham Road, Newtown and Piccadilly. Hunt had his reasons for choosing his own route, and Bamford – who was already finding the nimbus fading from his one-time hero – after a short disagreement soon complied. Besides, the Newtown diversion afforded Bamford's procession the opportunity of being cheered by the Irish community of Manchester. The green flag and the band's playing 'St Patrick's Day in the Morning' drew loud and emotional support from the inhabitants of the district, leaving, as Bamford describes them: 'those warm-hearted suburbans capering and whooping like mad'.[23] Despite the suggestion made by Bamford's phrase, the casualty lists show that there were a good number of Irish immigrant workers amongst the demonstrators at Peterloo.

Plaque commemorating the Peterloo procession from Oldham and surrounding areas. (Author's collection)

On St Peter's Field, the Oldham, Lees, Crompton and Saddleworth contingents had already arrived. The cavalcade had left Bent Green soon after 8 a.m. with its cap of liberty and ELECTION BY BALLOT banner held high. Among them was 22-year-old John Lees, already a Waterloo veteran at 18, who was known as an outgoing, happy person who worked in his father's cotton mill. He was an enthusiastic participant who was spotted by a friend running to join his fellow marchers before they set off. His father had watched him leave the house 'as hearty then as ever he was since he was born'.[24] Another member was 62-year-old Thomas Buckley of Burnley Lane, described by a fellow townsman as 'a person fanciful to the fruit garden, a staunch patriot, an enemy to oppression'.[25] Within a matter of weeks both Thomas and John would be dead from wounds received on that day.

The procession from Oldham, which contained around 150 standard-bearing women,[26] was swelled yet further when Failsworth was reached, where they were joined by groups from Royton (with their Women's Reform Society banner) and Chadderton. Here the gathering had been organised on the main road, by the Political Pole. With one of those wrong-footing ironies that history supplies now and again, the original 1793 Pole had been erected 'to demonstrate the loyalty of the township and its hatred of Tom Paine, and all his works'. In gold lettering there could be read the dedication to 'the King, Church, and present glorious Constitution'. Nonetheless, adding to the tone of ingenuous celebration on the day, the Failsworth contribution included a banner-carrying troop of twenty-four young women dressed all in white.[27] One of their number, a Mrs Dunkerley, would fight hard to hang on to her red and green silk flag when a Yeoman tried to cut it out of her hands later that day.[28] Another of the Failsworth women, Ellen Brindle from Dob Lane, would be forced by the crowd into a Windmill Street cellar, from where she was carried unconscious into a nearby house.[29]

During the rest period at a nearby inn (probably the Crown and Cushion, as this was closest to the Pole) 'Doc' Healey downed a noggin of gin, toasting 'success to the proceedings of the day'.[30]

Further down the Oldham Road the Newton Heath and Miles Platting group joined the procession. Their leader was the 16-year-old silk weaver Elijah Ridings, whose uncle had been arrested by Nadin in the Ardwick spy-plot incident of 1817. Young Elijah was to have a narrow escape that day.

At New Cross, by which time this contingent had grown to 6,000, it was decided to jettison any sticks deemed unnecessary.[31]

Eastwards of Manchester there was the weaving centre and market town of Ashton-under-Lyne, surrounded by its industrial settlements of Charlestown, Hurst, Taunton, Dukinfield, Smallshaw Green, Boston and Little Moss. All of these places contributed support, forming a contingent of around 2,000, of whom at least twenty would receive serious injuries that afternoon. The outlying Pennine mill communities of Stalybridge and Mossley also sent a deputation via Ashton, with 65-year-old Nancy Prestwich carrying the banner at the front of the column. Nancy, a Mossley woman, was noticeable in her crimson dress and black bonnet, in which she wore the laurel sprig of peace. Uniquely among the processions, though, it was the group from Ashton that did not contain any women who travelled as members of a Female Reform Union.[32]

Joseph Prestwick, a weaver from Old Street in nearby Droylsden, was part of a group of six or seven which also walked along the road from Ashton, but separate from the main group. It was the promise of a spectacle which attracted this small band to St Peter's Field, as the expectation was: 'It will be a grand sight.'[33] Joseph would receive a sabre slash on his hand, and William Thornley, also from Droylsden, would be trampled on and cut on the head.[34]

The Stockport procession, having assembled at the by now usual meeting place of Sandy Brow, set out along the old Roman road (the London coach road) to Manchester. Among their estimated 1,500 number were some forty members of the Female Reformers of Stockport. 'Mrs. Gaunt...wearing a white dress and cap of liberty'[35] was prominent, as was fellow reformer Mary Waterworth. Mary would be described in one of the trials as 'a profligate amazon',[36] showing once again the male's discomfort with women who did not conform to one of the currently accepted stereotypes.

James Moorhouse, accompanied by his six-month pregnant wife, overtook the marchers in his carriage about 2 miles north of the town. The procession passed him again as he was watering his horses by the Midway House inn, and he took the lead once more at Longsight, entering Piccadilly some ten minutes before them. Moorhouse's estimate of numbers was 'near one thousand men and boys, and near one hundred women and young girls'. He described their demeanour as 'perfectly peaceable'.[37] The suggestion that Moorhouse hire out the roof of his coach at a shilling a time for those who wished to get a better view of proceedings in St Peter's Field was overruled, on the grounds of potential damage to the vehicle. Moorhouse then made his way via the field to Deansgate, where he met up with Hunt's carriage.[38]

Francis Philips described the Stockport procession in a similar vein:

On the 16th August I went on the Stockport Road about 11 or a little after, and I met a great number of persons advancing towards Manchester with all the regularity of a regiment, only they had no uniform. They were all marching in files, principally three abreast. They had two banners with them. There were persons by the side, acting as officers and regulating the files. The order was beautiful indeed.[39]

When the Stockport faction reached the White Bear pub in Piccadilly, their fellow marchers from Ashton-under-Lyne were visible,[40] and the two groups joined together for the final walk down Mosley Street. They had been the first contingent to arrive at around 11.30 a.m., and London reporter Charles Wright, already on the hustings cart, described the order of the procession:

Martial music.
A deputation of 12 maiden reformers with white caps.
Two banners each of which was surmounted with a cap of liberty. One of these banners bore the inscription of *Annual Parliaments* and *Universal Suffrage*, on the reverse, *Vote by ballot*. The second banner had an inscription *No Corn Laws*.

Mosley Street in 1819. The Portico is on the left, and St Peter's Church is in the distance. (Portico Library)

Women next marched in procession four abreast, generally with handkerchiefs slung over their heads, and tied under the chin. In two or three instances, I observed these women had infants lashed to their backs.

Next followed females four and four of all ages and sizes, from ten years of age and upwards.

The men closed the rear, marching four abreast, generally arm in arms with walking sticks. This party was more than twenty minutes in coming on the ground. They took their stations in an orderly manner, the women forming the inner circle round the cart.[41]

The 5,000-strong Salford contingent had assembled from across the Borough, including from scattered townlets such as Pendlebury, Barton-on-Irwell, Eccles, Irlam o' th' Height, and Pendleton. The procession converged on New Bailey Bridge with its 'high parapets of dull red stone',[42] at the time the only viable pedestrian and vehicular crossing of the Irwell from Salford to the Deansgate and St Peter's Field area of south Manchester. The column would have passed the grim fortress of the New Bailey prison on the right, and a few hundred yards upstream the Collegiate Church of St Mary's – the Cathedral from 1847 – would have been visible beyond the riverside slum dwellings and warehouses.

James Crompton from Barton-on-Irwell would not survive his injuries received that day. He would be trampled on by Yeomanry horses during the dispersal of the crowds.

Judith Kilner and her friend Martha Partington were both from King Street, Eccles. Judith, mother of five children and pregnant at the time, would sustain a dislocated hip during that afternoon's mayhem.[43] According to a couple of sources, there is a poignant detail from the Salford march into Manchester: during a stop in a pub Martha stood with a drink in her hand and toasted the success of the day, adding that she hoped to God she might never return home alive if the meeting were to achieve nothing.[44] From the moment that she lifted her glass, the 38-year-old mother of two children had less than four hours to live.

An estimated 3,000 walkers had assembled on The Square in the centre of Bury, leaving for Manchester between 8 and 9 a.m. The procession, which contained 'a great many women and children',[45] centred on the weaver William Entwisle of King Street, who carried the single Bury banner. It would be alleged at the Hunt trial that the flagpole was crowned with 'a bloody dagger'. This view was modified by Matthew Cowper, an accountant and lawyer's secretary, who saw it as 'a barbed point…painted red'. William Burns described the addition as a fleur-de-lys, and claimed that he had painted it red solely because he had done so late on the Saturday night previous to the march, and there had been no time for him to replenish his stock of yellow paint.[46]

The Bury contingent kept mostly to the main road into Manchester, passing through Cheetham Hill, where an observer remarked on their 'very orderly' deployment.[47] Some small groups took the hill paths, especially from the outlying village of Tottington, 2 miles to the north-west of Bury centre. These minor groups included weavers William Haworth and Samuel Kaye, both of whom would receive 'severe' sabre cuts later that day.[48]

The bulk of the Bolton contingent – most of them weavers – would probably have assembled on Dr Taylor's field, a 300 x 80 yard stretch of open ground alongside Moor Lane, roughly in the space now occupied by the County Court and the Market Hall.[49] There were smaller groups, however, such as the one from Little Bolton, the hamlet north of the river Croal. This group of four contained Joseph Hindle from Duncan Street, who would be cut by a sabre and forced by the crowd into a cellar. His fellow marcher William Cheetham would be attacked by Meagher the Yeoman trumpeter on Peter Street. William Thompson, a weaver who lived on a street opposite Dr Taylor's field, would lose an eye that day after receiving a blow from a sabre.

Little is known about the marchers from the south-west axis of Altrincham, Sale and Stretford. There is a record of one Thomas Chadwick from Stretford injured at Peterloo,[50] and there may not have been support from the towns further down the Chester Road. There is peripheral contemporary evidence of 'constantly increasing pauperism' in Altrincham, partly alleviated by a well-established system of charity and the dreaded Broadheath workhouse – about which there were 'sinister rumours as to its management'.[51] Just up the road in Sale, poverty and hunger were rife, and a common crime among the poorer people at the time was the stealing of potatoes by uprooting them from farmers' fields. There was a fear of seditious influence from Manchester, as a few years beforehand the local innkeepers were advised:

> …to discourage all conversation tending to inflame the public mind, and as it is suspected that evil-disposed persons are travelling about the country to excite a spirit of discontent and uneasiness, they are requested to be particularly watchful of all strangers who may enter their houses.[52]

Given this context of poverty and murmurs of agitation, it is possible that a group would have walked to Peterloo from these townlets, although the smaller populations would have meant a comparatively minor participation. The same qualifications apply to any assumed contingent from Wigan and the towns of Westhoughton, Atherton and Leigh; but it should be remembered that Wigan and its surrounding settlements would hold its own 20,000-strong reformers' rally in November.

Much was to be made by the authorities of the marchers allegedly carrying 'clubs' or 'bludgeons': but were these implements really nothing more than walking sticks? The majority view was that there was nothing threatening about them. After all, as we have seen, both Hunt and Bamford had expressly forbidden the carrying of any weapon, and many sticks had been jettisoned en route.

At the John Lees inquest, John Shuttleworth, a Unitarian cotton dealer, stated: 'I saw in the hands of the people common walking sticks and nothing else. It did not appear to me that more than one or two in ten even had a walking stick.'[53]

William Michelroyd of Silk Street, an Irishman who had lived in England for thirty-one years, insisted that the sticks he saw were 'no bludgeons or shillelaghs'. Another Irish expatriate, the weaver Alexander Anderson, described the staffs as 'small rods'.[54] Edward Baines, the *Leeds Mercury* reporter, saw them as 'walking sticks; and sometimes lighter'. Even warehouse owner Francis Philips, one of the loyalists' most ardent apologists, conceded at the Redford vs. Birley trial that they were 'such as countrymen walk with'. There is also a telling detail given by Ann Jones, a witness at the same trial: she saw men throwing down their sticks in a bid to beg for mercy from the rampant cavalry.[55]

Philips, however, also joined the chorus of loyalists who saw something sinister in the carried sticks. He had ridden with a friend to Ardwick Green to monitor the arrival of the Ashton contingent, and observed the following:

Nearly half of the men carried stout sticks, many had them shouldered, and one man particularly attracted my notice, from his audacious appearance, having on his shoulder a club, as thick as a wrist, rough, newly cut, with the bark on, and many knots projecting: my eye being directed to him, he shook his club at me, in a menacing manner.[56]

This business of shouldering the staves would be pinpointed by the magistrates and their supporters, firstly as proof that they were not being used as walking sticks, and secondly to emphasise the supposed military deployment of the marchers. Some reports – admittedly mostly the rhetoric of the right-wing oligarchy and its supporters – stressed the sturdy nature of the 'cudgels' and their potential as weapons. However, the accusation attempted by *Wheeler's Manchester Chronicle* the following Saturday (repeated in the official Magistrates' Statement the following year) had a whiff of desperation about it: 'many of the Reformers having shouldered large sticks and bludgeons, as representative of muskets'.

Another embellishment to the cudgels tale was the imagined morph of the weapons into pikes. A letter to *The Times* from a Manchester correspondent on 24 August poured scorn on the idea:

> I have myself seen several cabinet collections of these formidable weapons, and I yesterday [Monday 23 August] examined the grand police depôt of them in the Infirmary. This…arsenal contains 45, but not *one* of them is pointed or fitted for a pike-head. Two hundred sticks were collected in the area by the inhabitants of Windmill Street and the police, and they all assure me that *not one of them was so constructed*.[57]

Were other weapons brought by the marchers to St Peter's Field? The vast majority of eyewitness reports say not. However, although the Reverend Stanley's account of that day's clash was largely on the side of the people, he could not avoid reaching the conclusion that 'some were armed'. After the demonstrators had been dispersed a constable showed him 'taken in the fray: a couple of short skewers or daggers fixed in wooden handles'.[58] But whether these implements were intended to be used as weapons or as picnic utensils we will probably never know for sure.

What were the marchers hoping the day would bring, as they converged on Manchester on that warm and sunny summer morning? The mood was jaunty and optimistic, and the effects of the distances travelled on foot were rendered negligible by the effect of the sheer numbers of well-deployed and well-attired people, the music of the bands, and the caps of liberty and the flags. There was a feeling of 'something in the air', and although the majority of participants may not have had the political voice to give effective articulation to their hopes – Hunt, Bamford, Mary Fildes and her Committee, Carlile, Wroe, John Knight and the other middle-class movers and shakers were expected to fulfil that duty – the day would be one of momentous change, of that they were certain. Surely the vast crowds attending would make Lord Liverpool's government sit up and take notice? At the very least, they were hoping for a wider awareness of their plight, and the tabling of reforms which would alleviate their poverty and bring some fairness to the grossly top-heavy political and economic system.[59]

The Times reporter John Tyas – no particular fan of Hunt, if truth be told, and 'no friend to popular reform'[60] – was to recall the following from St Peter's Field:

> I had several conversations with different persons belonging to the reform party, who said they only wished a restoration of their rights, and above everything else, were desirous to preserve order and tranquillity.[61]

There were many whose motive for joining the marchers was non-political. Middleton farmer William Elson, for example, cites 'curiosity'; significantly, he allowed his three children to badger him to accompany him on the march: 'I should not have allowed my children to go to the meeting, had I apprehended any disturbance or riot; nor would I have gone myself, had I entertained such a fear'.[62]

John Smith, the reporter for the *Liverpool Mercury*, observed the buoyant mood, noting the 'good humour in every countenance'.[63]

This upbeat feeling gained expression in some bullish remarks made by a small number of the marchers to some of the more well-heeled onlookers. Roger Entwisle, a solicitor, was watching the arrival of the Stockport contingent when one of the crowd called out to him: 'Thou hast got a good coat on thy back; before the day is over, I'll have as good a one as thee.'[64] James Heath was in the dining room of his house on Bury Road, Cheetham, when he heard the procession pass outside. He went to his garden gate, where he was informed by one of the crowd, 'You will not sleep in that house tonight.'[65] Thomas Sharp, an iron merchant from Rusholme and former Boroughreeve, was with some friends on Mosley Street at around 9 a.m. when told by one of a group of early arrivals, 'You've had your way long enough, it'll be our turn before night.' Sharp overheard a snatch of conversation from the group as it passed by the Portico Newsroom and Library: 'I'd love to see the inside.' 'Patience and you will before night, and many another building, and many another house.' Sharp immediately went home and loaded a brace of pistols.[66]

Francis Philips claimed he overheard the following (although he omitted to mention where, when, or who the speaker was): 'It will soon be settled; and when our strength and numbers are known, people of consequence will join us.'[67]

Needless to say, these mostly throw-away remarks would be highlighted later by loyalists wishing to find evidence of the seditious intentions of the marchers. Although the threat of violent revolution on the day was most implausible given the peaceable context and mood of the processions and the gathering, it was rather these blunt and scattershot expressions of egalitarian ideas which helped feed the apprehension amongst Manchester's mercantile class.

Whilst Bamford and the Middleton contingent were approaching St Peter's Field via Oldham Street, Piccadilly and Mosley Street, Hunt's carriage took a circuitous route to St Peter's Field. The 'Orator' and his cavalcade descended St George's Road (formerly Back Lane, and now Rochdale Road) past the field where the 1808 weavers' demonstration had been held, crossed the Swan Street junction and entered Shudehill. From here they passed through Withy Grove, Hanging Ditch, Market Place, and St Mary's Gate, to emerge on Deansgate. He finally reached the field from the west, via the end of Peter Street.

There was method to Hunt's meanderings. First port of call was Withy Grove, where James Murray lived. The confectioner 'Gingerbread Jack' Murray was at home recovering from his roughing-up on White Moss the previous day. He heard the noise from the passing procession and hobbled to his bedroom window, from where he recognised Hunt and Johnson on the barouche, as well as a 'young and smart lady' who was carrying a banner. The crowd went slowly past his house, pointed up at him and 'hissed, hooted and groaned'. They then pointed to Hunt and gave a cheer.[68]

On nearby Long Millgate the head teacher of the Manchester Grammar School, Dr Jeremiah Smith, had closed the school at 10 a.m. and sent the day pupils home. He had locked all doors and put up the shutters, feeling apprehensive about the 'great influx of strangers into the town'. Unable to go home because of the crowds, he repaired to the Star Inn (No. 251 Deansgate), from where he saw Hunt's contingent pass, repeating the display of hissing and hooting.[69] However, if the target of the jeering was the assembly of magistrates, the birds had flown, since the lawgivers, having breakfasted at the Star, had already left for Mr Edmund Buxton's house at 6 Mount Street, which overlooked St Peter's Field.

Market Place. Market Street leads off to the left, and the Cotton Exchange and St Mary's Gate are on the right. (Stockport Local Heritage)

The procession halted in Old Mill Gate, where several shopkeepers were quick to close their shutters. There was a shout from the crowd reassuring the shopkeepers that they were meant no harm and that they need not be afraid. This had no effect, and the shutter-closing continued.[70]

The purpose of reaching Deansgate via St Mary's Gate was to pass in front of the Cotton Exchange. Hugh Cholmondeley from Knutsford, described as a 'gentleman of leisure' and nephew of Lord Delamere, was standing on the Exchange steps when Hunt and his entourage passed. He reported: 'There was an amazing shouting.' Cholmondeley also recalled the near ghost town: 'All business seemed to be suspended. I observed the shops… shut.'[71] In an attempt to illustrate Hunt's supposedly sinister sway over the mob, during the Redford vs. Birley courtroom proceedings one of Birley's defence lawyers, a Sergeant Hullock, made reference to the ease with which Hunt ordered the procession to halt in front of the Exchange – 'with as much facility as you, gentlemen, could order your servants'.[72] Once more the mention of 'servants' indicates the target audience of the comment. We may also note the condescending tone used when referring to the lower classes, and by implication, their lack of political credibility. It may also have been a somewhat ham-fisted attempt by Hullock to drive a wedge between Hunt and his working-class followers.

John Tyas the reporter, although not in the best of health, had been on St Peter's Field from around 8 a.m., determined to send a detailed account of the day's proceedings to his newspaper. As the crowds grew and grew, he decided to leave the field and walk down Deansgate to meet Hunt's carriage. He met Hunt outside the Exchange, where he asked the Orator if a place could be found for him on the hustings. Hunt told Tyas to stay close to the carriage, and this would be arranged. It was round about here that Moorhouse also joined the barouche.[73]

On Deansgate, innkeeper John Barlow had decided not to open his pub The Coach and Horses 'about 60 yards from the police office', and on seeing the passing procession, closed the doors and shutters and sat in candle-lit gloom until the noise had passed.[74] Thomas Styan, a gunsmith who had his shop near the bottom of Market Street near the Exchange, closed up at 11 a.m., fearing theft from his stock of firearms and gunpowder.[75]

There was more shouting as Hunt's vociferous, but well-controlled, entourage passed the end of Back King Street (now Lower King Street) as that was the site of the Police Offices. It was another token show, as by now the majority of the regular force and the 300 Special Constables had already assembled in Saint James's Square, and were taking up their positions on St Peter's Field. The commanders of the 15th Hussars stationed on Byrom Street, Lt-Col L'Estrange and Colonel Townsend, had trotted up Quay Street to Deansgate to watch the procession go by. Hunt saw the uniforms, stood up in the carriage, and waved his white top hat. The crowd 'answered with shouts, apparently of defiance'.[76]

Lieutenant William Jolliffe (later Lord Hylton), at the time already an officer at age 18, has given a clear description of the gathering crowds as the mustered Hussars watched and waited:

> The two squadrons with which I was stationed must have remained dismounted nearly two hours. During the greater portion of that period a solid mass of people continued moving along a street [Deansgate] about a hundred yards to our front on the way to the place of meeting. Other officers as well as myself occasionally rode to the front (to the end of the street) to see them pass. They marched at a brisk pace in ranks well closed up, five or six bands of music being interspersed, and there appeared to be but few women with them. Mr. Hunt,

with two or three other men, and I think two women dressed in light blue and white, were in an open carriage drawn by the people. This carriage was adorned with blue and white flags; and the day was fine and hot.[77]

Hunt's open carriage was about to turn into Peter Street. Some 250 yards away across the field the hustings wagons and the double line of Special Constables were in place, surrounded by a crowd already in excess of 50,000. This included a substantial ring of spectators watching from upper floor windows in the adjacent houses, from the top of the high wall that surrounded the Quakers' Meeting House, and from the raised ground towards the eastern end of Windmill Street. As Hunt entered the field, the bands played 'See the Conquering Hero Comes' and 'God Save the King'. The crowd gave vent to a massive cheer, which many of those present declared was the loudest they had ever heard. On that sunny August day Henry Hunt had brought the people hope.

It was around 1 p.m.

2

Powder Keg
(1 p.m.–1.30 p.m.)

As Hunt's arrival was heralded by the bands, the exultant crowds and the banners resplendent in the sunlight, the authorities' preparations for the day – no less assiduous than those of the demonstrators – so far had gone largely unnoticed.

A good number of the 300 policemen had been sworn in that morning as Special Constables. They were from the same social strata as the Yeomanry: middle-class shop owners, tradesmen, innkeepers and suchlike. As Chief Constable John Moore put it, they were 'persons of considerable respectability, and of property'.[1] Unlike the regular policemen with their uniform and black stovepipe hat, they had no official outfit, but each of them had been issued with a truncheon as badge of authority.[2] Fifteen inches long and with a circumference of 6in at the business end, the regulation stave was decorated with the King's name and the Royal Coat of Arms. As Thomas Schofield put it with a devastating irony at Hunt's trial: 'I saw some peace officers, but did not know them as such until they began to use their bludgeons.'[3]

The military and paramilitary back-up, ready and waiting for the command to get involved, was out in force. Besides the mounted Hussars and Yeomanry and field cannon already mentioned, 160 men of the 88th Infantry from the King Street barracks, with fixed bayonets, were deployed quietly and out of sight in Dickinson Street. Their commanding officer was Lt-Col McGregor. A few blocks to the north, in Brazennose Street, 250 soldiers of the 31st Infantry Regiment under the command of a Lt-Col Tonyn were awaiting orders. Including the constables, the estimated total of the forces available to the magistrates was over 1,500, all armed with bayonet, pistol, sabre or truncheon.[4]

The truncheon which belonged to Special Constable Richard Owen at Peterloo. (Author's Collection/Greater Manchester Police Museum)

One of the major factors in the ensuing disaster was the lack of specialised crowd-control training for the Yeomanry's horses. There are three elements in the crowd situation that are more or less guaranteed to spook an untrained mount: separation from the rest of the troop, sudden and unexpected noises from an unidentifiable source, and a rider whose panic is communicated to the animal. All three elements were present on St Peter's Field that day, and the panic element would have been aggravated by the growing alarm felt by the tightly packed crowd. Only a long process of temperament assessment and then acclimatisation would have prepared a horse for the extreme demands of Peterloo – a process that was signally absent in this case.[5]

The reaction of a horse suddenly confronted by a large gathering with its noise, movement and colours was aptly illustrated by Reverend Stanley's mount when met on Mosley Street late in the morning of the 16th by the arriving Ashton/Stockport contingent: 'Though my horse showed a great deal of alarm, particularly at their band and flags, [the people] broke rank and offered no molestation whatever.'[6]

Moreover, hardly any of the Manchester and Salford Yeomanry on duty that day could claim professional connections to horsemanship skills. Out of the force of approximately fifty riders who made their way to St Peter's Field, the following figures have been given:

13 publicans or innkeepers

8 saddlers or similar horse-related professions

7 cotton or textiles manufacturers

4 cotton merchants

4 butchers

2 tobacconists

2 watchmakers

2 attorneys

2 surgeons

2 cheesemongers

A painter

A candle maker

A corn dealer

A surveyor

A gentleman's servant

A quack doctor

A dancing master[7]

Bruton includes in the list of 'small manufacturers' ironmongers, tailors, calico-printers, and butter makers.[8] The modern Socialist author Krantz calls them 'the local business Mafia on horseback',[9] and the left-wing organ the *Manchester Observer* had been even more scathing, effectively throwing down the gauntlet just a month before Peterloo:

> The stupid boobies of yeomanry cavalry in the neighbourhood have only just made the discovery that the mind and muscle of the country are at length united, and during the past week have been foaming and broiling themselves to death in getting their swords ground and their pistols examined … The yeomanry are, generally speaking, the fawning dependents of the great, with a few fools and a greater proportion of coxcombs, who imagine they acquire considerable importance by wearing regimentals. … Half a dozen hungry, angry weavers would eat up a whole corps of Yeomanry Cavalry.[10]

This letter from William Fitton no doubt had the same stinging effect on the Yeomanry as Bamford's dialect poem had had on the mounted Special Constables and militia who had been repulsed by the crowd's sticks and stones at Sandy Brow back in February. So, adding to the virulent undertow of class-based acrimony, there were specific scores to be settled.

There is evidence that Saxton, the *Observer* sub-editor and publisher of the above, was targeted at Peterloo.

It is certain that the troop's sabres had recently been sharpened. Daniel Kennedy was employed by Richardson the cutler of 21 Deansgate, and one of his jobs in July 1819 had been to grind the Yeomanry's swords. They were 'ordered to be made very sharp.' Each sabre had a label, indicating the name of the weapon's owner.[11] The whole purpose of the crescent shape of the 33in (84cm) blade was to inflict the maximum damage, by creating as long and as deep a cut as possible – much more so than was possible with a straight blade. Some indication of its potentially lethal sharpness may be inferred from George Swift's observation of the neat slash made by one of the sabres in Saxton's clothing, causing a wound to the thigh: 'The sword that cut it must have been sharp as a rasor [*sic*] or it could not have cut it so clean.'[12]

The sabre was relatively light and easy to manoeuvre, but with a weighted tip to the blade, which further enhanced the cutting action.

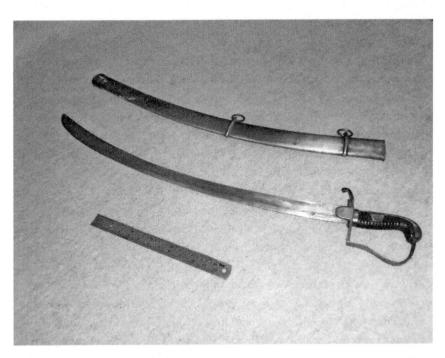

Regimental sabre and scabbard, standard issue for the Hussars and the militia. (Author's collection)

Members of the Yeomanry whose names were to gain some notoriety because of Peterloo included: Major Thomas Joseph Trafford, officer in overall command, landlord of large estates in Lancashire and Cheshire. He did not, however, accompany his troops to the field; Captain Hugh Hornby Birley, renowned for his strong reactionary views, owner of a large textile mill on Oxford Street on the banks of the Medlock; Captain Richard Jones Withington, a warehouse owner from Tanner's Lane, Pendleton; Lieutenant Edward Vigor Fox, of Cannon Street; Sergeant Major William Gregson, of Back King Street; Edward Meagher the Trumpeter, a tailor by profession, who led the charge on his piebald horse; Alexander Oliver, an innkeeper of Shudehill; Edward Tebbutt of Pool Street, a candle manufacturer and dealer; George Burgess, landlord of the Hen and Chickens Inn, later a gentleman's servant; Thomas Shelmerdine; John Hulme of Cannon Street, a calico printer; Richard Meadowcroft Whitlow, an attorney; Robert Sharp, an iron dealer of Market Street; James Moon, a cotton dealer; James Hamnet, an attorney's clerk from Salford; Samuel Street, of Bridge Street, a land surveyor; William Carlton, a horse breaker, innkeeper of the Sign of the Fox, Deansgate; William Bowker, innkeeper of the King's Head, Old Shambles; Thomas Barnes of Ardwick Green, a cotton dealer; Samuel Harrison of Miles Platting.[13]

These troops were under the direct civil authority of the magistrates, and not the military. Most of them were local men, known to many of the crowd.

On the subject of law and order, was the Riot Act read? If so, when, by whom, and how many times? According to *Wheeler's Manchester Chronicle* – the report was repeated the following week in the *London Mercury* – 'The Riot Act had been twice read, once by the Revd Mr. ETHELSTON, and once by JOHN SILVESTER, Esq.'[14]

The former reading was described by the Reverend Hay (who had supplied several cards with the Act printed on them) as being delivered by his friend the Reverend Ethelston in a carrying, operatic baritone. Hay at least was convinced that the reading was clearly audible:

He read it with his head very far out of the window… He leant so far out, that I stood behind him, ready to catch his skirts for fear he might fall over. Mr. Ethelston is a gentleman whom I have occasionally heard sing, and he has a remarkably powerful voice. When he drew back his head into room, after having read the proclamation, I observed to him 'Mr. Ethelston, I never heard your voice so powerful.'[15]

Ethelston agreed: 'I exerted myself in every possible manner.'[16] Nevertheless, the Reverend Stanley, at the time in the room above, says he never heard the reading. Manchester salesman James McKinnell, who claimed to be standing on the steps of Buxton's house from 12.30 p.m. until 'the end', had no recollection of hearing it either. James Harmer, the solicitor who would be representing the Lees' family interests in the John Lees inquest, and who was in the vicinity of No. 6 Mount Street between 11.30 a.m. and 1.30 p.m., did not hear it.[17] The opinion of members of the crowd (and indeed, the reporters and others on the platform) as to whether it was read may not be 100 per cent reliable, as there would have been plenty of distractions as the various contingents with their musical bands and the accompanying cheers, and then Hunt's barouche, and then the Yeomanry, arrived on the scene. When John Benjamin Smith was in an upstairs window alongside Buxton's house, watching Hunt's speech to the silent crowd around 100 yards away, he 'could hear his voice, but could not understand what he said'.[18] So if the exact words of 'Orator Hunt's' typically fortissimo delivery were unclear at that distance, it was unlikely that the bulk of the assembly would have heard the gist of a Riot Act being read from an upstairs window on Mount Street – if indeed it was ever read at all.

The opinion of the foreman of the jury at the John Lees inquest was unequivocal: 'I beg to say for myself, and my brother Jurymen, we have heard sufficient evidence to convince us that the meeting was peaceable, and that the Riot Act was not read.'[19]

Perhaps the comment by *The Statesman* the following Thursday captures the crux of the matter: 'It will not be enough that it was read from a distant window, or gabbled over in the corner of a field.'[20] And even the ultra-right-wing Francis Philips was to concede, 'It was heard only very partially' – whatever that may mean.[21]

According to Hay, the timing of the reading was just after the arrival of the Yeomanry on the field. Hay's words at the Redford-Birley trial were: 'It was read just at the time, I think, in the interval between the Yeomen coming up, and whilst they were forming – just as they began to form.'[22] However, this does not tally with Hay's statement in his 16 August letter to Lord Sidmouth, which appears to claim that the Riot Act was read whilst the arrests were being made, which was significantly later (see Appendix 6). Whichever may be true, in either case the stipulated hour's grace which was supposed to be the crowd's legal deadline to leave the field was totally ignored. There are serious doubts about the second reading, supposedly by Colonel Silvester. Ethelston was to state that he was unaware of any reading other than his own.[23] An attempt at a reading by Silvester is suggested by James Jacques, the brother-in-law of the Mr Buxton whose house was being used by the magistrates, and who was in the room with them. Jacques says that Silvester left the room with one of Hay's printed cards and went down into the crowd. He returned after five minutes, looking dishevelled: 'He appeared to have been in the dirt – to have been knocked down.'[24] So I think we can conclude that Silvester's attempt had not met with too much success.

Aston's Exchange Herald stated that the Act had been read at noon by the Boroughreeve Edward Clayton,[25] but this has no corroboration from any primary source. The *Leeds Mercury* report flatly contradicts the claim, giving valid reasons for doing so, and Clayton was busy otherwise from noon anyway, organising the double row of Special Constables.[26]

The actual spoken delivery of the Riot Act took about forty-five seconds at most. Here is the full official text:

> Our Sovereign Lord the King chargeth and commandeth all persons, being assembled, immediately to disperse themselves, and peaceably depart to their habitations, or to their lawful business, upon the pains contained in the Act made in the first year of George the First, for preventing tumults and riotous assemblies, God save the King.

When all is said and done, it may be argued that the reading of the Riot Act was inappropriate anyway. For the Act to be read, according to the official recommendation, there had to be a gathering of twelve or more people who 'unlawfully, riotously and tumultuously assemble together to the disturbance of the public peace'. The assembly had not been declared illegal: the careful wording of Hunt's proposal for the meeting's theme, following the ban on the one originally planned for 9 August, had appeared to cover that base. And one of the most striking aspects of that vast crowd as it gathered and grew was its controlled placidity, the very opposite of the 'riotous' and 'tumultuous' prerequisite for the reading of the Act. John Benjamin Smith, watching the arrival of the crowds from his upstairs room, is again a useful source, with this much-quoted passage:

> It seemed to be a gala day with the country people who were mostly dressed in their best and brought with them their wives, and when I saw boys and girls taking their father's hand in the procession, I observed to my Aunt: 'These are the guarantees of their peaceable intentions – we need have no fears.'[27]

The report from the *Manchester Courier* agreed:

> [The crowd had the] appearance of a large village party going to a merry making than that of a body of people advancing to the overthrow of the government...[28]

John Brattargh, a wharf owner from Pendleton who was watching the processions from a first-floor window near the field, noted that 'the women were tidily dressed: apparently in their holiday clothes'.[29] Archibald Prentice related his experience of the gathering:

> The 'marching order' of which so much was said afterwards, was what we often see now in the processions of Sunday-school children and temperance societies ... if the men intended mischief they would not have brought their wives, their sisters or their children with them. I passed round the outskirts of the meeting, and mingled with the groups that stood chatting there. I occasionally asked the women if they were not afraid to be there, and the usual laughing reply was – 'What have we to be afraid of?'[30]

John Jones, a fustian-cutter who lived and worked at No. 14 Windmill Street, was an observer from the second floor of his house. Both he and his wife Ann agreed that the arrival and gathering of the various contingents was 'very peaceable'. Further along the same row Samuel Slack, owner of the house from the second floor of which he was watching proceedings, declared that he 'felt no alarm for the safety of his property'. This unintimidated view was shared by Robert Hyde Gregg, a merchant who owned a Manchester warehouse and who would later be the proprietor of Quarry Bank Mill, Styal. Gregg's vantage point was the knoll at the eastern end of Windmill Street. Reporter John Smith observed that, before the Yeomanry's appearance: 'I saw not the slightest apprehension of danger.' James Scholefield, the dissenting minister who gave evidence at Hunt's trial and who had had a viewpoint some 10 yards from the lines of Constables, spoke of the crowd's 'utmost regularity, jocularity, and good humour'. John Shuttleworth, a cotton and twist dealer, was to assert at the John Lees inquest: 'No riot, tumult, or disorder, not the slightest had taken place.' The Reverend Stanley, who had arguably the clearest and most comprehensive view of all ('I looked down upon it like a map') described the 'sullenly peaceful' mood of the approaching crowd, and claimed that he saw no resistance with sticks or stones as the Yeomanry made

their advance.[31] The *Leeds Mercury* report, written by eyewitness Edward
Baines Jnr, the editor's son, included the observation:

> The Reformers, who seemed determined to make this a splendid day, were
> equally on the alert, not indeed in preparing arms, for of those they were
> totally destitute, but in preparing flags and small bands of music… It is evident,
> however, from the great number of females, and even children, who formed
> part of the procession, that nothing was anticipated that could involve them in
> the least degree of peril…[32]

The report in *The Times* that Wednesday stated:

> Whether the Riot Act had been read, I am not enabled positively to say, but I
> affirm, from actual observation, that not the slightest breach of the peace had
> been committed, or appeared, as far as I can judge, likely to take place; and
> most certainly, instead of an hour being allowed after proclamation, for the
> people to disperse, not twenty minutes had elapsed, after.[33]

Hunt himself was to score a nice point on the opening day of his preliminary
hearing at the New Bailey Courthouse on the Friday of the following week.
Magistrate James Norris was presiding, and as he began his address, at the
mention of High Treason the crowd behind the dock made their disapproval
known, loudly. Hunt to Norris: 'I can't hear. There was more order at the
meeting the other day than here.'[34]

It would appear that it was this very calmness, control and self-assurance
displayed by the Peterloo gathering which put the wind up the watching
magistrates. This was no 'swinish multitude', an inferior breed that could be
spooked and cowed by a show of force. At one point in Hunt's trial, Hulton
gave as one reason for his feeling of alarm: 'the extraordinary way in which
the people approached'.[35] Shades of a future widespread and organised
insurrection, rendered more present and threatening by the authorities'
scaremongering, were imagined to be walking among the confident, level-
headed and serried ranks of the workers with their emblematic laurel sprigs,
bold embroidered banners, slogans and caps of liberty.[36]

From about noon around 300 of the Special Constables had been set up
in two lines between No. 6 Mount Street and the hustings carts. The avenue
thus formed seemed to state the magistrates' intentions from the off: arrests
were being prepared for, once the meeting got under way. Then the crowd

grew and grew, each new contingent's arrival being greeted with hearty cheers. Another cart was added to the platform, and the wagons were moved 'six or eight yards' yards further away from the constables, and the space was filled by the crowd.[37] Thus the line of communication between the magistrates and the hustings was broken.

The cry of 'Make way for the female reformers!' ensured that the area closest to the stage was occupied by a large number of the women marchers with their banners and caps of liberty.[38] At least five of them would be invited onto the platform. Observing this development, the reporter from the right-wing *Wheeler's Manchester Chronicle* cloddishly – yet typically – missed the point with the remark: 'Females…with a demeanour the reverse of everything that man delights to see in woman.'[39]

There was a lively commentary on the bovine Nadin and his cohorts as the Deputy Chief Constable patrolled the space between the double cordon of police:

'That is Joseph. He has a great guts, he has more meat in his belly than we have.'
'This is the black mob [the uniformed constables].'
'They have very good coats to their backs, they have better coats than we have.'[40]

Jemima Bamford's narrative gives an indication of how densely packed the crowd was close to the platform. Jemima had lost track of her husband Sam during the approach along the northern part of Mosley Street, and would see him again but briefly on the hustings. The heat and the crush were beginning to have an effect on her:

The crowd seemed to have increased very much, for we became insufferably pressed. We were surrounded by men who were strangers; we were almost suffocated, and to me the heat was quite sickening.[41]

Feeling most unwell and almost fainting, she tried to make her way out of the crowd. She found this nearly impossible, and managed to leave the crush only by locating the double row of policemen and making her way between them.[42] She then turned right to pass in front of the Mount Street houses and ended up on the Windmill Street knoll, which she reached just as Hunt's carriage was arriving.

The multitude was packed solid around the stage, and raised on poles over the inner crowd there were visible sixteen banners and nine caps of liberty.[43] Robert Jones (a mechanic and rag-dealer employed to help erect the hustings), 'Doc' Healey, Saxton and the young George Swift ('with great vehemence of action and gesture') had made brief warm-up speeches which were tolerably well received,[44] but it was obvious whom those present really wanted to see and hear. Hunt's carriage worked its way through the crowd, and the Orator, conspicuous in his white top hat, climbed onto the platform to lengthy, tempestuous cheers. (By this time Bamford had left the stage in search of some 'refreshment'.)[45] Without much ado, Hunt was proposed chairman by Johnson, and having cleared the hustings of surplus elements such as the odd musical instrument (and those persons deemed political supernumeraries) and achieved silence from the multitude, he began his speech.

The identity of the people on the platform may be inferred with a fair degree of certainty, thanks to overlapping evidence from various sources. According to the J. Evans print (see p.150) there were more than fifteen atop the two adjoining wagons, which is many more than is shown on other representations of the scene, but accounts by George Swift, the reporter Charles Wright, Carlile and the Dolby transcript of Hunt's trial seem to corroborate this number, at least at the moment of Hunt's arrival:

Henry Hunt	John Knight	Richard Carlile
John Thacker Saxton	Joseph 'Doc' Healey	George Swift
John Tyas	Edward Baines Jnr	Charles Wright
Robert Wylde	Robert Jones	

Mary Fildes, plus at least four women[46]

However, the fewer number on other pictures – usually around eight – reflects Hunt's action of clearing the hustings of those he deemed to be surplus to requirements.[47]

John Knight held the list of the meeting's resolutions – which were presumably very similar to the ones that had been read out by Hunt at the Smithfield rally on 21 July – but during the ensuing havoc this list would be snatched from his hand by Nadin, never to be seen again.[48]

From the window in Buxton's house, Hulton had been following proceedings with the help of a pair of opera glasses.[49] Unnoticed by the vast majority of those present, the authorities had been building their own response to the day's events.

Over the course of a couple of hours during the morning more than thirty of the local worthies – 'gentlemen of highest respectability'[50] – had petitioned Hulton with the insistent opinion – and a written and signed note – that 'the peace of the town is endangered'.[51] The atmosphere of increasing alarm in the magistrates' room made it almost inevitable that soon or later a warrant for the arrest of Hunt and the other occupiers of the hustings carts should be drafted, despite the fact that the meeting had at no point been declared illegal, and that proceedings so far had been peaceful and orderly. The gist of the document was that Richard Owen, a Special Constable and pawnbroker by profession, had 'made oath before us' that 'the town is in danger', and the further necessary nine names were added so as to make the warrant legally valid:

William Hulton
Revd C.W. Ethelston
Revd William R. Hay
John Silvester
Richard Wright
Thomas W. Tatton
Robert Teddon
William Marriott
Ralph Fletcher[52]

The document – timed at 1.15 p.m. – was handed over to Nadin. The Deputy Chief Constable, no doubt eyeing up the sweet trolley of arrestable radicals on the hustings, promptly declared that he would need military assistance to deliver the warrant to Hunt. His view was shared by many of the magistrates present.[53] The Reverend Stanley, however, was to assert that in his opinion military intervention was 'premature and unnecessary'. This concurs with the assessment of Carlile that it was 'unprovoked and unnecessary'.[54] Needless to say, it was the magistrates' view which held sway.

Hulton wrote two identical notes, and simultaneously dispatched the riders bearing them. Reverend Stanley, looking out of the back window of Buxton's house, saw them disappear out of the rear garden gate, one turning left to go to Portland Street, and two others turning right down the southern part of Mosley Street, to reach the Byrom Street muster via Fleet Street. The notes read:

Sir, as Chairman of the Select Committee of Magistrates,
I request you to proceed immediately to Number 6, Mount Street, where the
Magistrates are assembled. They conceive the civil power wholly inadequate
to preserve the peace. I have the honour, etc.,
    William Hulton.[55]

The relatively young and susceptible Hulton was under pressure to make
a firm and prompt decision, but still, admittedly with hindsight, one may
question the wording of the note. That phrase 'wholly inadequate to
preserve the peace' must have been like an alarm bell to the waiting cavalry,
suggesting that it was kicking off on St Peter's Field. And the sending of
the two messengers simultaneously looks like the first spasm of real panic.
Someone in the chain of command should have realised that professional
soldiers – the 15th King's Hussars – with properly trained men and horses
should have been contacted first, with the Yeomanry kept as a distant reserve.

The Yeomanry at Pickford's timber yard on Portland Street were, crucially,
closer than the professional cavalry stationed across Deansgate on Byrom
Street. Thomas Withington was one of the two riders who delivered the note
to Lt-Col L'Estrange and the Hussars, and the troop of the Prince Regent's
Regiment of Cheshire Yeomanry, who, because of the crowds, could only
be reached via a circuitous route. Byrom Street was also where the two field
cannon were in readiness, with Major Dyneley in command.

Joseph Birley (Hugh Hornby's brother) rode to Pickford's yard, just 500
yards and a couple of blocks away from Mount Street. Here he delivered
his note to Major Trafford. Captain Hugh Hornby Birley looked over
Trafford's shoulder and read the missive at the same time.[56] Around sixty of
the Manchester and Salford Yeomanry, with Captain Birley in command,
mounted up and set off at speed for St Peter's Field.

Thomas Padmore described their departure: 'The Yeomanry galloped
furiously towards St. Peter's Field. They appeared as if they were mad…'[57]

There has been much debate as to whether the Yeomanry had been drinking
before or during the muster in Pickford's yard. Mrs G. Banks, in *The Manchester
Man*, comes right out and says it: 'yeomanry fired with drink…were let loose
like barbarians on a closely-wedged mass of unarmed people…'[58]

Leading radical Sir Francis Burdett was equally forthright when he spoke
in the House of Commons on 15 May 1821, asserting that the 'wretches
who had perpetrated the massacre at Manchester were at the time in a state
of intoxication'.[59]

A couple of comments made by eyewitnesses reinforce this impression. William Harrison, cotton-spinner:

> I saw a sword held by the first man who came down [Meagher?] … He came into the crowd on gallop. He was fuddled, I reckon. He could hardly sit on his horse, he was so drunk; he sat like a monkey.[60]

Peter Drummond, a weaver, observed:

> …the Cavalry appeared angry…and I think there was a good deal of intoxication among them, because I saw them roll about on their horses.[61]

And it is certainly tempting to suppose that even if the company had not spent the morning in the pubs, around noon on a hot day, with a high number of innkeepers in the troop, as part of a group-bonding process (and perhaps for a dash of Dutch courage) they might well have passed the bottle round whilst waiting for the orders to arrive. It may be relevant, though, that there was a public source of spring water not 400 yards from Pickford's yard, at the top of King Street (near the site of the present Spring Gardens), and there would have been a plentiful supply of drinking water, at least for the horses.

Thomas Preston was in Cooper Street when he saw the Yeomanry pass on the way to St Peter's Field. He was none too impressed:

> He met [the Manchester Yeomanry] going at a sharp trot. He remained some time stationary, and saw them rush in a broken and irregular line towards the hustings. He observed the riders jolting in their seats, as if their horses were proceeding in unsteady motion.[62]

He makes no mention of a smell of alcohol as the troop clattered past (and nor do any others who got physically close to the Yeomanry, such as Thomas Padmore in the yard, and John Robinson at the corner of Mount Street) but this may not mean anything, as street-level and equine odours may have masked it.

It is true that the following appears in a pamphlet published in September 1820, presented as part of a Preston Yeoman cavalryman's diary:

At this moment we came athwart a public house, and after having enlivened ourselves with a bumper of cognac, we joined our squad half as full of *spirit* as we carried with us to Peterloo.[63]

It should be noted, though, that this is an extract from a near-deadpan, and very funny, lampoon. The tip-offs include the pen-name of the author 'Squib', and the cast of bumbling Yeomanry characters with the proto-Dickensian names of Whistlepig, Big Sam, Maggot, and Thickdick.

William Norris Buckley, a Manchester tradesman who lived in Derby, was on the steps of St Peter's Church when he saw the Yeomanry pass on their way to Mount Street: 'They went at a gallop, pell-mell, with drawn swords. I observed they looked remarkably pale.' This pallid aspect of the riders' faces was a detail which was corroborated by others. Peter Drummond observed that 'they looked very pale'. Joseph Barrett, a cotton manufacturer from Newton Heath, who was watching the scene from an upper floor window in Windmill Street, noted: 'The Yeomanry looked very pale & frightened.'[64]

Was the paleness down to alcohol, or was it indeed fear that showed on their faces as they made their way, unsure and unbriefed, to deal somehow with the 50,000 plus crowd? If fear to any degree, we may be certain that the emotion would have been communicated to the horses.

It was on Cooper Street that the backmarker of the Yeomanry, hurrying to catch up with the rest of his troop 'at a gallop', caused the first fatality of the day. A Mrs. Ann Fildes was crossing the street carrying her 2-year-old son William when the horse sent her flying, knocking the child to the ground and killing him.[65] It was a foretaste of what was to follow on St Peter's Field: the undisciplined haste, the tunnel vision, and the poorly controlled deployment of force. It would also be an indication of the attempted cover-up policy, as when the report of this incident was filtered through official channels, cause of the child's death was given as 'died from a fall from his mother's arms'.[66]

On the platform at the far end of St Peter's Field, Hunt was several minutes into his address, delivering it to a rapt and silent crowd. It is worth repeating the speech in full here:

My friends and fellow countrymen, – I must entreat your indulgence for a short time; and I beg you will endeavour to preserve the most perfect silence. I hope you will exercise the all-powerful right of the people in an orderly manner; and if you perceive any man that wants to raise a disturbance, let him instantly be put down, and kept secure. For the honour you have done me, in inviting me a second time to preside at your meeting, I return you my thanks; and all I have to beg of you is, that you will indulge us with your patient attention. It is impossible that, with the utmost silence, we shall be able to make ourselves heard by this tremendous assembly. It is useless for me to relate to you the proceedings of the last week or ten days in this town and neighbourhood. You know them all, and the cause of the meeting appointed for last Monday being prevented. I will not therefore say one word on that subject; only to observe that those who put us down, and prevented us from meeting on Monday last, by their manifest exertions have produced twofold the number today. [*Applause*] It will be perceived, that in consequence of the calling of this new meeting, our enemies, who had flattered themselves they had gained a victory, have sustained a great defeat. [*Applause*] There have been two or three placards posted up during the last week with the names of one or two insignificant individuals attached to them. One Tom Long or Jack Short, a printer —

This is the text that appears in Wroe, p. 3. Much was made by the loyalists of Hunt's use of the phrase 'put down', arguing that this was evidence of the radicals' aggressive, even murderous, intentions. It was arguably an unfortunate choice of words, but Hunt accompanied the phrase with a quelling, downward gesture of the open hand, which seems to suggest a desire for quiescence.[67] He uses the same expression later in the speech, and here it is obvious that a violent context was not intended.

As an indication of how language may be doctored to fulfil specific aims, it is interesting to compare Hunt's actual words with the different emphasis in the version given at the Redford vs. Birley trial by George Read from Congleton:'He said, that if the enemies shewed any symptoms against them, they were to put them down, quiet them, and keep them down.' Then there was the variant supplied by solicitor Roger Entwisle later on at the same trial:'If they attempt to molest you, you will knock them down, and keep them down.'[68] Even more damning was the paraphrase given by an unnamed source to the *Liverpool Mercury* of 20 August 1819 before being corrected by eyewitness reporter John Smith:'…if they considered [a person approaching to be] an enemy, to put him under their feet, and to keep him there.'

Hunt's speech was here interrupted, as a disturbance occurred beyond the Mount Street houses, at the far end of the wall which surrounded the garden of Cooper's Cottage. The irruption was first noticed by the spectators on the Windmill Street knoll, and their reaction was almost immediately communicated to the crowd around the hustings. Thoughts that this was the arrival of latecomers from the Blackburn contingent or venerable reformer Major Cartwright[69] were soon scotched as around sixty mounted members of the Manchester and Salford Yeomanry burst into view to fill the space by the corner of the wall. There was a cry of 'The soldiers! The soldiers!' and people in the crowd turned to look or began to drift away from the edges.

Manchester merchant John Robinson was standing on Mount Street, near to the wall corner, when he saw the Yeomanry suddenly appear with a speed which took him by surprise:

> They came at such a rate, that I had great difficulty in getting out of their way, and had almost fallen in the effort to save myself from being run over. Two persons were knocked down, about ten or fifteen yards from me.[70]

Most onlookers' accounts agree that the troop was 'in extreme disorder'. John Shuttleworth judged their approach to be 'hasty, irregular and violent'. Hunt remarked with a withering irony: 'There is a pretty sight for you', and so ramshackle did the muster appear that he was overheard to say, 'This is a trick. Stand firm.'[71]

Hunt, sensing a lessening of the crowd's concentration and courage, decided to rally them by proposing three cheers. *The Times* reported that this was 'to show the military that they [the people] were not to be daunted … by their unwelcome presence'.[72] Or as *Liverpool Mercury* reporter and junior editor John Smith, also on the platform, put it: 'There was a little alarm manifested at the outskirts, and he gave the shout to re-inspire confidence – that was all.' Mary Yates, who had walked part of the way from Middleton arm-in-arm with Jemima Bamford, had a slightly different view:

> I thought the soldiers were come to calm the uneasiness that might arise by the presence of so many people. I heard the words 'Give them three cheers!' The noise made was a sound of rejoicing; I huzzaed as well as the rest. We were all very comfortable together. The women sometimes shouted as well as the men.[73]

Onlooker Thomas Sharp, however, noticed a significant tone to the cheers:

> They faced about toward the Yeomanry, and immediately set up a most tremendous shout, accompanied with hootings and hissings. It was a shout which differed very materially from the cheers that had been given to the parties on the ground; it appeared to me to be an act of defiance.[74]

The exhortation to 'stand firm' was carried out allegedly by several rows around the hustings linking arms.[75] However, *Leeds Mercury* reporter Edward Baines, after having jumped down from the hustings on the opposite side to the Yeomanry's advance, saw no evidence of this locking of arms.[76] The question of whether those people surrounding the platform really did link arms – thus denying the police and the Yeomanry clear access to the stage – would be a subject of lengthy debate at Hunt's trial. Whether this human shield was deliberately put into place or not, it was obvious that the cavalry would have difficulty in reaching the platform in any case – 'deterred from proceeding by the solid mass through which they must force their way'.[77]

The Yeomanry, perhaps goaded by a perceived mockery in Hunt's huzzahs, replied with three cheers of their own. Francis Philips states that the constables joined in.[78] There followed a hiatus of a minute or so, during which time Chief Constable Andrew spoke to Birley, and Birley spoke to his troops (and according to Hay, Ethelston read the Riot Act, leaning out of the first-floor window of No. 6 Mount Street). Andrew's and Birley's words were presumably orders as to how to proceed, and judging from the subsequent botched manoeuvre, the instruction would have been to surround the platform and ensure the arrest of Hunt and his company. Meagher's bugle sounded the attack and the would-be cavalry surged forward towards the crowd, their drawn and raised sabres gleaming in the sunlight.[79]

3

'That Horrid Confusion'
(1.30 p.m.–1.45 p.m.)

Before we follow the Yeomanry's attempted encircling manoeuvre and the subsequent catastrophe, some time should be spent on the allegation that they were assaulted first, by stones, brickbats and cudgels.

As reports vary greatly, the evidence concerning the crowd's throwing of stones and half-bricks appears full of contradictions. On the one extreme we have the testimonies which claim stones aplenty were hurled soon after the

A drawing by Cruikshank illustrating the Yeomanry's charge. A detail from this image is featured on the Britons Protection pub sign on Great Bridgewater Street (see p.180). (Working Class Movement Library)

Yeomanry arrived, and *before* their movement into the crowd. On the other there is the complete denial of stone-throwing from start to finish. The truth would appear to be somewhere in between.

The perennial question here is what happened first: the Yeomanry's cutting or the people's throwing of missiles? Sergeant Hullock, in his opening defence address at the Redford vs. Birley civil action, had no doubts:

> …long before they [the Yeomanry] reached the hustings…they were assaulted by brickbats and stones innumerable.[1]

This view, that the slashing with sabres was the Yeomanry's reaction to being attacked by the crowd, although backed up by Hulton,[2] is firmly contradicted by the majority of eyewitnesses. Thomas Hopkins, carver and gilder, stated that the gathering was peaceable before the Yeomanry started cutting at heads and raised arms, and that no stones were thrown before that.[3] Yeoman George Burgess was of the same opinion: 'no stones were thrown until after the arrests were made'.[4] This seems to agree with Joseph Nadin's view: 'When we came on the outside [of the mob, i.e. after the arrests] we were peppered with stones.'[5] Reporter Jeremiah Garnett (who was to switch his allegiance from the right-wing *Wheeler's Chronicle* after Peterloo) asserted that 'no stones were thrown betwixt Mr. Buxton's house and the hustings'.[6] John Smith, the *Liverpool Mercury* reporter on the hustings, stated: 'I saw no brickbats or stones thrown till the close of the dispersion, when I saw one stone thrown.'[7] Mr Sergeant Blackburne, in the course of examining Reverend Stanley at the same trial, put the following question: 'Did you see either sticks or stones, or anything of the kind used against the cavalry in their advance up to the hustings?' Stanley's reply: 'Certainly not.'[8] Another man of the cloth, Reverend Hindmarsh, a dissenting minister from Salford, made the observation from near the Quakers' Meeting House:

> From the first to the last I saw nothing done either to intimidate, or insult, or oppose the military…I saw no stones, brick bats or sticks hurled in the air, or at the cavalry.[9]

Thomas Worrell the Assistant Surveyor of Paving claimed that he had cleared the field, its periphery and the surrounding streets of stones early in the morning,[10] but this does not quite tally with the evidence given by Robert Britton, a merchant's agent who lived near to St Peter's Field. Britton was to affirm that he checked the field at 8 a.m. on the morning of the 16th, and whilst the 'greater part' of the open space itself was 'perfectly clear of stones brickbats and missiles of any description' he spotted 'some few brickbats' in the vicinity of the Quakers' Meeting House.[11] To be fair, Worrell claimed to have put in another hour later (9 a.m.–10 a.m.), but work at this time would have been restricted, as by then the crowds had begun to arrive.

Birley gave a carefully worded version of events during his speech the following April at the King's birthday celebrations. He related that as he approached the hustings he was aware of a movement in the crowd, which 'appeared to be intended to throw an obstacle in the way of our advance'. The statement is feebly ambiguous, and therefore unconvincing. Bruton's opinion of Birley's apologia was that it was 'a very lame affair'.[12]

The clinching argument for there being no missiles thrown from the central crush may be based on an observation made by a Special Constable. John Barlow, the Manchester merchant, had noticed: 'They [the crowd] could not stoop for them [the stones], they were so very dense.'[13] Extrapolating from this, we can only conclude that the crowd was so closely packed around the hustings that it would have been well-nigh impossible to manoeuvre the arms so as to deploy stones (or sticks, for that matter) in an aggressive way. At Hunt's trial, Thomas Schofield, a cotton carder from Shelderslow (a hamlet a couple of miles east of Oldham), made the same observation:

> I saw no brick-bats or stones thrown, nor sticks lifted up against the cavalry. The people were so jammed and crowded together, that they could not do so, even had they been inclined.[14]

Wheeler's Manchester Chronicle of 21 August alleged that a number of demonstrators wore 'long brats that contain pockets. These pockets were all filled with stones.' However, this is a detail which has not been widely corroborated. Jonathan Edward Taylor assessed it as 'too ridiculous to obtain credit', arguing that if a worker could afford such an expensive apron or overall, he would also have the wherewithal to buy 'some more efficient weapons of offence, than a pocket full of stones'. He also poured scorn on the assertion that two wagon-loads of stones were cleared from the field *after* the dispersal.[15] In any case, the point about the central crowd being unable to throw missiles because of the crush is still valid.

So, if stones or brickbats were thrown, it was from the periphery of the field, and after the central crowd had been scattered by the cavalry's initial attack. As we will see, there is some evidence of the demonstrators defending themselves in this way.

One of the more censorious narratives telling of the crowd's aggression and the Yeomanry's and Constabulary's forbearance – leaving aside for the moment the versions supplied by hardline loyalists such as the Reverend Hay, Hulton, Birley and Sergeant Hullock – was in a letter sent by a Special Constable, one Robert Mutrie, a merchant who lived on Union Street, to his brother-in-law in Scotland. The brother-in-law, named Archibald Moore, was steward to the estate of the Marquess of Bute on the Isle of Rothesay. This letter was first made public in 1988, and it was at once held up as showing the flashpoint violence of Peterloo in quite a different light. Mutrie tells of 'people coming on the green in regular military order with monstrous clubs over their shoulders'.[16] The Yeomanry, 'using only the backs of their sabres' charged the crowd, and at one point in the confusion 'in one moment upwards of 100 of us [constables] are laid on our backs'. Mutrie goes on to boast: 'I got to the Hustings and in the scuffle for plunder I got hold of a very grand cap of liberty from off one of the standards.' Most of the letter deals with the ferocious and lengthy confrontation that evening across town at New Cross, but for the moment it is the St Peter's Field details as seen by Mutrie that concern us. The 'military order' and the 'monstrous clubs' are discussed – and largely dismissed – elsewhere in this book. The 'backs of the sabres' can be easily disproved by looking at the casualty lists, and the sight of several dozen prostrate policemen would have afforded a memorable spectacle – yet this appears in not a single other eyewitness account.[17] The word 'plunder' is revealing, suggesting a victory in a military engagement, with Mutrie helping himself to the spoils of war. One gets the idea that the constable is trying to impress his brother-in-law, who in his capacity of estate steward (or 'factor' in Scottish terminology) would have been on at least nodding terms with the landed gentry. The letter was not intended for publication but was just a private communication between family members. Mutrie seems to want to paint himself as some sort of war hero, by emphasising the violent potential of the crowd, the restraint of the civil and military forces, and his own dash of courage in a skirmish.

So the bugle sounded and the Yeomanry launched into their charge, sabres drawn. The Reverend Stanley related that a woman who was unable to get out of the way fast enough was knocked to the ground 'to all appearances lifeless'. She remained there until the field had been cleared, when two men picked her up and took her into Buxton's house.[18]

As the Yeomanry blundered onwards into ground zero the charge inevitably lost its impetus as the cavalrymen were swallowed by the crowd, and the troop lost its formation as the horses became separated from one another in the crush. Unable to cope with this unexpected turn of events, both riders and horses started to panic, and the sabres were put to use.

The Yeomanry could have used the flat of their swords to disperse the mob, but in most cases it was the freshly honed blade that was used. The Bees' analysis[19] of the number of women cut when compared to the number of men leads them to the conclusion that, since there were far fewer women cut by sabres, this proves that the Yeomanry were discriminating in their choice of target. I would suggest that it proves nothing of the sort. Bush has calculated that the proportion of men to women at Peterloo was 8:1, whereas the proportion of men wounded or killed to women wounded or killed was 3:1. This includes injuries or deaths by weapon, trampled by horses, or crushed by the crowd.[20] I propose reasons for this high proportion in the following pages: chivalry had nothing to do with it.

Local publicans, mill owners and shopkeepers on terrified horses, hemmed in by a hostile crowd in a situation in which they were clearly out of their depth, may – possibly – excite some sympathy. Far more blatantly culpable, though, is the Yeomanry's subsequent activity, once the crowd had started to attempt to flee. Birley, amongst others, later tried to minimise the effects and number of the sabre cuts,[21] but the list of wounded and dead tells a vastly different story.

In the wake of the horsemen, in the space thus forced, there walked the arresting party of Clayton the Boroughreeve, Chief Constables Jonathan Andrew and John Moore, and the bulky figure of Nadin, to whom the warrant had been given. The arrests of the speakers on the hustings were soon carried out, but the Yeomanry almost immediately showed that their purpose was wider and more brutal:

> As soon as Hunt and Johnson had jumped from the waggon, a cry was made by the cavalry, 'Have at their flags.' In consequence, they immediately dashed not only at the flags which were in the waggon, but those which were posted in the crowd, *cutting most indiscriminately to the right and to the left* in order to get at them. This set the people running in all directions, and it was not until this act had been committed that any brick-bats were hurled at the military. From that moment the Manchester yeomanry cavalry lost all command of temper.[22]

John Thacker Saxton, Editor of the *Manchester Observer* and publisher of the previous month's 'stupid boobies…fools…coxcombs' barrage of insults to the Manchester Yeomanry, was spotted on the hustings wagon. He was immediately singled out by two of the Yeomanry:

> Two privates rode up to him. 'There,' said one of them, 'is that villain Saxton: do you run him through the body.' 'No,' replied the other, 'I had rather not – I leave it to you.' The man immediately made a lunge at Saxton, and it was only by slipping aside that the blow missed his life. As it was, it cut his coat and waistcoat, but fortunately did him no other injury.[23]

It was not just the radical newspapermen who appeared to be targeted:

> Among the wounded were several girls dressed in white, who had been on the hustings. One young woman who held a colour, resolutely stuck to it until cut down; and when the staff was wrested from her, she kept hold of the drapery, and as she fell, twisted it round her waist.[24]

Joseph Wrigley from Oldham stated at the John Lees inquest: 'I saw them [the cavalry] cutting at the carriage in which there were some women'.[25]

Why were there so many women amongst the casualties? One reason was the result of the deployment of the processions en route to the meeting: many of the contingents deliberately placed the female marchers at the head of the column, so naturally this section of the parade would be closest to the hustings when the crowds started to fill up the field.[26] It is also likely that the Female Unions each carried at least one banner, so that there were proportionately more flag-carrying women than men. Given the fierce obsession of the police and militia with seizing and destroying the standards and caps of liberty, this is a significant detail. Moreover, the attacking of the women was the obvious conclusion of the current male attitude. Men felt threatened by women who were seeking autonomy, and who therefore did not conform to the accepted role of mere bystanders and passive supporters. If these female reformers were going to apparently neglect their domestic duties and march in ranks with the men and carry standards with provocative slogans, they were seen as fair game, and if they received blows from sabres or truncheons, they only had themselves to blame.[27] The report in the *Manchester Observer* of 21 August included: 'The women seemed to be the special objects of the rage of these bastard soldiers.' 'Bastard' here has the nuance of 'false' or 'counterfeit'. This callously unrepentant attitude was evident in the alleged mindset of one John Brown, 'gentleman', who according to his brief obituary in the *Northern Star* of 15 March 1845, had 'openly and exultantly boasted that he had severed a woman's breast off with his sabre at the ever-memorable Peterloo massacre'. It is possible that the woman was the believed fatality Margaret Downes, who was 'dreadfully cut in the breast: secreted clandestinely, and not heard of, presumed dead'.[28]

By now L'Estrange and the 15th Hussars, followed by the Cheshire Yeomanry, had arrived from Byrom Street. The field artillery had rattled along in their wake. They had been obliged to take the long way round because of the crowds: south along Deansgate, then along Fleet Street – whose narrowness, plus (according to some contemporary maps) a tight chicane near the Deansgate end, would have further slowed them down – to emerge on Lower Mosley Street, thus entering St Peter's Field by the south-east corner. It was a journey well over half as long again as that taken by the Yeomanry, whose route to the field had been much more direct, along the straight and relatively broad thoroughfares of Nicholas and Cooper Streets. Moreover, professional cavalry following military protocol would have taken

A Cruikshank image, sponsored by Carlile, of the militia's attack (see p.179). (Manchester Central Library Archives+ (M01563))

longer to mount and move off in rank and file than was the case with the headlong posse which, by all accounts, characterised the Yeomanry's passage to the field.

Had the professional cavalry got there first, quite another denouement may be imagined. As it was, by the time the Hussars arrived – a crucial several minutes after the Yeomanry – the scene was screaming chaos, partly obscured by the rising clouds of dust. In his account of the day Lt Jolliffe of the Hussars gave his assessment of the situation:

> I saw that the Manchester troop of Yeomanry…were scattered singly or in small groups over the greater part of the field, literally hemmed up and hedged into the mob so that they were powerless either to make an impression or to escape…and it required only a glance to discover their helpless position, and the necessity of our being brought to their rescue.[29]

L'Estrange drew up his men in front of the row of houses on Mount Street, whereupon Hulton gave the famous command: 'Good God, Sir, don't you see they are attacking the Yeomanry? Disperse the meeting!'[30]

At this stage it could be argued that no clear-cut impression was emerging from 'that horrid confusion'[31] on the field, but more than likely Hulton saw what he wanted to see – often a symptom of unchallenged power – in order to justify his summoning and sending in the mounted troops. Jolliffe observed the situation differently: the Yeomanry had ridden themselves into a tactical cul-de-sac where terror reigned, but Jolliffe makes no explicit mention of their being attacked in any way at this time. Moreover, the vast majority of eyewitness testimonies dispute Hulton's assessment.

Almost as Dickens swathed the Chancery intrigues of *Bleak House* in his all-pervading London fog, the cloud of dust kicked up by the horses and fleeing humans on St Peter's Field rendered precise observation problematic. Of course, the shroud of dust was not a fiction writer's metaphor, but a real factor in the confusion, and one of the possible reasons why reports of the confrontation differ. The dust and its obfuscating effect are mentioned by several of those present.[32]

However, there was one aspect which could not be denied: dust or no dust, sticks and stones or no sticks and stones, the Yeomanry's sabres were seen raised and glittering in the sunlight, and their razor-sharp blades were being put to brutal use. Cries for help and mercy were ignored, and 'sabres were plied to hew a way through naked held-up hands and defenceless heads;

and then chopped limbs and wound-gaping skulls were seen.'[33] Details of
the soldiers cutting at the people are legion, and the list of causes of injuries
features a significantly high number of sabre wounds.[34]

Following Hulton's shouted instruction, the Hussars formed themselves
into a line in front of the Mount Street houses and swept the field from
east to west. The immediate area would be effectively cleared within ten
minutes,[35] as the people fled to the periphery of the field and into the
surrounding streets. At least it was not deemed necessary to order the field
artillery into action.

L'Estrange's professional soldiery appear to have brought some semblance
of order to the dispersal. Hunt was to mention in a letter to the *Manchester
Observer* (6 September 1819) the 'Hussars' steadying influence'. The *Leeds
Mercury* (21 August 1819) agreed: 'The Hussars conducted themselves with
great propriety … as far as we could learn.' Nevertheless, there is evidence of
some of their members plying their sabres with a will.

On the credit side, John Jones, a resident of Windmill Street, saw one of
the Hussars actively restraining the Yeomanry's assaults on the populace with
the much-quoted exhortation: 'For shame! For shame! Gentlemen, forbear,
forbear! The people cannot get away!'[36]

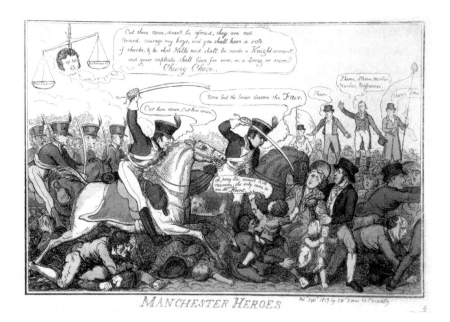

Another Cruikshank cartoon. (Working Class Movement Library)

One of the first detailed lists of casualties to be published contains the following entry concerning the injuries to a Samuel Allcard, an 18-year-old plasterer who lived on Portugal Street: 'Right elbow and head cut severely, his finger nearly cut off by the sabre of a Yeoman, thrown down and trampled on… This youth was saved by one of the 15th reg., who threatened to cut the Yeoman down if he struck him again.' Just five entries lower down on the alphabetical list, however, we read that iron founder William Allcock from Heaton Norris had his 'right arm much hurt, by a blow from a sabre… This was done by one of the 15th Hussars.'[37]

Mary Dowlan, a charwoman who lived on Lad Lane, a back street running parallel with the western end of Peter Street, recounts that she was about to be cut by a Yeoman (identified as Edward Tebbutt) on the far side of the hustings, towards Windmill Street, when she believed that the intervention of a Hussar saved her life. Mary was to return home shortly after that, where she dressed the wounds of fourteen men. She was to compare her home to 'a slaughter house'.[38]

The young Elijah Ridings, who had led the Newton Heath and Miles Platting contingent, considered his escape from injury or worse on St Peter's Field to be due to the help of a Hussars officer, who called out to him: 'Be quick young man, this way,' pointing out to him with his sword a way out of the mayhem.[39] We should remember, though, that the uniforms of the Yeomanry and the Hussars were very similar, and it may be impossible to arrive at comprehensive conclusions as to who was doing what. Several of the Yeomanry were positively identified as they rode about cutting at the people – of that at least we may be certain.

It is worth returning to Jemima Bamford's narrative now. We left her on the Windmill Street knoll, just as Hunt was arriving on the field.

I thought if I could get to stand at the door of one of those houses [on Windmill Street], I should have a good view of the meeting, and should perhaps see my husband again; and I kept going further down the row, until I saw a door open, and I stepped within it, the people of the house making no objections. By this time Mr. Hunt was on the hustings, addressing the people. In a minute or two some soldiers came riding up. The good folks of the house and some who seemed to be visitors, said, 'The soldiers were only there to keep order; they would not meddle with the people,' but I was alarmed. The people shouted, and then the soldiers shouted, waving their swords. Then they rode amongst the people, and there was a great outcry, and a moment after, a man passed without his hat, and wiping the blood off his head with his hand, and it ran down his arm in a great stream. The meeting was all in a tumult; there were dreadful cries; the soldiers kept riding amongst the people, and striking with their swords. I became faint, and turning from the door, I went unobserved down some steps into a cellared passage; and hoping to escape from the horrid noise, and to be concealed, I crept into a vault, and sat down, faint and terrified, on some fire wood. The cries of the multitude outside still continued, and the people of the house, upstairs, kept bewailing most pitifully. They could see all the dreadful work through the window, and their exclamations were so distressing, that I put my fingers in my ears to prevent my hearing more… The front door of the passage…soon opened, and a number of men entered, carrying the body of a decent, middle aged woman, who had been killed. I thought they were going to put her beside me, and was about to scream, but they took her forward, and deposited her in some premises at the back of the house.[40]

With the clearing of the hustings, the seizing or destruction of banners, and – some of the militia giving vent to a pointless spite – the hacking at abandoned musical instruments,[41] the job of suppression would have seemed complete. Unfortunately, the aggressors' vindictive streak did not stop with the smashing of flags, drums and bugles.

Gauntlet
(1.45 p.m.–3 p.m.)

On the northern edge of the field the Quakers' Meeting House would be a scene of fierce resistance to the mounted troops, with the inevitable bloody outcomes.

As the Yeomanry's beleaguered horses charged the people and the sabres flashed and cut, the prime viewing spot of earlier in the day was suddenly transformed into a possible place of refuge for the fleeing crowd. And amongst the pieces of timber below the 10ft-high surrounding wall, there were stones to be had:

> Being pressed by the yeomanry, a number…defended themselves with stones which they found there. It was not without difficulty, and after several were wounded, they were driven out. A young married woman of our party, with her face all bloody, her hair streaming about her, her bonnet hanging by the string, and her apron weighed with stones, kept her assailant at bay until she fell backwards and was near being taken; but she got away covered with severe bruises.[1]

Joseph Prestwick, a weaver from Droylsden, was to testify at the Redford vs. Birley proceedings that it was amongst the timber below the Meeting House wall that Thomas Redford was cut on the shoulder by Yeoman Alexander Oliver. Bamford gives a similar detail: Redford held up the green and gold flag until the staff was cut from his hand, and 'his shoulder was divided by the sabre of one of the Manchester Yeomanry'.[2] Prestwick also named one Samuel Harrison as striking at an old man and woman.[3]

Mr William Norris Buckley, the tradesman who had been on the steps of St Peter's Church when he had seen the arrival of the Manchester and Salford Yeomanry, ran into the graveyard of the Meeting House when the Yeomanry charged into the crowd. From here he saw the cavalry overtake some of the people, whose escape was hampered by the timber. He witnessed the Yeomanry 'cut five or six – they were indiscriminate'. He recognised several of the attackers: Robert Sharp, Mr Whitlow the attorney, James Moon, and a Mr Fox, all 'striking under the wall'.[4] Buckley escaped over the far wall into Dickinson Street, where he saw another assault, described below. James Slater, a weaver from Stockport, tried to hide in a small outhouse in the chapel grounds, but finding it full, had to abandon the idea and make a run for it. He was chased round the trees by four cavalrymen who 'cut his hat to tatters'.[5]

There were other obstacles baulking the protestors' flight into Dickinson Street. The barrier across Mount Street and the narrowness of the gap between the Quakers' School and the Meeting House hampered an easy passage,[6] and besides that, the infantry with their fixed bayonets in Dickinson Street prevented access to the streets beyond.[7]

If any of the fugitives thought that the chapel and graveyard would be respected as sanctuary, the military failed to share their belief. Francis Philips stated that the outer graveyard gates were 'burst open by a private soldier with a musket'.[8] William Jolliffe, the young Lieutenant in the Hussars, related:

> At the very moment I reached the Quakers' meeting-house, I saw a farrier of the 15th ride at a small door in the outer wall, and to my surprise his horse struck it with such force that it flew open. Two or three Hussars then rode in, and the place was immediately in their possession.[9]

At the John Lees inquest, Ann Booth would accuse two of the Yeomanry – Edward Meagher and John Hulme – of cutting at two people, one in the yard and another on the steps of the front gate. She claimed that Hulme was 'murdering his fellow creatures. I can call it nothing else.' William Butterworth claimed he was pursued by John Hulme all the way from near the hustings to the Quaker chapel, where Hulme wounded him with his sabre.[10]

Two further incidents that, according to Bush, 'reveal the predatory aggression of the Hussars'[11] were to emerge from the Lees inquest. Charles Washington told of the entry of six Hussars into the Quaker graveyard, where they cut at the fugitives. Peter Warburton was pinned against the chapel wall and received seven sabre and bayonet wounds.[12]

A somewhat different view of the battle that raged around the Meeting House was given by Francis Philips and the Hussars: much was made by the loyalists of the injuries sustained by the militia and the police. John Hulme – a 'gallant youth' – was struck in the face with a brick.[13] Hulme was later seen being carried on a makeshift stretcher down Dickinson Street. Eyewitness John Railton wrote in a letter to his wife dated 16 August that Hulme 'was taken to the Infirmary, and is not expected to survive the night'.[14] Lieutenant Frederic Buckley, an officer in the Hussars, saw 'a great many people…upon the wall, below the wall, and within the wall', all throwing stones, 'acting in concert', and shouting 'Pelt them! Pelt them!' Lieutenant James McAlpine saw a member of the Yeomanry lying on the ground 'apparently senseless'. Private William Rooke says he was attacked by a man with what looked like a gardener's hook; there were 'a thousand with sticks' in and around the Quaker chapel.[15]

William Brockbank, a Quaker who wrote the history of the old Meeting House in 1865, recorded the following:

> During the Peterloo massacre, many of the mob took refuge in this Meeting House, and were pursued into it by the soldiery – the trees in the graveyard being hacked by their swords – the green palings spattered with blood, and the floor of the house being stained in many places.[16]

The bloodstains on the Meeting House floor would prove well-nigh impossible to eradicate, even with the planing of the wooden surface.[17] The building would be demolished in a few years, and the current one built in 1829. The wall which at present surrounds the Mount Street Meeting House and yard is the same one which dates from Peterloo. It is a formidable 10ft-high barrier on the outside, so it is unsurprising that some of the pursued demonstrators, trapped there amongst the timber, turned and fought.

The Yeomanry would prove themselves far keener than the Hussars in their harrying of the fleeing crowd. John Robinson, the Manchester merchant who had nearly been knocked over by the Yeomanry's arrival on the field, stated that he saw the volunteer soldiery 'galloping after men, women and boys, in every direction'.[18]

Abraham Wrigley, a cotton-spinner from Oldham, saw the cavalry chase some people as far as the junction of Windmill Street and Lower Mosley Street, at the south-eastern corner of the field. He saw 'blood flowing

The wall surrounding the Quakers' Meeting Hall is still there. In the distance, down Bootle Street, is the Abercromby pub, home of the graphic Peterloo mural. (Author's collection)

very copiously from the heads of some of the people, after their hats were struck off'.[19]

Anne Jones, a resident of Windmill Street, was 40 yards away from the speakers' platform at the time of the Yeomanry's attack:

> I saw the cavalry cutting and slashing men on their way to the hustings. After getting to the hustings, they turned their horses round, and rode over the people in all directions, still cutting and slashing.[20]

Anne's husband John saw two of the Yeomanry he recognised – Withington and Bowker – cutting at everyone within reach. Anne then pulled people into her house – 'to save their lives' – but at one point they were pursued by a policeman who 'with great triumph' shouted, 'This is Waterloo for you! – this is Waterloo!' A railing in front of the house gave way from the pressure of the crowd, causing serious injury to a woman who fell into the cellar.[21]

Several eyewitnesses asserted that the Special Constables were lashing out with their truncheons. Jonah Andrew, a spinner from Lees, testified at the John Lees inquest:

> I saw several constables round him [John Lees], and beating him with their truncheons severely. One of them picked up a staff of a banner that had been cut with a sword, and said, 'Damn your bloody eyes. I'll break your back,' and they struck at him for a considerable time with their truncheons and the staff of the banner.[22]

This does not seem to have been an isolated incident. William Harrison observed: 'I saw plenty of constables striking with their truncheons'. At the same inquest, James Mills stated: 'It was peace officers that jobbed at me.' ('Jobbed' is here used in the older sense of 'struck or stabbed suddenly'.) Harry Kirkman, a weaver, claimed he saw one of the magistrates, Ralph Fletcher of Bolton, 'strike several people with a staff which he had in his hand'.[23] After Abraham Wrigley the Oldham spinner had been pursued hatless to the corner of Windmill Street, he turned round to retrieve his hat, and saw 'the constables striking some people who had got away, infirm people'.[24] At least one of the fatalities, Sarah Jones of Silk Street, mother of seven children, allegedly lost her life through truncheon blows: 'severely beat on the head and much bruised'. Sixteen-year-old Thomas Dale of Jersey Street was also hit about the head by police truncheons. He did not die, but was 'disabled about one week'.[25] According to one account Arthur Neil (or O'Neil/O'Neale), a weaver from Pigeon Street, Ancoats, suffered bruising from the constables' batons before being knocked down and crushed to death by the stampeding crowd. The constables seem to have been as free with their truncheons as the Yeomanry were with their sabres: among the several women struck by the police, Ann Peel of Thomas Street, having been beaten on the head, remained unconscious for a week, and thereafter suffered from chronic headaches; Ann Hall, a 52-year-old widow from Shudehill, was 'severely beat about the head and shoulders'.[26]

At the same time, two of the Special Constables were killed in the Yeomanry's charge. John Ashworth, landlord of the Bull's Head Inn, was sabred and ridden over, and William Evans, a carter of Queen Street, Hulme, trampled on by the cavalry charge, probably died within a few days.[27] Two Special Constables badly injured by the horses were Samuel McFadden ('left collar-bone broken and shoulder dislocated; three horses went over him') and John Routledge of Chorlton Row – 'a respectable man, a master mason' – who had his shoulder dislocated when trampled on during the charge. Three more constables were sabred by the militia, two of them suffering severe head wounds. Once again this gives some indication of the chaotic, reckless character of the Yeomanry's attack.[28]

Thomas Preston saw some of the crowd flee in the direction of St Peter's Church, but they were caught and struck at by the cavalry at the corner of the wall of Cooper's Cottage.[29]

Even if the fugitives managed to escape the cavalry and the Special Constables, there were still the bayonets and rifle butts of the infantry to contend with. The 88th Regiment, who had been waiting in Dickinson Street, and the 31st Infantry, who had moved in from Brazennose Street, were responsible for a number of assaults on the fleeing crowd. The MCC Report notes eight people with bayonet wounds on the head, thigh, stomach or back. One of them, John Pimblet, had his left arm skewered to his body. Thomas Bowker of Crumpsall was bayoneted in the belly near to the Quaker's chapel, before being knocked down and trodden on by a Yeomanry horse. Mary Evans was stabbed in the back of her leg, and her niece who was accompanying her had her clothes slashed. The two women were saved from further harm by another soldier.[30]

A panoramic view of the dispersal (see p.178). (Manchester Central Library Archives+ (M07592))

At the opposite end of St Peter's Field, facing Watson Street, next to the New Jerusalem Church, there was a narrow enclave. A group of people was pursued there by a cavalryman with a drawn sword. A hundred yards or so away, in Roger's Row, a cul-de-sac off Jackson's Row, a similar incident took place. Captain Richard Withington appeared at the end of the entry brandishing his pistol, shouting the order, 'Come out or I'll blow your brains out.'[31]

The pursuit continued into the surrounding streets. William Cheetham related that he was in a group of four or five people in a street a quarter of a mile from the field when Yeomanry bugler Edward Meagher came upon them. Meagher gave the order, 'Damn you, disperse. Damn you, I will cut your head off.' He then gave Cheetham a sabre cut below the ear 'three inches long and one inch deep'.[32] Meagher was found not guilty of this and other witnessed assaults, including one on 71-year-old Alice Kearsley,[33] in the ensuing court action.

William Norris Buckley, having made his escape from the Quakers' graveyard over the wall into Dickinson Street, there saw a Yeoman striking down a man on a crutch.[34]

In a nearby street Elizabeth Farren, her baby at her breast, saw and recognised a Yeomanry horseman as her former neighbour from Camp Street, Edward Tebbutt the candle maker. Tebbutt slashed at her with his sabre, cutting a 3in-long wound on her head. The baby was knocked from her arms, receiving 'a severe contusion on the head'. Elizabeth was knocked unconscious, and came to 'in a strange cellar'.[35] Tebbutt was instantly recognisable, from Elizabeth's description: 'he was a great dark man, with great Black Whiskers, he rode near the Trumpeter'.[36]

Tebbutt was involved in another similar attack. Mr William Gillmore – 'a respectable tradesman' – was having dinner in his house on Quay Street when he heard the noise from St Peter's Field. He left the house to have a look, and saw people being chased by the Yeomanry into his street. He turned around to go back home, and 'within twenty-five paces of his own door' a Yeoman – again positively identified later as Tebbutt – struck at Gillmore's head with his sabre. The first blow was blunted by the hat Gillmore was wearing, but after the hat had been knocked off, Tebbutt struck again at his bare head, inflicting a wound.[37] Tebbutt was cleared of this and other charges of assault in the ensuing inquests.

One poignant and much-cited incident once again reflects the furiously scattershot nature of the Yeomanry's attack on the people. Margaret

Goodwin, an elderly widowed neighbour of Yeoman Thomas Shelmerdine who had known him from childhood, recognised him as he charged towards her. Her remark 'Tom Shelmerdine, thee will not hurt me, I know,' failed to save her from injury as she received a sabre cut to the head and was trampled by the crowd.[38]

Robert Keymer, an officer in the local militia of Failsworth – who were not directly involved in the confrontation – gave evidence at the Redford vs. Birley civil action that he saw a couple of brickbats thrown at the Yeomanry: one close to the New Jerusalem Church, and the other across Deansgate on Quay Street. Although this seems to prove that there were stones lying around on the periphery of St Peter's Field, it also shows the extent of the Yeomanry's hounding of the fleeing crowd.[39]

Recent research has confirmed the scale of the law enforcers' pursuit. James Richardson of Salford, who had not even been at the meeting, was sabred – 'his nose cut down to his face' – outside his father's house on Jackson's Row; John Foster, a Salford man, was attacked by a posse of Special Constables on Deansgate, causing bruising on his head and body; John Hargreaves, a 61-year-old labourer, was ridden down by cavalry near the Piccadilly Infirmary; Patrick Reynolds, a weaver of Newtown, was charged into a lime-hole, where his legs were badly scalded; and Richard Wilde, aged 14, from Coop Street, Manchester, was cut in the back of his head as far away as Oldham Street. Mary Jones received a blow from a sabre a mile from St Peter's Field.[40]

It appears that a large group of people was chased as far as Bridge Street, which is along Deansgate, over a quarter of a mile from the hustings. Martha Partington from Eccles was killed here by a fall into a cellar, caused by pressure from the crowd. For such a crush to occur at this distance from the field, the harrying by the soldiers must have continued this far. One report of Martha's death records 'thrown into cellar'; another states 'crushed to death in a cellar-hole'.[41] The inquest returned a verdict of 'accidental death'. The coroner's comment almost beggars belief: he and the jury 'lamented the great indiscretion of women in wantonly putting themselves in the way of harm, and said that they must, under the circumstances, take the consequences'.[42]

On the subject of distance from the hustings, at the John Lees inquest James Harmer wished to call as witness the keeper of a toll gate 'near a mile distant' from St Peter's Field. The evidence given would have been to show the terror of the fleeing crowds: in order to pass more quickly through the gate, even at this distance they were willingly throwing down sixpences and half-crowns for the penny fee, without waiting for change. The coroner deemed the detail inadmissible, however, and the gatekeeper was not called.[43]

As to whether gunshots were fired during the dispersal, the evidence, although considerably less copious than on other matters, is still available, although just as equivocal. Small firearms of the day were single-shot pistols, like the newly popular duelling weapons. As they took some time to reload, giving the enemy every opportunity to retaliate, they were used sparingly, if at all, in battle. Co-ordinated and successive volleys from ranks of trained musketeers or riflemen – 'platoon firing', which was used in battle and to disperse the rioters at New Cross that evening – were of course a different matter. The mounted 15th Hussars were issued with regulation flintlock 'Brown Bess' carbines, but they were rarely used in action, and there appears to be no evidence of them being fired at Peterloo.

William Norris Buckley stated that he saw the Manchester and Salford Yeomanry loading their pistols in Pickford's Yard,[44] whereas it would appear highly unlikely that the vast majority of the crowd was so equipped. There was the expense, for one thing: a musket or duelling-style pistol, plus upkeep, powder and shot, would have been beyond the means – and practical usefulness – of most of the impoverished workers present. Unsurprisingly, the right-wing press thought otherwise, 'Not a single shot was fired by any of the Military, although they were fired upon, several times, by the Reformers and their abettors.'[45]

Lieutenant-Colonel L'Estrange concurred in his letter to Major-General Sir John Byng, written later that evening: 'not a shot...has been fired by any of the military, though several have been fired by the populace against the troops'.[46] Hay said as much in his narrative of the day's events in his letter to Lord Sidmouth, written a couple of hours later (see Appendix 6). This view is firmly rebutted by Jonathan Edward Taylor, however, who quotes inquest evidence to back up his conclusion that 'all the firing yet alleged [has] been *traced* either to the 88th or to the Yeomanry'.[47]

In any case, it would have been difficult to pinpoint the source of a small and momentary flash and bang, especially in the midst of a panicking crowd, but eyewitness reports seem to prove that some shots were fired. Reverend Stanley wrote: 'I...distinctly heard four or five shots...on the opposite side of the square...but nobody could inform me by whom they were fired.' The various recorded opinions of the source of these shots are: 'out of an upper window near the New Jerusalem Church'; 'out of the [Quaker's] Meeting Place yard'; 'from the top of a house below the Windmill'; 'at the end of

Jackson's Row, from a window near the Quakers' Meeting House wall…
betwixt the dye-house and the gates [on South Street]'. The last witness,
Robert Hall, a Salford cotton salesman, was convinced that Yeoman John
Hulme was the target. He also stated that a shot issued from a window of
a house on Watson Street, and that a foot soldier returned the fire. These
depositions give the impression that at least one radical sympathiser had
access to a small firearm.[48]

There is, however, more to say on the matter, even before we consider
the shootings by the troops at New Cross that night. Once again the John
Lees inquest is our source of information. Ann Rayborn, the daughter of
the landlady of the lodging house at No. 1 Watson Street, gave evidence
that around 2.30 p.m. – so during the 'mop-up' operation – two shots were
fired *into* one of the upstairs windows, smashing the glass. A posse of police
and soldiers then entered her house, where they accused a Mr Wilson of
throwing stones from the roof. (Given the steeply sloping roofs of the Watson
Street houses, this action would have been very difficult, if not impossible.)
Nevertheless, Wilson was arrested and taken away. Both Ann and her mother
Elizabeth denied that any stones or gunshots had issued from the house.
They asserted that the soldiers, however, once inside the house, had fired a
third shot, on the landing of the stairs.[49]

The information contained in the Police Office handbill of 21 July calling
for an 'Armed Association' (see Appendix 1) suggests that it was much more
likely that the supporters of the civil authorities carried firearms on the day.

In most cases, though, like Major Dyneley's field artillery, the primed
pistols were not intended for use, but were rather seen as an intimidating
presence and a token of official power.

Meanwhile, back at the hustings, the major arrests had been made. The
Reverend Stanley – from his vantage point 100 yards away – made the
observation: 'Hunt fell, or threw himself, amongst the constables, and was
driven or dragged as fast as possible down the avenue which communicated
with the magistrates' house; his associates were hurried after him in a
similar manner.'[50]

Hunt, running the gauntlet of hisses, groans and dismissive blows from
the lines of policemen,[51] was closely followed by Captain Withington
who waved a cocked pistol at his back. On the steps of Mr Buxton's house
General Officer Clay struck him a double-handed blow on the head with a
truncheon, the ferocity of which was fortunately minimised by the Orator's
white top hat, which was forced down over his face.[52] Hunt's own account

of his passage from platform to house is colourful (see Appendix 5) and we are perhaps safer to follow others' narrative at this point. He was certainly assaulted, but probably not to the extent suggested by his later version of events. In an 1831 speech to reformers, he mentioned the 'sabre wound on the hand and about sixty blows from the constables'.[53] If this is true, the truncheon blows cannot have been too violent, or he would never have survived the walk to the house. George Swift, present with Hunt later that afternoon at the New Bailey prison, relates that Hunt was unable to lift his injured left arm very far, but no more serious injuries are mentioned by the young shoemaker.[54] Also, Hunt was able to walk unaided the three-quarters of a mile to the New Bailey, where within a few days he had penned several cogent and strongly worded letters. In them he declared himself 'in tip-top spirits' and 'in high health'.[55] However, when in 1885 Oldham demonstrator James Cooper gave a lecture on his experiences at Peterloo, he described Hunt in Buxton's house thus: 'as pale as death… His clothes were torn off his back; his coat, vest, and even shirt were torn to ribbons.'[56] This may be an embellishment though, especially as Cooper also relates that he escaped quickly from the field and was cornered in a doorway a quarter of a mile away by a mounted Yeoman, so he may not have had the time or the opportunity to register precise details of Hunt's condition.

It would appear that Hunt had Nadin to thank for protection from some of the worst blows. According to Hunt's version, the Orator manoeuvred the Deputy Chief Constable, who 'yielded like a child', into the way of the most fearsome blows (see Appendix 5). Considering Nadin's bulk and natural obduracy, this is somewhat hard to believe, and the truth seems to be that Nadin willingly effected Hunt's safe passage to the house. The motives may not have been as praiseworthy as they appear; Nadin was notoriously capable of great unpleasantness towards those he deemed his social inferiors, but Hunt the moneyed landowner was seen to deserve at least a modicum of respect. Furthermore, the arrest of the talismanic reformer was set fair to be the jewel in the crown of Nadin's career, and it could be argued that the Deputy Chief Constable was simply protecting his investment, as it were. A martyred or grievously wounded Hunt would have been no use to either Nadin or the anti-reform lobby.

No doubt emboldened by the military presence, Nadin also claimed to have dragged Joseph Johnson off the platform by his legs.[57] Apart from these incidents, the shifting of detainees from hustings to Buxton's house, and then on foot to the New Bailey prison, seems to have been carried out expeditiously enough. The real horrors had taken place, and were still taking place, on the field and in the surrounding streets.

The Reverend Stanley, coming face-to-face with Hunt in the hallway of the house, noted an interesting detail: 'I thought I could perceive a smile of triumph on his countenance.'[58] Perhaps getting himself taken into custody had been among Hunt's objectives all along, since being put on trial in such high-profile circumstances would give him a national platform for his ideas of reform. In one of his letters from the New Bailey prison, he wrote that he was 'looking forward to trial...before an honest jury'.[59] His response to Nadin's, 'Sir, I have a warrant against you, and arrest you as my prisoner' had been, 'I willingly surrender myself to any civil officer who will show me his warrant.' Nadin, conceivably playing a power game of his own, had not produced the warrant but had simply said, 'I will arrest you: I have got information on oath against you.'[60]

The *Liverpool Mercury* and *Wheeler's Manchester Chronicle* published a list of those detained (see Appendix 8). Bamford, Joseph 'Doc' Healey, Carlile and the injured Mary Fildes were among those who had slipped through the net, albeit temporarily in the men's case. Mary, having sustained some truncheon blows 'about the face and head', had jumped off the platform at the same time as Hunt was apprehended.[61] Her account of the subsequent skirmish, according to the People's Museum in Salford, runs as follows:

I was standing on the speakers' platform when the soldiers attacked. I tried to leap to the ground, but my dress got caught on a nail. As I was trapped in mid air, a yeoman slashed me with his sabre and stole my flag. He didn't take the red Cap of Liberty on top of the flag pole and I snatched the red and white plume from his hat.

Having made her escape, Mary then made herself scarce for a couple of weeks, whilst the police searched her house on Comet Street, and the legal machinery concerned itself with those considered to be bigger fish. By keeping a low profile and possibly by virtue of her gender, Mary managed to avoid arrest. The silk banner stolen by the Yeoman would become a *casus belli* later that day, at New Cross.

The list of around thirty detainees given in the *Liverpool Mercury* included: Henry Hunt, John Knight, John Tyas, John Thacker Saxton, George Swift, Mary Waterworth, Sarah Hargreaves, Eliza Grant [*sic*],[62] Joseph Johnson, and James Moorhouse. Moorhouse was to insist that he was not on the platform when the arrests were made. This was true, as he had made a swift exit to the Windmill pub before the speeches started (see Appendix 12). He was arrested later that day anyway as he continued his libations in the Flying Horse on Market Street, where he had met up with his six-month-pregnant wife. Among those later discharged were reporter John Tyas and Stockport reformer Mary Waterworth.[63] The seriously injured Elizabeth Gaunt, astonishingly, and to Hunt's fury, was imprisoned for twelve days before being released on the first day of the initial hearing at the New Bailey.

Bamford's harrowing description of the field after the dispersal is justly famous:

> In ten minutes from the commencement of the havoc the field was an open and almost deserted space. The sun looked down through sultry and motionless air. The curtains and blinds of the windows within view were all closed. The hustings remained, with a few broken and hewed flag-staves erect, and a torn and gashed banner or two dropping; whilst over the whole field were strewed caps, bonnets, hats, shawls, and shoes and other parts of male and female dress trampled, torn and bloody. The Yeomanry had dismounted – some were easing their horses' girths, others adjusting their accoutrements; and some were wiping their sabres. Several mounds of human beings still remained where they had fallen, crushed down and smothered. Some of these were still groaning, others with staring eyes, were gasping for breath, and others would never breathe more. All was silent save these low sounds, and the occasional snorting and pawing of steeds.[64]

Although this was almost certainly not an on-the-spot report – Bamford by then had quit the field – and one might look askance at the detail 'several mounds of human beings' who 'still remained where they had fallen', Bamford's picture of devastation is corroborated in many important respects by Lieutenant Jolliffe:

> The field and the adjacent streets now presented an extraordinary sight: the ground was quite covered with hats, shoes, musical instruments, and other things. Here and there lay the unfortunates who were too much injured to move away, and this sight was rendered the more distressing by observing some women among the sufferers.[65]

The Reverend Stanley recalled his impressions of the scene:

> Some were seen bleeding on the ground and unable to rise; others, less severely injured but faint with the loss of blood were retiring slowly or leaning upon others for support...[66]

Joseph Barrett, a warehouse owner from Newton Heath, had watched events from the second floor of a house on Windmill Street, next door to the pub. He concurred with Bamford in that he remembered there were 'heaps of people lying, who seemed dead, but had got into this state, by being stuck & frightened, though many of them were wounded'. He also recalled an unnamed Cathedral Minister 'high in office' strutting about the scene of devastation 'like a cock that had beaten his opponent'.[67]

Jonathan Edward Taylor observed a detail which 'smote his heart': the Yeomanry had re-mustered in front of Buxton's house, waving their swords and cheering 'in token of triumph'.[68]

Bamford had left St Peter's Field with the fleeing crowd 'carried, I may say almost literally, to the lower end of the Quakers' meeting house, the further wall of which screened us from observation and pursuit',[69] from where he escaped by the back streets. He then made his way via King Street and Market Street to the road back to Middleton, continually asking about the whereabouts and safety of his wife. He received news that she was safe, and they were to have an emotional reunion later that day on the main road near Harpurhey. Jemima had heard various rumours that Samuel had either been killed, or wounded, or imprisoned.[70] Bamford had taken care to hide the sprig of laurel inside his hat in order to avoid recognition and arrest. His reprieve, however, would last less than ten days; Nadin and the magistrates considered him too big a prize to fly the coop for long.

Very few of the demonstrators' flags and caps of liberty survived. Time and again, obsessively, the banners, symbols and mottoes of reform and liberty were prime targets: the Yeomanry with their cry 'Have at their flags!'; the pride of Mutrie in plundering his 'very grand cap of liberty'; Nadin who claimed at the Lees inquest to have bagged himself 'a green flag'; Nathan Broadhurst who picked up a cap of liberty and refused to surrender it to the Yeomanry, whereupon he was pursued with the cries 'Damn him, cut him down!'; James Walker the dyer of Edge Street, who jumped off the hustings holding 'a coloured flag': 'I had the flag trailing behind me; and the Cavalry trod upon the staff, and broke it...'; the observation from William Harrison:

'The constables first attacked the colours…they were tearing the banners from the people'; and the telling detail supplied by John Fell, a shopkeeper from Union Street:

> I saw one of the Yeomanry Cavalry, at about fifteen or twenty yards from the hustings, take a standard from one of the people; he turned his horse's head, and rode a few yards towards the house, and waved the flag in the air, by way of triumph.[71]

There was the gloating report in *Wheeler's Manchester Chronicle* the following Saturday, stating that two of these captured standards were to be publicly burnt in Stockport market place.

During his return to Middleton later that day, Bamford and some stragglers were overtaken by a troop of Yeomanry riding along the Collyhurst road. One of the cavalry was wearing a 'broad green band, or sash, across his shoulder and breast'. Bamford correctly guessed that this was a fragment of the SUFFRAGE UNIVERSAL banner – the one originally carried by Thomas Redford – sported now 'for the gratification of the vanity of the captor'.[72]

Such compulsive targeting is a clear indication that, more so than the huge crowd and the presence of so-called demagogues, what really frightened the authorities and the middle-class-based powers was the fashioning of libertarian and egalitarian *ideas* into a newly organised, visible force.

The roads into Manchester that had been filled with happy processions a couple of hours earlier now saw a straggling rout of refugees fleeing in the opposite direction. Archibald Prentice, having returned to his home in Salford before the arrival of Hunt, was shocked by what he saw:

> I had not been at home for more than a quarter of an hour when a wailing sound was heard from the main street, and, rushing out, I saw people running in the direction of Pendleton, their faces pale as death, and some with blood trickling down their cheeks. It was with difficulty I could get any one to stop and tell me what had happened.[73]

A spectator in a house in St Ann's Street was to recall many years later:

> I saw them running past like a flock of frightened sheep, many with clothes half torn off their backs, some had lost a shoe, and half of them were without hats.[74]

From the upstairs window of his house on Mosley Street, John Railton observed: 'constantly coming past in carts, coaches and on boards persons dead or sadly hurt, and others limping along that had met with some accident or other'.[75]

And yet not all was terror and despair – at Newton Heath a man from Copster Hill, Oldham, had collected hats and shoes from the empty field and was handing them out to stragglers who had lost theirs.[76]

The speed with which the Hussars cleared the field is further proof of the crowd's lack of weaponry and aggressive intentions. Just a few seconds' rational thought is enough to reveal the absurdity of the accusation typically expressed in the *Wheeler's Manchester Chronicle* report:

> The whole assemblage had every appearance of military array... The rebellious nature of the Meeting; its numbers and threatening aspect; the warlike insignia displayed; the order of march and military arrangements...[77]

A couple of witnesses at Hunt's trial retained a markedly different impression. Sidney Walker, lieutenant in the Bengal native infantry, stated: 'The persons assembled were not in military order...they did not look like soldiers.' Firmly contradicting Francis Philips's observation on the Stockport marchers, Thomas Brooks observed: 'The people were walking in a straggling way, not at all like military.'[78] And obviously, to cram the bulk of your so-called force (which included women and children) into a densely packed, highly visible and un-manoeuvrable mass with no organised defensive resources would have been military suicide. If armed insurrection had been planned, this would have been an insanely incompetent way to go about things.

One has only to compare the afternoon's rapid dispersal to the pitched battle which took place on the streets around New Cross throughout the coming night. Here the workers *were* armed with stones and brickbats, which they freely used, and, after the violent injustice of earlier that day, they were in a far from pacific mood.

5

Nightfall
(3 p.m. onwards)

Richard Carlile, having escaped minus his hat, took refuge in a house on Windmill Street. He arrived on the doorstep with a wounded woman, and the occupier, thinking he was a doctor, allowed them entrance.[1] He was to stay there until evening, by which time he had sent out the house tenant to buy him a replacement hat. Most shops being shut, this took several hours, and it was 6 p.m. before he was able to make plans for a speedy return to London. Carlile reasoned that he would be far more useful publishing his report in the capital rather than tarrying in Manchester, and there were other reasons for an imminent departure which became clearer as the night wore on. After a visit to James Wroe to tell him of his intentions, Carlile set about making his way back to London. It proved to be a more involved process than he had envisaged.

The following extract from Carlile's narrative is given verbatim and in full. Not only is it a grand cloak-and-dagger tale, it captures the pervasive atmosphere of disquiet, occasionally erupting into panic, that beset Manchester and beyond in the hours and days following Peterloo:

I resolved to leave by the first mail, but my portmanteau was still in the enemies' quarters. A person in Mr. Wroe's house undertook to bring me to a coach stand, and having got into a coach, I ordered the man to drive me to the 'Star' Inn, to the door of which we had great difficulty in getting owing to the pressure of so many mounted yeomanry. I got out boldly, and told the coachman to wait, and went into the travellers' room. I made sure of being known, as we had driven past the inn in the morning in the open barouche, and were seen by all the servants, who did not fail to hiss a little as their house was the rendezvous for the enemy, a circumstance I did not know when I went there. On calling the waiter he was quite sullen, saying they had

The Star Inn, Deansgate, where Carlile stayed during his time in Manchester. The magistrates breakfasted here on the morning of Peterloo, and the final session of the abortive John Lees inquest was held here. (Simpkin, Marshall, Hamilton, Kent & Co.)

kept me a bed at a great inconvenience to other customers. I pacified him by telling him to charge for it, but I had to ring again and again before the bill and the portmanteau were brought, and all the time I thought there was something brewing for me. At last a different waiter came, and then my things were soon brought and my bill settled. Having pleased the waiter beyond his expectations, I slipped on a greatcoat and a pair of white gaiters, and he ushered me to the coach with a great deal of ceremony, and the yeomanry in front were requested to make way for one whom they had been sent to kill in the morning. While I had been waiting so long for my bill, etc., my coach had to move on to make way for another, and so I was shown to the wrong coach and drove off to the 'Bridgewater Arms', from whence the mail coach started. I had just got out and paid the man when there was a hue and cry after me by the first coachman I had hired, and unknowingly left behind at the 'Star' door. My first impression was that the police had scent of me, but I soon found my mistake, paid the man, and all was right. At three in the morning the coach left, and great was the terror of the coachman, guard, and passengers that it would be stopped by the Reformers before it got to Stockport. I had nothing to fear on this head, but was not free of apprehension that one of my fellow-travellers was a police officer in disguise set to watch me, or to keep at my heels at any rate. He was despatched from Manchester as an express agent to London, either to the Government or some mercantile house. There were four of us in the mail, two were friends of the master of the 'Bridgewater Arms', and had been there on a visit, and appeared to be coach-masters themselves living somewhere between Macclesfield and Derby. Those two worthies were well filled with wine, but a bottle was brought to the coach door by the master to have a parting glass, when to every glass was the toast, 'Down with Hunt!' One of them would insist on my taking a glass as a fellow-traveller to join in the sentiment of 'Down with Hunt!' To pacify the fools and disarm suspicion as far as possible, I drank the glass of wine with 'Down with Hunt!' which was considered the proof of my being a good fellow and a fit companion for them. The panic which prevailed in all the towns from Manchester to Northampton can scarcely be conceived, and it fell to my lot to detail the particulars of the massacre at each town we passed through, as nothing but post-horse expresses had passed through till the arrival of our mail coach.[2]

Whilst this drama was being enacted, and even as the Reverend Hay was penning his summing-up of the day's events in his letter to Lord Sidmouth (see Appendix 6), there were nocturnal riots in the New Cross area of Manchester. The blue touch paper was lit when Mary Fildes's silk banner – the one with the woman holding the scales of justice and treading on a serpent – which had been taken from her on the hustings, was displayed in the Oldham Street grocer's shop window of a Mr Tate. A mob gathered outside the shop and smashed the windows. Some constables and a troop of the 15th Hussars were quickly on the scene, but the stone-throwing crowds proved difficult to quell, partly because, once confronted, they ran through houses and passageways to reassemble in the next street. Eventually the Riot Act was read, and the riflemen of the 88th Regiment opened fire on the crowd, leaving three or four persons on the ground.[3] William Bradshaw from Whitefield and 17-year-old Joshua Whitworth from Hyde – the latter shot in the back of the head – were killed, and Salford man Samuel Jackson was shot in his left knee and had to have his leg amputated. Elizabeth Green of Withy Grove had her ankle smashed by a bullet.[4] Troops of cavalry and Special Constables patrolled the streets throughout the night:

> Sudden alarms from different quarters, the escorts of prisoners down to the New Bailey, occasional reports of fire-arms, the sounds of horses' feet, the rattling of the drum, and the strains of the trumpet, kept the inhabitants in constant trepidation, and it was not till an early hour on the Tuesday morning [4 a.m. according to Jolliffe] that these things ceased, and temporary quiet restored.[5]

The radical James Wroe put a different emphasis on the night's events:

> It is impossible to depict the feelings of distress and consternation visible in the countenances of the people during the remainder of Monday; nor was the conduct of the *authorities* calculated to allay those feelings. Every where might be seen parties of cavalry, headed by the civil power, scouring the streets with a savage ferocity never before witnessed; and towards evening things were in a yet worse condition…many were wounded, and some lost their lives… The night of Monday and nearly the whole of Tuesday were one continual scene of tumult and alarm.[6]

Special Constable Robert Mutrie, who had been in the double line of policemen on St Peter's Field earlier in the day, was now on horseback. He included the following in the letter to his brother-in-law:

> Mr. Norris was very averse that we should commence hostilities and with great reluctance gave his consent that it [the Riot Act] should be read. The moment it was read Captain Booth ordered the Infantry officer to form a hollow square in the centre of the Cross, we all took shelter in the square when the word was given to fire in all directions – the square then opened and the horse charged every way upon the crowd – my mare grew quite mad

and carried over the back of many a poor Devil. – two people were shot in the first charge just opposite my room window. You may be sure I was (as was my Mare) very thankful to get relieved at 3 o'clock in the morning…this does not look like peace.[7]

As the next day dawned, a stunned and uneasy quiet had fallen on the town.

The following is an extract from a letter written within a couple of hours of the St Peter's Field dispersal by Major Dyneley, commander of the Royal Horse Artillery that had been waiting with the pair of cannon on Mosley Street:

> The first action of the Battle of Manchester is over…and I am happy to say has ended in the complete discomfiture of the Enemy… I was very much assured to see the way in which the Volunteer Cavalry knocked the people about during the whole time we were on the ground; the instant they saw ten or a dozen Mobites together, they rode at them and *leathered* them properly.[8]

The tone of the extract is one of entirely inappropriate triumphalism, betraying either an unforgivable ignorance of events, or a near-sociopathic delusion. One could argue that it was written in a heated, unguarded moment, with feelings still running high from the conflict, and intended only as a private communication, like Mutrie's letter to his brother-in-law (Dyneley apologises for 'the hurried way in which I am writing'). However, the authorities were quick to make public a purportedly more in-depth, considered version of the same: already early in the morning of the 17th their broadsheets were appearing in the Manchester streets. The following extracts will suffice to give an impression of the content:

AN ACCOUNT OF THE MANCHESTER MEETING, WHICH TOOK PLACE ON THE 16TH OF AUG. 1819

> …The events of yesterday will bring down upon the name of Hunt, and his accomplices, the deep and lasting execrations of many a sorrowing family, and of the well-affected numbers of society at large. With a factious perverseness peculiarly their own, they have set at open defiance the timely warnings of the Magistracy, and having daringly invited the attendance of a mass of people, which, as it respects yesterday's muster, may with much reason, be computed at 100,000 individuals, they proceeded to address them with language and

suggestions of the usual desperate and malevolent character... The first notable object in the procession was a board exalted above the crowd, bearing the specious inscription 'Order'; next came a miserable band of musicians; and in about the centre of the phalanx, the odious instigators of the day's calamity, viz. Hunt, Johnson, Knight...

...the red cap of liberty held a prominent place in the procession, and several flags with the usual inflammatory sentences were displayed.

...the bugle sounded, and the Manchester and Salford Yeomanry Cavalry... advanced in full charge through the multitude... The 15th Hussars and the Prince Regent's Regiment of Yeomanry Cavalry next approached, and routed the throng, with the utmost dismay in all directions.[9]

Typical of the radical riposte was the following from the *Manchester Observer* the next week:

Just published – No. 1 – price twopence – of PETERLOO MASSACRE containing a full, true, and faithful account of the inhuman murders, woundings and other monstrous Cruelties exercised by a set of INFERNALS (miscalled soldiers) upon unarmed and distressed people.[10]

And the Home Office's pre-emptive response to *that*:

As the 'Peterloo Massacre' cannot be otherwise than grossly libellous, you will probably deem it right to proceed by arresting the publishers.[11]

The war of words – which has continued with varying levels of intensity and degrees of polarity ever since – had begun. The government, however, had another, potentially more malignant weapon: that of silence. This manifested itself not simply with the selective *omertà* of the magistrates or the volunteer or regular troops, nor only with the government's repeated refusal to respond to petitions asking for an enquiry, but also in the widespread gagging tactics employed by the powers in the land. This policy was to culminate in the infamous draconian Six Acts, which were to turn the kingdom into a virtual police state.

PART THREE
Aftermath

An artist's impression of the New Bailey prison, viewed from the bridge over the Irwell (based on a contemporary print). (Author's collection/Rob Hall)

1

War of Words and Silence

On the right bank of the River Irwell, not far from where Salford Central Station is now, stood the formidable structure of the New Bailey prison. Demolished in 1872 when it was replaced by Strangeways on the Bury Road, this forbidding institution – the 'Manchester Bastille' – in its day served many purposes, containing courtroom, holding cells, and facilities for punishment and execution. Bamford described it thus:

> A building of sombre appearance, with flanking towers and shot-holes, and iron spikes jutting above high walls, and ponderous black fetters hung above the barred windows and grated portal.[1]

In 1819 the flogging of women was still a possibility in the prison, and the treadwheel and mangle were still in use if it was thought a prisoner needed to be kept busy. Solitary cells were 7ft 3in (2.21m) by 5ft 9in (1.75m), beds were hard, and there were no heating facilities. To give some idea of the standard of food, the treat of the week was the Sunday stew, made from cow's head. One head fed twenty men, or forty women. Regular fare was stale bread, pea soup, gruel, and potatoes.[2]

It was here that Hunt and the others were held while awaiting their court hearing. From 5 p.m. on the day of their arrest they were placed in solitary confinement, so that they could not communicate with one another. The weapon of silence was already being deployed. Hunt claims that on several occasions he asked to see the warrant for his arrest, but this was refused, as was bail.[3]

Nevertheless, some communication with the outside world was possible. Hunt wrote several letters from the New Bailey, which were all delivered to the intended recipient, but not before they were intercepted and copied by the magistrates. The relevant letters in the John Rylands collection are in Hay's meticulous hand, not Hunt's.[4] One is reminded of Bamford's request to Hay at the New Bailey after the Ardwick Bridge arrests in March 1817: Bamford was told that he would be allowed to write a letter to his wife, but he should leave it unsealed 'as it must be examined before it was forwarded'.[5] One suspects that Hunt knew that his missives would be read by the magistrates, as he is forthright in his description of the events of 16 August and where the blame should be laid. Four of these letters were published in the *Manchester Observer* of 28 August.

Elsewhere, the outspoken commentaries (and, more discreetly, the groundwork for litigation) continued unremittingly. An equitable view of Peterloo has been rendered more difficult by the fact that, almost from the beginning, passions were running high on both sides. Carlile, for example, may have risked alienating some neutrals with his emotive and colourful account – one of the first to hit the London streets, two days after the event – even though there are vital truths among the odd overstatement and the verbal pyrotechnics:

> The Yeomanry Cavalry made their charge with a most infuriate frenzy; they cut down men, women and children, indiscriminately, and appeared to have commenced a premeditated attack, with the most insatiable thirst for blood and destruction. They merit a medallion, on one side of which should be inscribed 'The Slaughter-men of Manchester', and a reverse bearing a description of their slaughter of defenceless men, women and children, unprovoked and unnecessary. As a proof of meditated murder on the part of the Magistrates, every stone was gathered from the ground on the Friday and Saturday previous to the meeting, by scavengers sent there by the express command of the Magistrates, that the populace might be rendered more defenceless.[6]

We have already sampled the rhetoric of the authorities' version of events, and with this febrile crossfire of recriminations it is perhaps not surprising that the town fell easy prey to rumour and panic. At 10.30 a.m. the following morning – Tuesday, 17 August – Chief Constable John Moore rushed into the Cotton Exchange 'in the utmost trepidation' with the following announcement:

...the Magistrates had ordered the Exchange, and all the shops and warehouses, to be instantly shut up, information just having been received at the Police-office, from a coachman, who came all out of breath, with the tidings that from 8 to 10,000 men, in regular array, armed with pikes, pistols, &c. were within half an hour's march of Manchester, determined to take revenge for the disasters of the previous day. Mr. Moore, therefore, requested that all the gentlemen present would repair to their respective warehouses, factories, workshops, &c. and state to the people in their employment, that the Magistrates wished all well-disposed persons to keep out of the way of the soldiers, as they really could not be answerable for the consequences of the apprehended conflict.[7]

The Exchange was immediately cleared and shut down. Visiting merchants hurried back home, shops and warehouses were closed, and the streets of Manchester were deserted.

A young lad, out walking with his father, would recall many years later:

When we were near to the Exchange-street end of the [St Ann's] square we met a whole troop of gentlemen, the old fat ones puffing and blowing and using their best endeavours to keep up with their juniors. They called out, 'Turn back! Turn back! They are coming in thousands, armed with guns and pistols and long pikes.' We, like the rest, turned tail and ran home [off Cross Street], locking and barring the doors behind us.[8]

The town braced itself for the invasion.

The Times takes up the story: 'Whispers at length began to circulate that the alarm was all a hoax.'[9] And a hoax was all it had been. Prentice could not resist the barb: the whole affair had been 'conjured up in the consciences of the guilty'.[10]

The edginess continued into the next week. There was an accidental explosion of gunpowder in a Market Street gunsmith's the following Monday, causing people to assume a reformers' attack and to run for Mr Norris and the soldiers. Taylor's sardonic comment echoes that of Prentice: 'Such are the operations of those whose conduct betrays a ridiculous compound of folly and fear.'[11]

Tuesday was normally market day, the town heaving with visitors intending to buy or sell. On this day, however, many shops and commercial buildings were closed, and the streets nearly deserted. Wednesday saw the posting of a large number of notices in the streets:

Caution – The Inhabitants of Manchester and Salford are requested not to be out of their own houses after nine at night, during the present disturbed state of these towns.[12]

Thoughts of genuine revenge smouldered for many a day, sometimes flaring into brief, uncoordinated acts of violence. Bamford relates that he spent the evening of Peterloo 'brooding over a spirit of vengeance towards the authors of our humiliation'.[13]

Special Constable Robert Campbell of Miller Street was attacked by a mob near The Angel inn on Newton Lane on 18 August: 'Several men seized him and beat him with a poker until there was no appearance of life, and threw a heap of stones on him as he lay on the ground.'[14] Jonathan Edward Taylor added the all-important detail: 'Hours before Campbell was attacked, he had been firing a pistol *loaded with ball* into the streets.'[15]

New Cross was the scene of two more riots before the weekend. *The Times* of 24 August reported the shooting of two women – apparently not fatally – by the 15th Hussars on the Friday night, despite the assurance from *Wheeler's Chronicle* that by the end of the week the town was mostly quiet and that nothing of 'particular consequence' occurred after Campbell's death.[16]

It was not only in Manchester that disorder erupted. On the Tuesday evening 'a large mob assembled in Oldham, and were guilty of very riotous conduct'.[17] Once again the military were called in to disperse the crowd and then to patrol the streets. A 'gentleman of high respectability' was in the wrong place at the wrong time, and narrowly avoided being shot by mistake.

On Thursday there was 'some tumult' at Rochdale. A troop of the 15th Hussars and a company of the 31st Regiment set off at speed for the town, and three demonstrators were brought back to the New Bailey by the soldiers.[18]

In Macclesfield on the night of 17/18 there were disturbances that culminated in a pitched battle. A 'numerous assembly of men and boys' gathered to hiss at the more well-to-do inhabitants as they passed in the street. Feelings escalated, windows of some of the more opulent houses were smashed, and when the Riot Act was read by a magistrate, this was ignored. In the absence of the regular soldiers, a combination of constables and civilians managed to overpower the rioters, of whom around fifty were in prison by 11 o'clock. There was sporadic trouble – including the hurling of abuse at passing London coaches – until all was declared quiet at around

3 a.m. Samuel Hardern, a 28-year-old wood turner from the town, was deemed the ringleader, and although he pleaded not guilty he was jailed for eighteen months. Ralph Wright, a veteran of Waterloo who wore his medal in court, was also adjudged to be involved, and was sentenced to six months. The disorder was definitely a reaction to what had taken place on St Peter's Field the previous day, as the political tone of the Attorney-General's courtroom speech made clear:

> Men deluded themselves if they thought their condition would be bettered by such kind of Reform as Universal Suffrage, Annual Parliaments, and Vote by Ballot; or that it was just that the property of the country ought to be equally divided among its inhabitants, or that such a daring innovation would ever take place.[19]

Tremors were spreading centrifugally throughout the land, creating diverse reactions. The Paisley riots of 11–13 September, during which windows 'particularly those of the clergy' were broken, were considered to be a direct result of 'the proceedings of the reformers at Manchester'.[20]

One of the first areas to register mass public sympathy with the Peterloo demonstrators was West Yorkshire. On Hunslet Moor on 20 September the gathering displayed a black flag with the legend 'We mourn for the Murder of our Manchester Friends'. Two weeks later on Skircat Moor near Halifax there was held aloft a yellow silk banner, on which was printed the stanza:

> *With heartfelt grief we mourn for those*
> *Who fell a victim to our cause*
> *While we with indignation view*
> *The bloody field of Peterloo*[21]

In Newcastle-on-Tyne a public meeting was called for 11 October on the Parade Ground, with the aim of 'taking into Consideration the late Proceedings in Manchester'. Those attending were urged to wear black 'in Memory of those who fell at Manchester, on the 16th August last.' At least 20,000 turned up to the teetotal and orderly assembly, at which it was resolved to start a fund for those injured at Peterloo. The pacific nature of the proceedings did not prevent the mayor from writing to Lord Sidmouth claiming that '700 of [the reformers] were prepared with arms (concealed) to resist the civil power'.[22]

As far north as Dundee, when a meeting of reformers was called in November, the printed notice of the aims included the paragraphs:

Also to express their sentiments on the late *unprovoked, cruel, and cowardly attack made on the people at Manchester*, while peaceably and lawfully assembled for a constitutional purpose.

A COLLECTION will be made at the entries to the place of meeting, in aid of the fund for obtaining justice for the Manchester sufferers.[23]

The meeting in the Magdalen Yard attracted a crowd of 10,000.

It was proving impossible for the authorities to quell the nationwide notoriety of the incident. At the other end of the country, in Chudleigh, Devon, one John Jenkins was arrested for owning a print depicting the Yeomanry's charge into the crowd at the moment of Hunt's arrest (see p. 150). It had been the local vicar, a magistrate, who had informed on Jenkins, who had bought the print (produced by J. Evans of London) in a stationer's shop in Weymouth. He was showing it to people via the medium of a magnifying glass set into a viewing box. The detailed, if inexpertly drawn, image captures the 'horrid confusion' of a frenziedly packed St Peter's Field, with over fifteen reformers crammed onto the besieged hustings carts, and the cavalry in the foreground frenetically chopping at and trampling the assembly, in which many distressed women are visible. Beyond the platform there is a sea of heads stretching to the distant line of houses on the periphery, where a line of infantrymen with fixed bayonets is gathering. In the middle distance a file of cavalry, sabres drawn, is forcing its way through the crowd. It was thought that the print was 'intended to inflame the minds of His Majesty's Subjects and to bring His Majesty's Soldiery into hatred and contempt'.[24] The print was seized by the Devon magistrates, and since Jenkins had spent over five weeks in prison awaiting trial, Lord Sidmouth considered this redemption enough.

John Knight chaired the 12,000-strong gathering at Habergham Eaves near Burnley in November 1819, where 'amidst the acclamations of the people' and wearing a red liberty cap he was an outspoken participant – despite being out on bail. One version of events asserted that the crowd were armed with 'pikes and pistols', and that there was talk of a 'universal rising'. Adding to the tension, a fire broke out in a nearby cotton mill, but it turned out to be accidental and was soon extinguished.[25]

In early November a crowd of 20,000, brandishing seven caps of liberty, fourteen flags, and life-size effigies of Hunt and Cartwright, met at Wigan.

J. Evans's print of Hunt's arrest at Peterloo. (Manchester Central Library Archives+ (M07590))

The theme of the assembly was 'Parliamentary Reform and the Massacre at Manchester'. It was almost a carbon copy of Peterloo, with its musical bands, banner-carrying Female Union and forty-odd Yeoman cavalry waiting in the wings – with one crucial exception: the cavalry were not called upon, and the whole thing passed off peaceably.[26]

At about the same time, ignoring the local magistrates' threats, Leicester radicals organised a meeting to which around 10,000 turned up. The Yeomanry had been ordered to 'stay close to their saddles' for at least a week before the appointed date, but once again their intervention was not needed, as the crowd assembled and departed without trouble.[27]

In Belfast *The Irishman* newspaper, to no great surprise, took the militant left-wing view: 'The spirit of Reform rises from the blood of the Manchester Martyrs with a giant strength!'[28]

The capital felt the reverberations too, as the editor of *The Times*, taking a more conciliatory tone, wrote on 26 August:

> I do not pretend to see farther into futurity than other people; but the result
> of the Manchester meeting has produced an effect on the public mind in

this quarter, which I cannot help thinking threatens us with mischiefs we could not otherwise have anticipated. The bursting smoke of the hitherto comparatively quiet volcano threatens us with an explosion, at no very distant period, if the utmost prudence be not employed to give gradual vent to the boiling lava, and thus allow it to spend itself gradually, otherwise it may sweep every thing before it.

There was some truth in the prophecy: the Cato Street Conspiracy, in which there was a plot to assassinate the whole of the Cabinet and create a provisional radical government, was just six months away.

In Manchester, repercussions were many and far-reaching, touching issues way beyond the immediate effects of the deaths and injuries. Yeomanry or Special Constables who owned shops or inns noted a sharp drop in custom. The businesses of Tate, the grocer who had displayed Mary Fildes's banner in his window, provoking to some extent the New Cross riots, and 'Gingerbread Jack' Murray, the confectioner and police spy, were especially boycotted.[29] Property values underwent a slump. In a letter from Chief Constables Moore and Andrew to Lord Sidmouth, mention was made of the difficulty of collecting rent from 'the lower orders'.[30]

Revenge on the authorities was much talked of. At around two o'clock on the very afternoon of Peterloo, 'hundreds' among the crowds fleeing St Peter's Field were already vowing that the next time they went to Manchester, they would go armed. This resolution was overheard on the toll road to Middleton and Rochdale by Sam Ogden, landlord of the Red Lion Inn. Sam, it will be remembered, had been serving refreshment to the joyful Manchester-bound processions some four hours previously.[31]

Richard Carlile, who was to fight for the crucial issue of freedom of the press, and whose statements were seldom couched in moderation, published a call to arms:

Every man in Manchester who avows his opinions on the necessity of reform, should never go unarmed — retaliation has become a duty, and revenge an act of justice.[32]

Easy enough to write such things in London, but the reality was considerably thornier. Once back home, Bamford's initial reaction was to organise some sort of mass reprisal. Indeed, he observed a small army of young Middleton men grinding scythes, axes, screwdrivers, nails and the like — 'anything which could be made to cut or stab'.[33] But without leader or agreed strategy, the army never got to march or use the weapons.

Bamford's rage and spirit of vengeance cooled once he realised that, having talked the issue over with a philosophical friend, such action would lead them down a dangerous road. Whom would they attack? If individual magistrates or those deemed to be perpetrators, were they contemplating assassination? Would not a violent reaction play into the hands of the authorities, who would surely use it as a justification of their own actions on the day? And what would the final result of an armed insurrection be? Once started, it could end in only one of two ways: the overthrow of the Manchester elite, and therefore retribution from central government, or, more likely, death by a bullet, a sabre, or the gallows. The arguments were persuasive enough to ensure that good sense prevailed.[34]

Specific tales of individual reprisal were rare, and in many cases, probably apocryphal. There were letters sent from Manchester to Lord Sidmouth in November 1819, alleging (a) a pistol ball fired into the sitting room of Robert Mutrie, the Special Constable who had given evidence at the John Lees inquest; (b) an 'attempted assassination of Mr. Nadin'. Taylor discredits the allegations, citing 'an almost unanimous disbelief' in the second one. He goes on to imply that the letters, respectively from James Norris, and the Boroughreeve and Chief Constables, seem to have been used as justification for the authorities' repressive measures, not least the upcoming Six Acts.[35]

Throughout the months following Peterloo the right-wing authorities, of course, had been far from idle. Typifying the swift closing of ranks – on top of the vigorous press, handbill and placard campaign – was the meeting called by the Manchester powers three days after the incident, the basic aim of which was to thank the magistrates, the special constables and the soldiers. It is significant that business was almost immediately adjourned from the Police Offices to the comfort zone of the Star Inn, and was equally promptly designated private. The first words of Chairman Francis Philips to the assembly were: 'If there be any persons present who do not approve of the objects of this meeting they are requested to withdraw'.[36] A petition disapproving of the closed nature of the proceedings and requesting a public one was ignored, despite being signed by 4,800 people. Just over a week later, Lord Sidmouth wrote his letter thanking the Manchester authorities for their 'prompt, decisive, and efficient measures for preservation of the public peace'.[37] In the House of Commons, two motions calling for a condemnation of the magistrates and a public inquiry about the events of 16 August were both heavily defeated.

As part of the early government clampdown, further arrests had been made. Another radical who had made his escape from Peterloo, Richard Carlile, would be tried and convicted of seditious libel and blasphemy in October. After his arrest in late August, he had been promised there would be no further proceedings against him if he agreed to stop circulating his vehement accounts of Peterloo.[38] This attempt at silencing him conspicuously failed, although the main indictment was for publishing Tom Paine's *The Rights of Man*. The government no doubt thought that incarceration would be an effective way of shutting him up. Not so; he continued to write his fiery radical texts whilst in Dorchester prison, and it was his wife Jane who published them in *The Republican*. Because of the publicity surrounding Carlile's case, sales of the newspaper rocketed. For continuing to sell seditious works, Jane was to join her husband in Dorchester prison in April 1822.

Sir Francis Burdett, a major reforming presence in Parliament, wrote a highly animated letter to the electors of Westminster on 22 August,[39] and chaired an open-air meeting at Palace Yard on 2 September, calling for the prosecution of the Manchester magistrates. Nothing came of it, despite the 30,000 attendees at Palace Yard, and before too long Burdett too found himself saddled with a custodial sentence of three months and a fine of £2,000. The charge, again, was 'seditious libel'.

One way or another, by the summer of 1820 all of the prominent supporters of the St Peter's Field meeting of 16 August, whether they had been present or not, would be behind bars. The octogenarian Major Cartwright was spared a jail sentence, but was ordered to pay a £100 fine for having spoken at the previous year's Birmingham rally.

Bamford, like Carlile, had escaped immediate arrest on the day of Peterloo. But the reprieve was even more temporary than that of Carlile. Nadin, in typical style, turned up at Bamford's house in Middleton at 2 a.m. on the Thursday of the following week, hammering on the front door with a backup of armed constables and a contingent of infantry hussars. The feisty Jemima shouted 'Hunt and Liberty!' at the visiting posse, whereupon one of the constables ordered her to shut up or he would blow her head off. Her unruffled response was: 'Blow away!'[40]

Bamford was taken to the New Bailey prison, where the next day he was to join the others for the initial hearing. Amongst those with him in the dock were Henry Hunt, John Knight, Joseph Johnson, Elizabeth Gaunt, Sarah Hargreaves, Robert Jones, Robert Wylde, James Moorhouse, Joseph 'Doc' Healey, George Swift, and John Thacker Saxton. Hunt had injured his hand in the Peterloo fracas, and Healey was suffering from a sabre wound on his back.[41] Hunt opted to conduct his own defence and cross-examination of witnesses. The nine presiding magistrates included several who had given their name to the arrest warrant on 16 August: William Hulton, Thomas W. Tatton, Richard Wright, William Marriott, and Ralph Fletcher.

This examination at the New Bailey less than two weeks after Peterloo gives clear indications as to how matters would progress.

The policy of imposing silence was exemplified by James Norris, the Chair of the magistrates, as he repeatedly forbade witnesses to answer Hunt's questions. Typical was the cross-examination of Matthew Cowper, an accountant. In each of the following instances, Norris interrupted Hunt's questioning with the instruction to Cowper: 'Do not answer the question.'

'Would you favour me with your particular address?'

'Is that [accountancy] your only profession?'

'Were you a Special Constable on Monday 16th, at the Meeting?'

'[Do you take reports of speeches] for the public Newspapers, or for your own private amusement?'

'Be so good as to state how you were employed in the interval [between hearing my speech and writing the full version of it].'

'You stated that the sticks you saw in the hands of the persons who came to the Meeting were more like threshing-flails than walking-sticks, pray what do you mean by a flail? And what is the difference between it and a walking-stick?'

'What did you consider as the dreadful part of the array?'[42]

In the post-Peterloo domain of litigation, battle lines were already being drawn. In a more flippant but nonetheless heartfelt manner, James Moorhouse refused to take off his white top hat whilst in the dock, showing his lack of respect for the bench. He argued that men who had so misconducted themselves had forfeited all title to deference and would receive none from him. He declared the hearing 'a farce', and one source relates that his face wore a contemptuous smile. His hat was, however, removed for him by a court constable, and he later apologised for his behaviour.[43]

Hunt was to get more and more exasperated as the hearing proceeded. At one point he addressed the bench: 'Say whether we are guilty of any offence, or if we are, whether we have not suffered enough.'

> In uttering this last sentence, Mr. Hunt evinced a considerable ardency of manner, which called forth great applause from the crowd behind. The Chairman indignantly commanded silence, and declared that if any tumult took place, he should be obliged to clear the court, and to commit the parties.[44]

Hunt reserved his most cutting scorn, however, when referring to the final discharge 'for want of evidence' of the severely injured Elizabeth Gaunt, who had been detained twelve days in solitary confinement, 'pale, emaciated, and almost fainting from weakness, in consequence of the wounds she had received at the meeting'.[45]

At Lancaster on 27 August the accused were charged with 'having conspired to alter the law by force and threats'.[46] The initial charge of High Treason – a capital offence – had been modified, possibly because the authorities were anxious not to create a martyr in this potentially explosive situation. The trial was set for the following March at York Assizes. Bail was granted to the radicals in the dock, and Hunt made a triumphal return to Smedley Cottage, in a carriage pulled part of the way by his supporters, despite the torrential rain. Feelings were running high: when Hunt stopped to give a speech outside a Preston inn, a coach arrived at speed, and the driver tried to strike Hunt with his whip. The crowd tried to 'tear the coachman from his seat', but Hunt ordered them to keep the peace, and the would-be attacker left unscathed.[47] The 'Orator' would be back in London by 9 September, where his arrival would be acclaimed by a crowd of over 300,000.[48]

Kicks and ha'pence, as they used to say in Lancashire: it was whilst being feted in Preston that Hunt received news of the death of his favourite horse, Bob, who had borne him up north three weeks previously. Rumours of the animal having been poisoned are unsubstantiated.[49]

2

Inquests

Edward Meagher, the Yeoman trumpeter and enthusiastic wielder of the sabre on 16 August, was to be involved in another fracas some weeks later. Having boasted, according to the *Observer*, of his actions at Peterloo, he had been an object of frequent public barracking in the town, and since he lived on Deansgate, it would only be a matter of time before the situation came to a head once more. At half past midnight on 3 October a crowd gathered outside his house, and Meagher, fearing for his safety and that of his family, fired a pistol from his upstairs window, injuring two people. He was brought to trial, and the verdict, given on 12 November, was a scaled-down facsimile of the outcome of the other court proceedings: the woundings were considered accidental, and justifiable since Meagher was 'defending his house, himself and his family when assaulted by a tumultuous [*sic*] of people at the dead hour of night'. The case was dismissed.[1]

Within a month or so of Peterloo, judicial inquests were held on several of the fatalities. The verdict on 17-year-old Joseph Whitworth of Hyde, shot in the back of the head during the New Cross riots, showed the typical official attitude:

> …the deceased was accidentally shot by the Military under the Command of the Civil Power in suppressing a Riot and disturbance which took place at New Cross.[2]

A similar shifting of responsibility was apparent in the verdict on the death of Edmund Dawson:

> On Saturday last [11 September] the Jury concluded their Inquiry as to the death of Edmund Dawson, and after the examination of witnesses (one of whom satisfactorily proved that the Riot Act was read) brought in the

following verdict: 'That it appeared the deceased died from a wound on the head, inflicted by a sabre or other sharp instrument on the 16th day of August last, at Manchester, but how such wound was given no satisfactory evidence was adduced.'[3]

John Rhodes had walked to St Peter's Field with Bamford's Middleton contingent. He received a sabre cut on the head and lost a lot of blood. He also suffered serious 'internal bruising', from what appears to have been either crowd pressure or being knocked down by a horse. He died from his injuries three months later. Incredibly, the coroner's inquest recorded death from natural causes. His father received just six guineas (£6.30) in compensation.[4]

The hope of bringing the Peterloo soldiery to justice for murder and assault appears to have been doomed from an early date. In October, Mr Williams the solicitor wrote the following:

> ...if, in the ordinary discharge of his duty, a soldier is directed to disperse an illegal meeting, and to charge & fire upon the meeting, and any death or other injury should arise to any of the parties so assembled, the soldier acting under orders cannot be responsible either for murder or any assault, or upon any other charge.[5]

The Reverend Hay, as might be expected, fully agreed with this legal opinion, throwing the weight of his Oxford Law Degree erudition into the argument by quoting the '5th Article of the 2nd Section of the Articles of War: the soldier is prohibited, under penalties, from disobeying the *lawful* command of his superior'.[6] Two objections immediately present themselves: firstly the 16 August meeting had not been declared illegal, and secondly it is highly debatable whether an Article of War may be justifiably quoted in connection with a peacetime demonstration, and it is even more debatable whether such an Article is relevant to the conduct of a body of civilian Yeomanry.

With the wind blowing in such an easily discernible direction, the inquest on John Lees took on crucial importance.

John Lees, an Oldham spinner and 22-year-old veteran of Waterloo, had suffered serious wounds from swords and policemen's batons on St Peter's Field. Eyewitnesses had seen him try to ward off the blows by interposing his stick, but he received sabre wounds on his elbow and shoulder, and many truncheon blows, the result of which was an injury to his spine. He managed to make his way to The Shears Inn at Newton Heath, where he was seen at around 5 p.m., his shoe torn, and with a cut on his shoulder. The next morning his father Robert saw him with 'his shirt all blood'. From being that of a young man of robust good health, his condition deteriorated rapidly. He began throwing up his food and lost the sight of his left eye due to the injuries to his spine. When his girlfriend Mary Fletcher came to visit him the following Saturday, she found him bedridden, and apparently unable to speak or even recognise her. He died on 30 August, his body in a 'state of putrefaction' and his 'windpipe full of blood'. It was declared after the autopsy that the necrosis had been caused by the wounds and bruises received at Peterloo.[7]

The inquest on John Lees lasted nearly three months. The venue was shifted twice: the proceedings which opened on 8 September at the Duke of York Inn, Oldham, were moved to the Angel Inn, Lees on 25 September, and thence to the Star Inn on Deansgate, Manchester on 7 October. Attorney for the Lees family was James Harmer from London, owner of the radical *Weekly Dispatch*. Thomas Ferrand was the Coroner.

It was perhaps a tactical mistake by Harmer to try to broaden the purpose of the inquest so as to accuse the entire troop of Yeomanry of wilful murder.[8] This gave the Coroner a perfect excuse to declare potentially damning details as inadmissible, as he insisted on hearing only evidence that pertained directly to John Lees, and would consider only what had happened in the immediate vicinity of the hustings.[9] Time and again he refused to accept identification of Yeomen who had been seen cutting the people with their sabres:

Alice Kearsley [aged 71]: A man saw the trumpeter give me the blow.
Coroner: This is not evidence – I will not hear it.[10]
Samuel Davenport: I saw Mr. Birley and the trumpeter cutting with their sabres.
Coroner: Stop, Sir, stop. I did not ask you whom you saw cutting; but what violence was done?
Samuel Davenport: I was going to tell you, Sir, that I saw Mr. Birley and the trumpeter.
Coroner: What do you mean by wandering from my questions, and telling me what you are not asked?
[*There followed an angry exchange between Mr. Harmer and the Coroner.*][11]
Harmer: State what you saw [on 16 August].
Coroner: I object to that.
James Walker: I saw Harrison and others of them cutting the people right and left, and —
Coroner: Stop! Stop! Sir, that is not evidence. Did you know John Lees?[12]

Harmer: Can you identify any of the Yeomanry who you saw attacking the people that day?

Martha Robinson: Yes; I can speak to some who cut several persons in the street where I live. [Roger's Row]

Harmer: Could you name them if you were allowed?

Martha Robinson: Yes, I could.

Coroner: I shall not let her name them.[13]

Harmer: [to Elizabeth Farren] Do you know who wounded you?

Coroner: Don't answer that – I forbid it.[14]

After several weeks of abortive and fractious verbal sparring the inquest was abruptly terminated on 1 December. The Court of King's Bench had declared the entire proceedings to be null and void because of a legal technicality. The following day Harmer wrote to the Coroner, asking if he intended to continue with the proceedings. Ferrand appeared to wash his hands of the affair, stating that the decision had not been his. Harmer wrote again, expressing astonishment at the 'extraordinary determination not to again resume the inquest'. Ferrand gave no reply, so Harmer left for London and matters came to a highly unsatisfactory end.[15]

Seven of the jurors wrote to Ferrand saying that their verdict would have been murder:

> We think it right further to declare to you, that from a careful and candid examination of the evidence hitherto adduced, we are of the opinion, that, in the case of JOHN LEES, a FOUL MURDER was committed…[16]

It was claimed by the *Observer* that the other five jurors had refrained from signing the letter simply because, since they were innkeepers, they were worried about possible loss of custom.

Robert Lees organised a petition for re-opening the inquest on his son – to no avail. It was par for the course that all Peterloo-related petitions were ignored by the government. It was either Wroe or Saxton, not bound by courtroom protocol, who gave vent to popular feeling in the *Observer*: 'the diabolical and unconstitutional attempt of smothering enquiry into the real cause of the death of John Lees'.[17]

The gagging of witnesses and the authorities' monolithic aloofness, however, was small beer compared to the Six Acts, hurriedly ratified in the weeks following the abrupt end of the Lees inquest.

Official attempts at silencing or trivialising the truth were never going to succeed forever. For most of the individuals involved, Peterloo cast an indelible, lifelong shadow. Many of the injuries sustained there had caused permanent or fatal disabilities.

Mary Heys from Chorlton Row, mother of six children and three months pregnant, was knocked down and trampled by the cavalry. As a result of her injuries she died in premature childbirth on 17 December, although the child survived.

Mary Smith from Failsworth, aged 46, 'had her left arm broken, her left leg dreadfully hurt, a large lump has risen on her throat, in consequence of its being trod upon'. This was recorded six months after the incident, and she was not thought capable of recovery.

Thomas Blinstone, aged 74, of Back Turner Street, had both arms broken, and was deemed disabled for life.

Ellen Wood, pregnant on the day of Peterloo, was knocked down and trampled on. Her child was born blind 'the doctor says, in consequence of her injuries'. Ellen received just £3 in compensation.

Owen McCabe, a 62-year-old weaver, had his ribs crushed and hip dislocated when knocked down by the Yeomanry horses. He was declared disabled for life, 'a poor distressed creature'. His unusually high £7 compensation is indicative of the seriousness of his disabilities.[18]

It was not only physical woundings which caused lifelong repercussions. Sixteen-year-old Mary Ward from Fallowfield had walked to St Peter's Field with her cousin, having heard that there was to be some sort of open-air party with musical accompaniment. She was wearing her new white dress which had been made by her mother. The two girls had been singing along to the bands until Hunt's arrival, after which matters took a sinister turn with the onslaught of the Yeomanry. Mary saw the cutting of a man close by her, and her dress was splattered with the man's blood. She went into shock, and the next thing she remembered was standing in Bootle Street, tearing strips off her dress to create makeshift bandages for the wounded. Although physically unharmed – apart from a minor scratch on her arm – the psychological damage would be profound. The post-trauma symptoms were so acute that her father had her committed to an asylum, and for the rest of her life she was unable to wear white and would become distressed whenever she saw a procession of white-clad people.[19]

3

For King and Constitution

It was the Establishment's firm intention now to demonise the reformers, and, with a similar purpose to that of the cavalry attacking the banners and musical instruments at Peterloo, to crush the spirit of reform by denying or trivialising the symbols of the movement. Hunt's trademark top hat, for instance, came in for some stick in reactionary circles. At the Wigan rally in November 1819, the Reverend Hall pulled a white hat from the head of a young lad, tearing off the strip of green ribbon.[1] Since September 1819, children had been banned from wearing the white top hat 'or other Badges which are now used by the disloyal and disaffected' to Anglican Sunday School classes.[2] *Wheeler's Manchester Chronicle* gloatingly recorded that thanks to the 'able measures adopted by our judicious government' the white top hat was no longer selling, and had had to be disguised by the addition of a soft black cotton covering in order for people to want to buy them.[3] The liberty cap came in for similar treatment:

> The mischiefs that had been hatched, engendered and perfected, under the ensign of the cap of liberty, had converted it into an emblem of disaffection. It was no longer the cap of liberty; it had degenerated into a badge of licentiousness.[4]

The 'able measures' mentioned in *Wheeler's Chronicle* were the draconian Six Acts, all of which received Royal Assent in December 1819. The officially defined purpose of these repressive new statutes was as follows:

(1) To prevent the training of persons in use of arms, and to the practice of military evolution and exercise;

(2) To authorise justices of the peace in certain disturbed counties, to search private houses and seize weapons collected or kept for purposes dangerous to the public peace, and to arrest their possessors;

(3)   To prevent delay in the administration of justice in cases of misdemeanour;

(4)   To prohibit the holding of political public meetings in larger numbers than fifty unless prior permission from a magistrate had been given, and to ban the use of music and display of banners at such meetings;

(5)   To ensure the more effectual prevention and punishment of blasphemous and seditious libels;

(6)   To subject certain publications to the duties of stamps upon newspapers, and to make other regulations for restraining the abuse arising from the publication of blasphemous and seditious libels.[5]

The iron fetters fell into place: there would be no more mass political gatherings, and the fourth Act, seemingly with an eye on the controversy surrounding the reading of the Riot Act at Peterloo, contained an article which stipulated that the time allowed for voluntary dispersal after the reading of the Riot Act was reduced from one hour to fifteen minutes. After that time had elapsed, the meeting, if still in evidence, was automatically deemed illegal. There would be no more idyllic countryside drillings. The stamp duty would render the purchase of left-wing newspapers more difficult for badly off workers. Any expression of dissatisfaction with the *status quo* would be more easily identified and punished.

The trial of Hunt and the other St Peter's Field reformers now took on crucial watershed significance: 'This important trial will be read and listened to with the liveliest interest wherever there is a spark of humanity or justice to be found'.[6] Hunt saw it too, and even allowing for his liking for the odd touch of melodrama:

The question involves more than a verdict of guilty or not guilty upon the defendants now on trial; it will decide no less a question than this: whether, hereafter, there shall be a particle of rational liberty left in the country.[7]

He was well aware, too, of the pivotal significance of St Peter's Field:

The day is arriving when we shall see whether Corruption has left any virtue in our Courts of Justice, or whether our Constitutional Rights were buried in the Tomb of Peterloo.[8]

Adding to the general atmosphere of trepidation had been the arrest of the Cato Street conspirators three weeks before the start of Hunt's trial. The eyes of the country were fixed on those ten days at York Assizes.

Having organised a fund to enable witnesses to travel to York, Hunt made the journey by coach. He was delayed at Rochdale, as the landlord of the Roe Buck Inn refused to supply Hunt with fresh horses, once he realised it was the rabble-rouser who had requested them.[9]

Bamford walked the whole way, accompanied by an entourage of around 120 supporters, via Blackstone Edge, Halifax, Bradford, Leeds and Tadcaster.

The courtroom was 'excessively crowded': on the first day (16 March) even before the doors opened at 8.10 a.m., some people had climbed an outside wall and entered the public gallery through a window. The press had been arriving since 6.45 a.m.[10]

Hunt insisted that all potential witnesses be removed from the gallery. (Nowadays, of course, it is standard procedure that witnesses are called into the courtroom only when required to give evidence.) The Reverend Hay, William Hulton, James Norris, Col John Silvester, the Reverend Ethelston, Lt Col George L'Estrange, and Col Ralph Fletcher left the room. The only one of these actually called for the prosecution was Hulton. It would appear that the presence of the others was a mere show of force – the authorities' power in reserve. Hay left York immediately, without waiting to see if he was needed.[11]

Hunt conducted his own defence, apparently relishing the opportunity to take centre stage and cross swords with his adversaries.

Bamford described the jury: 'They sat motionless, and like men who were asleep with their eyes open.' The impression of a *fait accompli* is enhanced by Hunt's suggestion that the York jury had been cherry-picked (or 'packed') under the supervision of the Sheriff.[12]

In the Thesaurus-driven style of such indictments, there were several counts, each amounting to much the same thing: a conspiracy to inflame the minds of His Majesty's subjects against the constitution, by creating a large, tumultuous and threatening assembly.

For a full account of the trial, the reader is referred to the Dolby text, which is available online. We will here mention several salient details which will give a general impression of the proceedings.

Justice Bayley made it clear early on that it was not the purpose of the trial to examine the conduct of the Yeomanry, but rather to consider the nature of the meeting, and the intentions of the designated leaders.[13]

The judge also gave his opinion that a gathering, although perhaps not of itself illegal, could be considered so if its great numbers were to create an alarm in the public mind. Also, a legal assembly may contain potentially unlawful intentions, which should be borne in mind. As to the banners, if they merely expressed an opinion rather than intent, they were not of themselves illegal.[14] In general, Justice Bayley's remarks show a commendable fairness.

Of interest is the duel of wits between Hunt and Hulton, in which the Orator sought to impair the Magistrate's testimony. The antipathy between them became evident when Hunt, tongue clearly in his cheek while questioning the apprehension Hulton said he felt on seeing the well-drilled contingents enter St Peter's Field, asked the magistrate: 'And this thing, which was so beautiful, created alarm in your tender heart?'[15] Hunt won this head-to-head contest, if such it was, in style.

There was an abrasive confrontation between Hunt and prosecuting counsel, the Whig MP James Scarlett: 'Mr. Hunt said, with great warmth, that Mr. Scarlett was continually putting words into the mouths of the witnesses.' The judge intervened, calling for 'no angry discussion'. At another point the judge tells Hunt: 'Let us refrain from personalities,' after Hunt called Scarlett 'unfeeling'. Scarlett accused Hunt of bringing a 'spirit of disorder and intimidation' into the court proceedings, and rebuked Hunt for his 'impertinence'.[16] At times their exchanges almost degenerate into acrimonious verbal tennis. Clearly, there was no love lost between the two men.

The jury were asked to consider not only what happened on the day, but also whether the Peterloo gathering implied any potential or preparation for a future uprising; whether the meeting was 'calculated to create a fear and terror of distant danger', and whether 'the public pulse was only to be felt on that day, and the full panic to be prepared for a future'.[17] Taking this on board, Scarlett suggested that Hunt's intention was to 'keep his people quiet until the proper occasion offered'. In a stunning display of doublethink, Scarlett pointed out that in Hunt's public notice of 11 August the phrase 'armed with no other weapon but that of a self-approving conscience', the word 'armed' was in italics, thereby sending a subtle contradictory message.[18] Although obviously there was no evidence to support this conjecture, at a stroke it shed an equivocal light on all of Hunt's pacific recommendations.

On the tenth day of the trial (27 March), the jury took less than five hours to reach a verdict. Although all ten defendants were found not guilty on all but one of the counts, it was on the crucial fourth count that, to general amazement, Hunt, Bamford, Knight, Johnson and Healey were convicted:

Guilty of assembling with unlawful banners an unlawful assembly, for the purpose of moving and inciting the liege subjects of our Sovereign Lord the King to contempt and hatred of the Government and Constitution of the realm, as by law established, and attending at the same.[19]

Bamford was deemed guilty (despite the emphasis on his peaceable approach) 'to the astonishment of the judge [who had spoken in Bamford's favour in his summing-up], the bar, and the audience'.[20]

The following month at Lancaster Assizes, Knight was also found guilty of going 'armed…for the purpose of hindering and obstructing the magistrates and peace-officers in the execution of their duty' at the Burnley rally of 15 November. Prentice was convinced that the only people who had taken firearms to this meeting were deliberately planted spies.[21]

The York jury seem to have targeted the most active, in other words potentially dangerous, defendants. Moorhouse's contrition and bible reading – plus the fact that his heavily pregnant wife had accompanied him to Peterloo – counted in his favour. Saxton was considered to have been there as a reporter, and the authorities already had their journalistic pound of flesh with the conviction of *Observer* editor James Wroe for seditious libel at Lancaster Assizes, at about the same time as the Hunt trial. Wroe was imprisoned for one year and made to pay a £100 fine. The role played by young Swift, Jones (who had merely supervised the erection of the hustings) and Wylde, a young man from Stalybridge (whose only misdemeanour seems to have been to encourage the people around the hustings to link arms) was not considered enough of a public threat to merit a 'guilty' verdict.

Hunt was sentenced to two and a half years in Ilchester prison. The others were confined to Lincoln prison for a year. Hunt's move for a retrial was unsuccessful.

The final paragraph of the Dolby document reads:

Mr. Hunt was cheered as he went home to his lodgings. He maintained, to the last, his wonted composure, and there was a calmness and respectful decorum in his manner at the close of the trial which excited much sympathy for his situation.[22]

On the reformers' side of the fence, the year or so after Peterloo saw two major trends: the collection of monetary aid for the wounded and bereaved, and the splintering and weakening of the radical ranks.

Contributions for the cause had poured in, not only from the Manchester area but also from London, Birmingham, Liverpool, Leeds and Norwich. A total of more than £3,400 collected was recorded by February 1820. However, less than a third of this amount was distributed to the victims, the rest being swallowed by legal fees and administration expenses. The actual amounts handed out to the wounded were meagre: mostly £2 or less in each case.[23]

Differences of opinion and arguments over political ways and means, personality clashes, and the repressive effects of the Six Acts were responsible for the enfeebling of the Reform movement. By December 1819 it was 'in a virtual state of collapse'.[24]

Support for King and Constitution, however, was gathering momentum. One month after the end of Hunt's trial, the birthday of the future George IV was celebrated in style in the Cotton Exchange Dining Room. Copious amounts of food and drink were consumed, and toasts were drunk – each one with 'three times three' cheers – to the new King, the Royal Family, the recently deceased George III, the army and the navy, the Duke of Wellington, the Lancashire and Cheshire Magistrates, the Manchester and Salford Yeomanry, the Cheshire Yeomanry, Francis Philips, Captain Hugh Hornby Birley, and various other notables. Hulton, Hay and Birley all made speeches, inevitably with reference to the previous 16 August. Now that Hunt and several of his close associates were safely behind bars, the garbled version of the Peterloo carnage – 'the peace of the town was in danger', 'only one person died of a sabre wound', '[the Magistrates'] conduct had been guided by plain common sense', 'the Meeting which had been suppressed was illegal', 'the…Yeomanry…and the 15th Hussars were obliged to use their sabres in self defence', etc., – was openly expressed, and to loud and rapturous applause. Two toasts that were drunk later in the evening were:

> May the *Dream* of Universal Suffrage and Annual Parliaments no longer disturb our *Repose*. May Radical Principles be speedily eradicated from the minds of the deluded.[25]

One week later, five of the Cato Street conspirators were hanged and beheaded in front of a large crowd at Newgate prison in London. Another five were sentenced to transportation for life. By the summer of 1820, the loyalists' star was overwhelmingly in the ascendant.

There may have been divisions and deterrents besetting the radical world at large, but the working classes continued to show a fundamental cohesion.

The first anniversary of Peterloo on Wednesday, 16 August 1820 was marked by processions, songs and speeches in towns across Lancashire: Bolton, Royton, Preston, Ashton-under-Lyne, Stockport, Blackburn, Middleton and, of course, Manchester itself. The *Manchester Observer* of 19 August devoted the whole of its front page to the topic. It described in detail the Manchester march – 'a great multitude who appeared to be filled with becoming feelings of solemnity and sorrow' – which started from the Union Rooms on George Leigh Street, returning there after a circular route which took in Piccadilly, Mosley Street, St Peter's Field, Deansgate, King Street, Fountain Street, High Street, Shudehill, and New Cross. At the spot where the hustings had been erected on St Peter's Field the crowd stayed long enough to sing a song and give three cheers for Hunt.

The procession contained a children's choir, which sang with a 'beautiful effect' on Deansgate during another one of the halts. On King Street, Nadin came out of the Police Offices to watch the procession go by. He was greeted with a brief outburst of jeering before the appropriate gravity was restored.

Once back at the Union Rooms, Saxton led the cheers for Hunt, Bamford and the others who had been imprisoned; and inspiringly, Mary Fildes's speech, which had been intended for the previous year, was finally read out (see Appendix 2).

Wisely, the soldiers, the militia and the police left the proceedings alone. Since the event was commemorative rather than overtly seditious, the 1,000-strong gathering was ignored by the authorities. The *Observer* report contained the 'strange and singular' detail of someone having deliberately placed a large number of brickbats on St Peter's Field overnight. This potentially catastrophic act came to nothing, and the identity and purpose of the brick-scatterer were never discovered.[26]

The *Observer*'s sensitive and discerning report was in marked contrast to the brief and dismissive article in the right-wing *Manchester Mercury*, which had devoted the whole of its front page that week to the dysfunctional royal marriage. The tone and highly selective content should not surprise:

Wednesday last, being the Anniversary of the notorious meeting of *Radicals* on St. Peter's-Field, in this town, they attempted by every means they could devise to muster all the forces in their power; about 12 o'clock, they began to assemble, and by one there was a considerable number on the field, but there did not appear to be any leader to the rabble, nor could they excite confusion, though dog-fighting and other incentives were resorted to. In the afternoon a number of children and full-grown persons, of both sexes, marched in a sort of procession over the field, and some of the principal streets of the town, singing what they termed an [*sic*] *Hymn*…[27]

One year on, the war of words had lost little of its animosity.

After the inquest on John Lees and the trial of Hunt and his fellow reformers, there was a third major litigation relevant to Peterloo. In April 1822, Thomas Redford of Middleton, who had been badly injured by a sabre cut to the shoulder, took out a civil action against four of the Yeomanry: 'between Thomas Redford, plaintiff, and Hugh Hornby Birley, Alexander Oliver, Richard Withington, and Edward Meagher, defendants, for an assault on the 16th of August 1819'.[28] Many of the relevant depositions on the subject of the volunteer cavalry's brutality have been mentioned above, but noteworthy here is the nature of the support for mill owner Captain Birley and the other three defendants, respectively an innkeeper, a warehouse owner and a tailor.

A number of statements from defence witnesses, given the overwhelming contradictory evidence from elsewhere, make one seriously doubt their veracity. Hulton repeated his assertion that stones were thrown at the Yeomanry as they approached the hustings.[29] James Andrews, Deputy Constable of Bury, stated that the stones 'appeared to come from the lower part of the hustings', a detail with which Joseph Bickley, a warehouse supervisor, concurred: 'the stones appeared to come from the centre of the crowd, where they were strongest'.[30] This has already been shown to have been virtually impossible, because of the press of the crowd.

The walking sticks and their use were presented in a similarly subjective light. James Jacques, brother-in-law of Edmund Buxton, claimed that he saw on the ground after the dispersal, 'a very large number of sticks, of very awkward appearance indeed…awkward in size and shape…as if drawn from the hedge that morning, a large proportion of them'. The implication being, of course, that these were anything but walking sticks, but had been brought in purposefully as weapons. Thomas Sharp saw a number of these sticks 'lifted so high above the horses' backs' that they 'rendered the horses more unsteady'.[31] Again, substantial doubt has already been cast upon these allegations by a host of eyewitness accounts.

In the two and a half years since Peterloo attitudes had ossified, resulting in possible tweaking of memories of events. Whether this fine-tuning was according to instructions or not, the fact remains that at the end of the five-day trial at Lancashire Assizes the 'special jury' took just six minutes to find for the defendants. Once again a tidal wave of evidence had been ignored.

4

A Gallery of Pictures

'History is a gallery of pictures in which there are few originals and many copies.'

Alexis de Tocqueville

The satirists had been quick to join battle.

The nowadays almost universally accepted sobriquet of 'Peterloo' first saw the light of day in the *Manchester Observer* on 28 August. Devised by James Wroe as an obvious play on 'Waterloo', it was the title given to a blistering parody of *The House that Jack Built*, and its final stanza ran:

These are the just-asses, gentlemen mild, who to keep the peace,
broke it, by lucre beguil'd, and sent Hurly-Burly, a blustering knave, a foe to
the poor, whom he'd gladly enslave, to lead on the butchers, bloodthirsty
and bold, who cut, slash'd and maim'd young defenceless and old, who met,
on the state of affairs to debate; in the field of Peter-Loo.[1]

The same accumulative format was used by William Hone in his *The Political House that Jack Built*. This bestseller was much longer than the *Observer* parody, contained drawings by George Cruikshank, and was a devastating swipe at the country as a whole. It was brought out in November and contains what look like two visual references to the Manchester incident: a possible Nadin as a jailer with his shackles and keys standing alongside three military figures; and in the background behind a group of destitute people, a cavalryman attacking a crowd with a sabre, in a scene which closely resembles another of Cruikshank's drawings of Peterloo.

The *Observer* had published what was claimed to be a handbill going the rounds in Manchester:

To be Sold by Auction, at the Police Office, on Saturday next, at 12 precisely, 39 pair of cavalry men's breeches; they are perfectly clean on the *outside*. N.B. They will be sold without reserve, as the parties are declining business. Also to be sold at the same time, 56 Constable's Staffs.[2]

The bogus Yeoman Cavalryman's diary, published in September 1820, has been mentioned already. As with the best satires, the grin beneath the deadpan mask peeps through almost unnoticed at first:

We have cotton-spinners and gin-spinners; iron-mongers, cheese-mongers, and commission-mongers (of the latter not a few). We have land-surveyors, and surveyors of King's taxes; dealers in waste, calicoes, hay, corn and bran – prince's mixture and common pigtail, – soap, pork, bacon, common law, and horse-flesh...

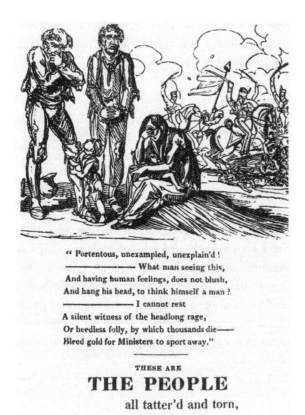

" Portentous, unexampled, unexplain'd !
——————— What man seeing this,
And having human feelings, does not blush,
And hang his head, to think himself a man ?
——————— I cannot rest
A silent witness of the headlong rage,
Or heedless folly, by which thousands die——
Bleed gold for Ministers to sport away."

THESE ARE
THE PEOPLE
all tatter'd and torn,

A page from Hone's *The Political House That Jack Built*. (Stockport Local Heritage)

...black pudding manufacturers, *gentlemen's* grooms, dyers, butchers, blue dippers, and all the customary *quantum* of tag-rag- and bobtail.[3]

Perhaps the most sophisticated of the parodies was Hone and Cruikshank's sham newspaper of July 1821: 'A Slap at Slop and the Bridge Street Gang', a wicked lampoon of John Stoddard's right-wing *The New Times*. Many of the barbs have long outlived their topicality, but two items from the plethora of fake illustrated adverts on the front page have attained lasting fame: the Peterloo monument and medal. The monument shows, atop a plinth decorated with skulls, a sabre-wielding horseman trampling a group of people which includes a woman carrying a child. Immediately below this item is the suggestion that Meagher's trumpet be melted down so as to make a number of medals to hand out to 'the warriors who distinguished themselves on the occasion'. The medal's design parodies Josiah Wedgwood's anti-slavery image, depicting a soldier about to bring down a bloodstained axe on a kneeling protestor. Underneath there is the exchange:

Q: 'Am I not a man and a brother?'
A: 'No! – you are a poor weaver!'[4]

On 30 October 1822 Hunt emerged from the Ilchester Bastille with typical ostentation: he wore his white top hat and the tartan cloak given to him by the Greenock reformers, and sported the gold medal and chain which had been presented to him by the Leeds Female Reformers after the York trial.[5] There were celebrations up and down the country, and unsurprisingly the Manchester loyalists attempted to pour ridicule on this allegedly dangerous character who was once more at large.

The *Manchester Comet: Or a Rap at Radicals* (clearly with *A Slap at Slop* in mind) was the reactionaries' satirical response, a one-off publication in the form of a newspaper which appeared on the same day as Hunt's release. For the most part the textual humour is well-worn, clunking and repetitive. There are deliberate misspellings of radicals' names: John Night, W. Coble-it, Mr Row, Hannah Saxon, and Peg Files. Johnson (constantly described as the brush-man) was reported to reside at 'Simpleton Cottage, Smedley'. Hunt's home base of Glastonbury was rendered as 'Glass-Tongue-Bury'. There was a belated crowing about the demise of the *Manchester Observer* (perhaps to mask the annoyance at the birth of the left-wing *Guardian*), which was referred to as 'the late MANCHESTER-LONDON-SAXTON-

Detail from 'A Slap at Slop'.
(John Rylands Library)

Advertisements.   35

VICTORY OF PETERLOO.

A MONUMENT is proposed to be erected in commemoration of the achievements of the MANCHESTER YEOMANRY CAVALRY, on the 16*th August*, 1819, against THE MANCHESTER MEETING of Petitioners for Redress of Wrongs and Grievances, and Reform in Parliament. It has been called a *battle*, but erroneously; for, the multitude was *unarmed*, and made no resistance to the heroes *armed;* there was no contest—it was a *victory;* and has accordingly been celebrated in triumph. This event, more important in its consequences than the Battle of Waterloo, will be recorded on the monument, by simply stating the names of the officers and privates successfully engaged, on the one side; and on the other, the names of the persons killed, and of the six hundred maimed and wounded in the attack and pursuit; also the names of the captured, who are still prisoners in His Majesty's goals; with the letter of thanks, addressed to the victors, by His Majesty's Command.

WOOLER-OBSERVER'. And of course, Hunt ('Saint Henry of Ilchester') came in for the most stick:

> At a little past twelve, Mr. Hunt arrived in a carriage drawn by four fine *jack-asses*…His appearance was very striking…with a large red night cap (tastefully decorated with little bells) on his head instead of a white hat.[6]

The cap and bells gag had been used five years previously, in the *Manchester Mercury*. If Hunt's white hat was supposed by the right-wing press to be past its sell-by date, then so were the *Comet's* jokes.

The best art – of whatever genre – has an inbuilt moral compass, a universally applicable guide to the higher reference points of the human spirit. There is no great Nazi art, and nor is there anything really uplifting from the post-Peterloo loyalist literary or visual bag of tricks. An example is the verse 'The Answer to Peterloo!', whose triumphal version of events, besides being slapdash with the facts (the Yeomanry did not assemble in St James's Square, there was no 'treason meeting', the peaceable crowd was not a 'REBELLY MOB', the woman on the hustings was neither Hunt's mistress nor his concubine, nor did she have 'her face closely shaven', etc.) is also technically poor, veering close to doggerel at times.[7]

Even worse was the piece published in *Aston's Exchange Herald* some three years after the event. The aggregation of barefaced untruths, set in an unsuitably jaunty metre, fair takes the breath away:

> *Though enrag'd by the strokes from the radical sticks,*
> *And the thick-flying missiles, the stones and the bricks,*
> *The Soldiers and Yeomen set bounds to their wrath…*
>
> …
>
> *The work of dispersion was done quite in mercy.*
> *There were three lost their lives – these were trampled to death,*
> *And one, from a sabre wound, yielded his breath.*[8]

Adding insult to the many injuries, part of this 180-line excrescence claims that the number of casualties had been exaggerated, either by the radicals trying to elicit sympathy for their cause, or by those trivially harmed by 'a bruise or a scrat' so as to make illicit money out of the compensation on offer.

Given the ethical swamp of such right-wing commentaries, it is no surprise that the anti-establishment stance had the best lines and most of the best graphic images; the targets were easier since more justifiable, a fact which was clearly in evidence in the well-known caricatures by George Cruikshank. Although sometimes an object of modern-day censure owing to his earlier depictions of political women, Cruikshank has at least partially redeemed himself with his views of Peterloo.

The two famous cartoons by Cruikshank (either George or his brother Isaac Robert) were supposedly separated by a month, but there are clear

Another Cruikshank cartoon. (Working Class Movement Library)

stylistic differences between them. The first, published in August 1819 (or so it was claimed) bears the title 'Massacre at St. Peter's, or 'BRITONS STRIKE HOME!!!'". It has as a frontal image a grotesquely obese cavalryman wielding an axe dripping with blood and charging at a woman with a baby at her breast. The appearance of the woman is more realistic than that of the Yeoman, and her raised arm and look of supplication recall one of the figures in Poussin's 'The Abduction of the Sabine Women'. The rest of the foreground is filled with sprawling, terrified wounded, and behind the fat Yeoman is an unbroken line of horsemen, all brandishing bloodstained axes. The background bristles with bayonets, and one of the soldiers is holding a flag on which we see:

LOYAL MANCHESTER YEOMANRY
Be Bloody, Bold, and Resolute
Span your proud horses &
ride hard in blood

The soldier on the left appears to be giving the orders:

Down with 'em! Chop 'em down! My brave boys, give them no quarter, they want to take our beef and pudding from us! – and remember the more we kill the less poor rates you'll have to pay, so go for it lads, show your courage and your loyalty!

Perhaps aware that the exaggerations in this drawing might be counter-productive in persuading the more literal-minded neutrals, one of the Cruikshank brothers produced another Peterloo cartoon: 'Manchester Heroes' (see p. 118).[9] The basic premise is the same – that of cavalry attacking defenceless civilians – but the axes have been replaced by sabres, the horsemen are more recognisably human, and there are more speech bubbles. We also see Hunt and other radicals on the hustings, shouting 'Shame, shame, murder, massacre'. There is a woman about to be struck by a sabre, but this time it is her child that is pleading with the Yeoman: 'Oh pray Sir, doan't [*sic*] kill mammy, she only came to see Mr. Hunt'. A gentleman is trying to pull the woman out of the way of the sabre's slash.

A chubby face in the sky risibly suggests some sort of divine intervention. The face, which bears a strong resemblance to the Prince Regent, is looking on with benign approval:

Cut them down, don't be afraid, they are not armed, courage my boys, and you shall have a vote of thanks, & he that kills most shall be made a knight errant and your exploits shall live for ever, in a song or second Chivey Chase.

Chivey Chase (more usually 'The Ballad of Chevy Chase') was a popular ballad at the time; its storyline told of a hunting party which segued into a savage battle with many killed – so the choice of song has resonance here.

Similar in style to the first Cruikshank cartoon is the drawing by John Lewis Marks: 'The Massacre of Peterloo! or a Specimen of English Liberty'. The chaotic savagery of the action is too compressed, and the porcine Yeomanry too close to pantomime villains, for the representation to have too many claims to realism, but nevertheless some telling observations are made, showing Marks's knowledge of precise details. The preparation of the sabres is alluded to by one Yeoman as he plunges his sword into a man's chest: 'D—n the fellow he has not made my Sword half sharp enough.' The magistrate, cup of wine in hand, is leaning out of the window and calling out: 'Cut away lads! the Riot Act is being read up in the Corner!' – a reference to the controversy surrounding whether the Act was read out or not. Behind him in the room, another magistrate with his back to us appears to be reading a paper to himself. A leering constable with a raised truncheon gloats: 'What a Glorious Day, this our Waterloo!', which is almost exactly what was shouted by the baton-wielding policeman who barged into Anne Jones's house on Windmill Street.[10] However, the constable's stamping on the head of a prostrate woman and grabbing his intended victim by the throat before landing his truncheon are details which are not corroborated by any eyewitness account, so possibly existed only in the artist's imagination.

The central figure of Marks's picture is the trumpeter on a rearing horse. In one hand he is brandishing a bloodstained sabre and in the other the trumpet which appears to be issuing the quatrain:

> *Raise up the Trumpet in high chearful [sic] Strain!*
> *Fill the goblets of <u>Rum</u>, to the <u>Legal Yeomen</u>!*
> *How Glorious our Ardour to lay down the lives*
> *Of defenceless Children, Husbands and Wives.*

But of course, there is only so much that satirical overstatement can achieve. Even though it could be argued that the grotesquerie of caricature is the most vivid and effective way of conveying the impression of an extreme experience, for many the horrors of Peterloo went way beyond the lampoon. The intended tone of the majority of the other famous visual representations of the flashpoint situation is serious and realistic.

The J. Evans print of Hunt's arrest 'Dreadful Scene at Manchester Meeting of Reformers' has been referred to above (see p. 150). Some details are incorrect: Buxton's house is in the wrong place, a couple of the reformers' banners are fictitious, and the distant part of the crowd is shown as a solid frogspawn-like mass of heads completely filling a space much bigger than the actual field. A series of letters appears on the drawing, referring to the key given below it: for example 'A' is Hunt about to be arrested on the platform by a Yeoman holding a sabre (another inaccuracy); 'B' is Johnson and 'C' is Saxton; 'D' is meant to be 'Sarah Hargreaves of the Female Union'; 'E' refers to the 'Soldiers pulling down the Flags of the reformers'; 'F' is 'the Yeomanry charging'; 'G' is supposed to be Buxton's house on Mount Street; and 'H' is the squadron of Special Constables.

A superficially similar, but more assiduously drawn, representation designed by a J. Slack started life as the design on a calico handkerchief, a copy of which may be viewed at the Working Class Movement Library in

J. Slack's design for a calico handkerchief (or headscarf). (Working Class Movement Library)

Salford.[11] It bears the title 'THE MANCHESTER REFORM MEETING DISPERSED by the CIVIL and MILITARY POWER Aug 16th 1819'.

The placing of the buildings around the field is correct, and again there is a guide to the most significant landmarks:

1. Society of Friends' School
2. St. Peter's Church
3. Mess. Pickfords and Co.'s Warehouse
4. Mr. Cooper's Cottage
5. House where the Magistrates sat
6. Mr P. Ewart's Factory
7. The Windmill Public House

The Mount Street houses are placed correctly at about 100 yards from the hustings. The edging is decorated with sheaves of corn and ribbon motifs which read, continuously:

Annual
Parliaments
and Election
by Ballot
Universal
Suffrage

The picture itself, as if viewed from the first floor of a Watson Street house, is a panoramic sweep of the fleeing multitude, in which there is a wealth of meticulous detail. The eye darts around the swirling mass of people to register the nest of sabres around the hustings and the banners; the eight or nine top-hatted reformers on the platform, an island amid the mayhem, with Mary Fildes holding the white banner and cap of liberty; closer to the point of view, more cavalrymen, sabres drawn, are turning this way and that in the solid crowd. Women are clearly visible, some of them having been knocked down, and there is a sinister hint in the three ownerless hats upturned on the ground.[12] In the immediate foreground a portly and well-dressed gentleman carrying a walking stick is trying to escape the havoc. It has been suggested that this figure was intended to represent a middle-class sympathiser, but it also implies the indiscriminate nature of the militia's attack.

Closer examination reveals more intimate details: the people watching from the Windmill Street rooftops and windows; the field cannon in front of Cooper's Cottage wall; the 'Britannia' image on Mary Fildes's flag; on the extreme right in the middle distance a woman holding a baby is being pursued by a horseman; a number of the men are carrying slim walking sticks, clearly not substantial enough to be considered weapons; and one notices how well dressed the people are: the men with hats, jackets and neckties, the women in bonnets, decent dresses and shawls. Overall, this picture is one of the most accurate representations of Peterloo.

'A View of St. Peter's Plain, Manchester on the memorable 16th of August 1819 representing the forcible dispersion of the people by the yeomanry cavalry' is another wide-angled view; it is an engraving by J. Sudlow taken from a drawing by T. Whaite, published in Manchester October 1819 (see p. 126).[13] Whaite claimed the drawing was 'taken on the spot', but once again sequential incidents are incorrectly shown as simultaneous. The foreground depicts the brutal dispersal of men and women, whilst one figure – presumably meant to represent Hunt, although the top hat he is wearing is black – is still standing on the hustings. In the middle distance a solid mass of people appears to be forced into the bottleneck between St Peter's Church and Cooper's Cottage. The buildings are accurately shown: from left to right we see the Quaker's Meeting House with its wall, beneath which a cavalryman is attacking a couple of stragglers; then to the right of the Church and the Cottage the block which contains Buxton's house; then on the far right the row of houses on Windmill Street.

Hunt, along with a number of other reformers, is usually shown on the platform in the images, even though the widespread assaults with sabres and truncheons by all accounts happened after the Orator's arrest and removal from the hustings. Each of the pictures attempts to fuse several elements into one impressionistic scene.

This is also true of another of the iconic Peterloo images: the hand-coloured aquatint 'possibly by Cruikshank'[14] published by Carlile with the caption:

> To Henry Hunt Esq., as chairman of the meeting assembled in St. Peter's Field, Manchester sixteenth day of August 1819, and to the Female Reformers of Manchester and the adjacent towns who were exposed to and suffered from the Wanton and Furious Attack made on them by that Brutal Armed Force the Manchester & Cheshire Yeomanry Cavalry, this plate is dedicated by their fellow labourer, Richard Carlile (see p.116).

Once again the foreground is taken up by the sword-brandishing Yeomanry driving their wild-eyed horses into the trampled and scattering crowd, some of whom lie bloodied and horror-stricken on the ground. Dominating the scene on the platform just behind the mayhem, holding banners and caps of liberty, are eight reformers, with Hunt and Mary Fildes again clearly recognisable. Just to the left of the platform a group of women is being attacked by a cavalryman, with one of the victims apparently skewered by a sabre. The picture is precisely drawn and up to a point – for example with the rendering of emotion on people's faces – realistic. However, once more, time and space have been compressed so as to achieve the maximum effect. On the far left we see the magistrates leaning out of a first-floor window, much closer to the hustings than they actually were. And as has already been established, the Yeomanry's hounding of the crowd happened after Hunt's arrest and the clearing of the platform. Also, the composition of the picture is a little too posed and contrived to convince utterly. Nevertheless, the impression given covers all the bases, and tells us much about what transpired on St Peter's Field.

The same classic symmetry is even clearer in another Cruikshank representation of Peterloo, a detail from which may be seen on the Briton's Protection pub sign on Great Bridgewater Street (see p. 110).[15] The central impression is of an eruption of sabre-wielding cavalrymen, identifiable by the 'MYC' banner. One of them – presumably intended to be Meagher – is carrying a bugle. The immediate foreground and left and right edges are peopled by men, women and young children being trampled on and attempting to flee the attack. One of the women is on the ground holding a baby, and her raised arm recalls the gesture of the woman in Cruikshank's 'BRITONS STRIKE HOME!!!' cartoon. A flag bearing the word REFORM and a cap of liberty is at an angle, toppling away from the central charge.

When the Free Trade Hall reopened in 1951, artist Mr H. Sherwood Edwards was commissioned to paint a commemorative mural of Peterloo. When the building became the Radisson Hotel in 2004 the painting was placed on a first-floor corridor wall, which is where it is today. The portrayal is considered by many to be too bland and ambiguous, the visual equivalent of the mealy-mouthed wording of the original blue plaque on the wall outside. It seems to go out of its way not to stir up too many emotions, and the attempt at photo-realism is certainly a world away from Cruikshank's and Marks's cartoon blood sport.

The artist of this mural may have had the wadding of 130 years and confusingly differing narratives to immure him from the reality of the deaths and the woundings. When Peterloo was still raw and bleeding in the memory, it was much more likely to be a powerful emotion that fuelled the response: it was in the grip of anger that Shelley wrote his poem 'The Masque of Anarchy'.

With its furiously terse lines, relentless drumbeat rhythm and nightmare images, 'Masque' leaves a visceral impression of a call to arms, a revolutionary incantation. The most inflammatory (and famous) stanza appears twice:

> *Rise like lions after slumber*
> *In unvanquishable number!*
> *Shake your chains to earth, like dew*
> *Which in sleep had fall'n on you:*
> *Ye are many – they are few.*[16]

So potent is the suggestion of insurrection here, that it is easy to forget that elsewhere the poem recommends non-violent resistance:

Stand ye calm and resolute
Like a forest close and mute,
With folded arms and looks which are
Weapons of unvanquished war…

And if then the tyrants dare,
Let them ride among you there;
Slash and stab, and maim and hew;
What they like, that let them do.

With folded arms and steady eyes,
And little fear, and less surprise,
Look upon them as they slay,
Till their rage has died away.[17]

The totally unfeasible reaction of 'folded arms and steady eyes' in the face of the Yeomanry's slashing sabres suggests here that Shelley has lost touch with reality. (Even though elsewhere in the poem the visions are replaced by hard facts: 'Such starvation cannot be/As in England now we see.'[18]) There are other fanciful touches in the 'visions of Poesy', such as a ghastly pageant in which Murder, Fraud and Hypocrisy are personified by members of the House of Commons. Home Secretary Lord Sidmouth and his duplicitous policies are captured with symbolic aptness:

Clothed with the Bible, as with light,
And the shadows of the night,
Like Sidmouth, next, Hypocrisy
On a crocodile rode by.[19]

Overall, the ninety-one stanzas tell us more about Shelley the wordsmith and political animal than about what happened on St Peter's Field. Nevertheless, for all its poetic licence and extravagance, 'Masque' is incendiary stuff and was given a compelling recital by Maxine Peake at the 2013 Manchester International Festival (see Appendix 14).

Unfeasible details or not, the basic premise of the poem is sound enough: whatever the horrors of the present, the future belongs to the multitude. It was this idea, deemed dangerously seditious, that kept the work from publication until 1832, thirteen years after its composition. By then, the political landscape had shifted considerably.

Back in the cauldron of late 1819, a lesser-known poem appeared in *Black Dwarf* on 22 September. The galloping rhythms of 'The Sword King' reinforce the terror of the cavalry's pursuit:

> *Who is it that flies in the tumult so fast*
> *When the yeomanry bugles are mingling their blast?*
> *The mother who folds her dear child to her breast,*
> *And screams, as around her expire the oppress'd…*

The vulnerable child figure becomes a symbol of the fledgling radical movement:

> *Base brat of reform, shall thy cries bar my way,*
> *To the laurels that bloom for the loyal today?*
> *Shalt thou live to rear banner, white, emerald or blue?…*[20]

The last line appears to refer to the two Middleton banners.

William Hone was in more serious mood, too, with his Byronic parody 'Don Juan Canto the Third'. The public was expecting the genuine article from Lord Byron, and the skilful pastiche of the poet's style might have fooled some. One of the themes of the multi-tasking poem was to highlight the futility of petitioning and speeches in the light of recent events:

> *But ne'er to* Speech *did the oppressor yield, –*
> *Already to their steeds the Yeomen sprung,*
> *And note of maddening charge their hollow bugle rung.*[21]

The Reverends Ethelston and Hay were the object of some poetic vitriol. The former was lampooned in the scathing 'Saint Ethelston's Day', the final stanza of which highlights the disingenuous role of the clergy:

> *'Cut away, my brave fellows, you see how they faint,*
> *They are the BLACKGUARD REFORMERS!' exclaimed the new saint:*
> *'Send them to the Devil, my lads, on your way,*
> *And, no doubt, they'll remember SAINT ETHELSTON'S DAY.'*[22]

Hay came in for similar treatment. Bamford went for the jugular in his depiction of the military-political-church hegemony which held sway at Peterloo, and Hay's key role in it:

> And here is a Barrack with soldiers enow,
> The deed which thou willest all ready to do;
> They will rush on the people in martial array,
> If thou but thy blood-dripping cassock display.

> And Mea***r shall ever be close by thy side,
> With a brave troop of Yeomanry ready to ride;
> For the steed shall be saddled, the sword shall be bare,
> And these shall be none the defenceless to spare!

> …

> Then the Prince too shall thank thee, and add to thy wealth,
> Thou shall preach down sedition and pray for his health;
> And Sidmouth, and Canning, and sweet Castlereagh,
> Shall write pleasant letters to dear cousin ***.[23]

Later in the century, Dickens lent his formidable presence to the debate with an article published in the *Manchester Weekly Times* in June 1867. The prolific writer, basing his narrative on Bamford's account and the report in *The Times*, helped in no small measure to keep the pot boiling. Another famous prose depiction is given in two coruscating chapters from *The Manchester Man*, a semi-fictional work by Mrs G. Linnaeus Banks, and one of the most heartfelt denunciations of the carnage. The original work was published in 1876, and the revised and illustrated edition twenty years later.[24]

Art and literature, of course, were but two of the aspects of the multi-faceted and continuing story. Peterloo would be a common point of reference in the great ideological battles of the nineteenth century, and the long crawl towards universal suffrage, people's rights, and a more genuine and workable democracy. To a greater or lesser extent, the Chartists, the Anti-Corn Law League, the Rochdale Pioneers (later to evolve into the Co-operative movement), the Trade Union Movement, and the Suffragettes[25] would keep alive the memory of St Peter's Field as a political and emotive touchstone.

5

Reflections

Was Peterloo a deliberately laid trap? There seems to be enough evidence to support the contention that the authorities' violence was premeditated. Carlile believed so (see p. 145) and many other contemporary writers at least acknowledged this possibility:

Dr. W. Cooke Taylor:

They [the magistrates] allowed the meeting of the 16th of August to assemble, hoping, by a *coup d'état*, to strike terror into the reformers of Manchester, and perhaps disposed to show their contempt for spinners and weavers, by arresting the leader in the midst of the assembly.[1]

Jonathan Edward Taylor:

I cannot but conclude, that it was *ab initio* intended to dissolve the meeting by force, and that the arrest of Mr. Hunt and his associates was merely the pretext by which the attack was to be justified.[2]

Archibald Prentice:

Did the magistrates…rather seek the opportunity of striking terror into the multitude assembled by arresting their leader, no matter at what risk of bloodshed, before their eyes?[3]

And the radical newspaperman Thomas Wooler was even more outspoken on the issue:

The proceedings at Manchester exhibited every mark of a deliberate intention to shed blood… [the authorities'] object was not to prevent the meeting, but to disperse it by force when assembled … to butcher a few, as a terror to the rest.[4]

This would be commensurate with the motives of the spies and *agents provocateurs* in previous years, in which the objective seems to have been not to stop the meetings and demonstrations, but rather to lure dissenters out into the open, so to speak, where, in this vulnerable position, they could be more easily identified and picked off. Cobbett in the *Political Register* of 16 May 1819, in his attack on Oliver the spy, spoke about the informer's 'traps' which were intended 'not to prevent, but to produce those acts [of dissension]'.

The *Manchester Observer* published a couple of assertions, which appeared to throw a sinister light on the whole affair:

> ...private enquiries were made, as to how many beds could be found in this institution [the Infirmary], just previous to the day of Meeting... Every patient in the Infirmary was literally turned out which could possibly be done, preparatory to the horrible butchery which took place on the 16th instant, in order to *prepare for the wounded which might be brought there for surgical aid.* This fact is almost conclusive that *something* was *previously* arranged, and of which the fruits were seen on that bloody day. ...all the surgeons, &c., of that institution were summoned to attend on that day.[5]

This suggests that the authorities were expecting carnage. At the Infirmary Weekly Board Meeting on 6 September, however, the allegations were emphatically denied:

> This board feels it a duty they owe to the subscribers and the Public to inform them that no summons whatever was sent to the surgeons &c., to attend *either* at the *Infirmary* or at St. Peter's previous to the meeting of the 16 August.[6]

As to the affirmation that beds were deliberately made available in anticipation of a bloodbath, the Infirmary published the following figures on 6 September:

Maximum number of beds: 120

Number of patients in Infirmary on the morning of 16 August: 116

Number of patients discharged on the same morning: 30 [not an unusually high number]

Number of patients admitted on the same morning: 22[7]

Nevertheless, there is a good deal of circumstantial evidence to suggest that Peterloo was indeed a deliberately created trap:

The 16 August assembly was never declared illegal beforehand, and there was no attempt to stop the processions as they entered the city along the main roads.

The meeting could easily have been prevented by the earlier arrest of the ringleaders, many of whom were highly visible in Hunt's barouche as it made the tour of the town beforehand.

Hunt had offered himself up for arrest on the previous Saturday, but the offer had been declined.

The military preparedness was markedly thorough: the sharpening of the sabres, the numbers of cavalry and infantry deployed, and the inclusion of two field cannon.

According to Jonathan Edward Taylor, a good number of the Yeomanry's sharpened sabres were not collected by their owners from the cutler's until Saturday, 14 August, which suggests the anticipation of a call for their use on the following Monday.[8]

The magistrates wrote to Lt-Col L'Estrange the day before, indicating that they would need military help at the meeting.

Magistrate Norris, in the letter he wrote to Lord Sidmouth the evening before, had stated that he did not expect peace the next day.

Hundreds of placards were posted in Manchester and Salford streets that morning, advising 'the peaceable and well disposed' people of the towns to stay indoors for the rest of the day.

The positioning of the troops out of sight in the surrounding streets suggests an intention to encircle and confine.[9]

The peaceable demeanour of the crowd was disregarded.

It appears unlikely that the Riot Act was read, or even if it was, the statutory one hour allowed for voluntary dispersal was not observed.

The Yeomanry pursued the fugitives to a great distance from the field.

Congratulations were sent to the magistrates and the militia from the Prince Regent and the Home Office (see Appendix 7).

Most of the country's leading radicals were imprisoned or awaiting trial within the next few months.

The repressive Six Acts were passed in November, mostly as a response to Peterloo.

Petitions from the reformers were resolutely ignored by the government, who repeatedly refused to hold a public inquiry.[10]

Robert Walmsley, in his hefty tome *Peterloo: The Case Re-opened*, reaches the conclusion that 'all were victims' in an unfortunate succession of accidents: magistrates, constables, crowd, radicals on the hustings, and soldiery were all equally disadvantaged in the same tragic and unavoidable shipwreck of circumstance.[11] A brief look at the future of several of the major players will cast serious doubts on this view.

William Hulton continued to grow rich from the seven coal seams beneath his land, paying his workers the lowest wages in Lancashire.[12] He became Chairman of the Bolton and Leigh Railway Co. in 1824, and founded the Hulton Colliery Co. in 1858, all the while opposing Trade Unions and political public assemblies. In 1831 he was involved in a conflict over wages and working conditions with the Colliers' Union, about whom he complained: 'You have wantonly injured me to the full limits of your ability, in my purse; and you have much farther wounded my feelings'[13] – which suggests that he was out of touch with reality, a feeling which is enhanced when one considers his long-term stance on Peterloo. He would remain ever proud of his contribution to the St Peter's Field catastrophe and would keep a captured cap of liberty in his study for the rest of his life. Despite overwhelming evidence to the contrary, he would always maintain that only two people lost their life at Peterloo: 'one, a woman, who, having impersonated the Goddess of Reason, was trampled to death in the crowd; and the other a special constable, who was cut down unintentionally by a private of a dragoon regiment'.[14] On the resignation of Major Trafford in May 1820, the Manchester and Salford Yeomanry expressed a wish that Hulton should be appointed their Colonel.[15] Hulton would remain unrepentant and unflinching in his hard-line approach to employees: in June 1836 he took three of his workers to court for breach of contract after they had refused to work because of dangerous mining conditions. They were found guilty and sentenced to three months' hard labour.[16]

In January 1820 the Reverend William Hay landed the sinecure of vicar of Rochdale, on a salary of £2,400 a year. Sources differ as to whether or not this was a reward for his role at Peterloo. He seems to have spent a good deal of his twenty years in the post fulfilling duties elsewhere, for when the succeeding vicar took over from Hay he found 'the Church in Rochdale…in a state of great collapse and stagnation. The previous vicar had been absent for the greater part of the year, and Church work, except for the most perfunctory kind, was dead.'[17]

The legislative career of magistrate James Norris suffered no impediment, as he was appointed Chairman of Salford Quarter Sessions in 1825, a position which he held until his death in 1838.

Hugh Hornby Birley was promoted to Major Commandant of his Yeomanry in 1820, then the following year elected to President of the Chamber of Commerce, a position which he was to hold for seven years. He continued to live in his extensive Didsbury house, and his Cambridge Street factory was visited by the Duke of Wellington in 1830.[18] Amongst the collection of awards presented to him was 'a beautifully engraved sword' from the NCOs and Privates of the Manchester and Salford Yeomanry (the irony seems to have been lost on all concerned); and from the Chamber of Commerce in recognition of his services, 'a valuable piece of plate' and 'a silver tureen weighing 240 oz'.[19]

Colonel Ralph Fletcher, already in command of the Bolton regiment of local militia, was another recipient of an array of glittering prizes: a number of gold cups, a sword, and two pieces of silver plate, in recognition of his services to 'the British Empire, its laws and constitution, its throne and its altar'.[20] Fletcher would be the Treasurer of the Grand Orange Lodge of England until his death in 1832.

Deputy Constable Joseph Nadin, having added to his fortune by ownership of the Queen's Theatre and several Manchester pubs, retired from his constabulary duties a rich man in 1822. He spent his twilight years as resident landowner of the extensive Orrishmere Farm in Cheadle, Cheshire. In his last will and testament, he describes himself as a 'gentleman'.

With a few exceptions, and despite the boycotting of certain shops and inns, the Yeomanry and special constables continued to enjoy their comparative affluence and did well out of the reinforced status quo.

In the end, once the metaphorical dust had settled and the prison sentences had been served, most of the prominent reformers also benefited in some way from Peterloo.

Perceived by many as the hero of the age, and after giving such a good account of himself at his trial, Henry Hunt was ultimately to gain political capital from Peterloo, being elected MP for Preston in 1831. He continued with his business interests with varying success: he invested in such widely diverse commodities as artificial coal, shoe-blacking, a cheese-dyeing additive, and a concoction that rendered clothes and shoes waterproof.[21]

He paid a return visit to Manchester in August 1832, heading a torchlit procession – a conspicuous innovation – and accompanied by drums, fifes and the odd celebratory gunshot.[22] He died in February 1835, and had a monument erected by the Reverend James Scholefield on the burial ground on Every Street, Manchester. Beneath the monument were extensive vaults, in which were deposited Hunt's memoirs, his letters written in Ilchester prison, and a history of Peterloo.[23] The monument, an 18ft-tall tapering obelisk topped with an unobtrusive statue of Hunt, fell into disrepair after a few decades, and the Open Spaces Committee ordered its demolition in 1888. The stones were sold off for a mere £3, and the documents which had been placed under the foundation stone were never found.[24] A less public memorial – that of a medallion bronze portrait – was presented to the Manchester Reform Club in 1908.

Sam Bamford lived to a grand old age in a cottage in Moston Vale. He earned a reasonable income from his writing and from the position of Charlestown postmaster, but suffered from failing eyesight and hearing in his later years. He died in 1872 aged 84, having survived Jemima by nearly a decade. The last photograph of the old campaigner shows him sporting the copious snow-white beard of a biblical prophet, his face serious but kindly.[25]

John Knight remained politically involved, as secretary of the National Spinners' Union in 1830, then as active supporter of the Society for the Promotion of National Regeneration, which sought to improve factory conditions and curtail the length of the working day. He was in the forefront

Bamford's monument in Middleton cemetery. (Author's collection)

of the campaign for Reform, memorably when he posted on the Oldham Constable's house wall 'a handbill of an inflammatory character attacking the Bishops and the Peers for their opposition to the Reform Bill'. He was entrusted with a salaried post of Treasurer for the Oldham Poor Relief Fund, not long before his death aged 76 in 1838. Around 2,500 people attended the funeral of the popular and energetic radical – 'the Cartwright of the North'.[26]

Mary Fildes returned to politics to help found the Female Political Union of the Working Classes, and would be active in the Chartist Movement. The Female Reformers of Manchester carried on unbowed after Peterloo, as is indicated in the letter written by Mary in collaboration with Susannah Saxton to reformer William Cobbett in November 1819:

> May these trifling tokens of our regard…prove more powerful than the sabres of the cowardly enemy, which we the Female Reformers of Manchester most of us narrowly escaped, and drive corruption to her pristine darkness; then shall the voice of war be heard no more, and our children reap the full fruit of their parents' labour.[27]

Later in life Mary Fildes left the radical front line and became landlady of a Chester pub. She died in her mid-eighties in 1876.[28]

The most notable exception to the success stories was Richard Carlile, who died in 1843 in extreme poverty, the result of crippling government fines, the purpose of which seems to have been to prevent him from publishing his radical texts.

Leaving Carlile aside, how does one equate the future of these luminaries, whether loyalist or reformer, with the fate of the people killed or maimed for life on St Peter's Field? Or indeed those who survived unscathed but who remained in dire poverty? Walmsley's conclusion that 'all were victims' – whether he meant on the day or in the long term – is baffling, to say the least.

And finally, the perennial question: was Peterloo a massacre?

The word was freely and emotively used in the liberal press in the immediate aftermath, and through constant repetition over the years the unexamined phrase 'the Peterloo Massacre' has been in danger of lapsing into a kind of routine and unreflective duckspeak. A number of historians have disagreed with the use of the word, quoting the dictionary definition and claiming that since the death toll resulting from St Peter's Field did not involve 'large numbers', the word is therefore a misnomer. For example, in 1890 Henry de Beltgens Gibbins wrote in his *Industrial History of England* that in this case the term 'massacre' was 'grossly misapplied'. Nearly seventy years later Donald Read also cast doubt on the word, although basing his argument on a debatable claim: 'Perhaps only in peace-loving England could a death-roll of only eleven persons have been so described.'[29]

But it is soulless pedantry to tally the bodies until one is satisfied that the supposedly correct demarcation is reached. I would maintain that a massacre is defined not solely by numbers killed, but also by the ferocity and indiscriminate nature of the attack, the inequality of the forces involved, and the intensity of the resultant public shock. In these terms, Peterloo deserves the epithet.[30]

Epilogue

The story is far from over.

The 200 years since the St Peter's Field carnage have seen the continuation of two conflicting trends: on the one hand, the movement to suppress or airbrush the truth; on the other, a desire to keep the memory, however distressing, alive.

Three moments spanning nearly a century will be enough to highlight the ongoing debate. In 1877 the new Town Hall was opened, artist Ford Madox Brown having been commissioned to paint a series of murals to illustrate iconic moments in the history of Manchester. Topics considered but ultimately rejected were Peterloo and the Lancashire cotton famine, the reason given being that the incidents were too contentious and upsetting.

In 1951, the rebuilt Free Trade Hall displayed the mural by H. Sherwood Edwards. This controversially cosmetic representation of the slaughter has been mentioned above. Since November 2017 a striking rejoinder to the Edwards painting has been on view a couple of hundred yards away in the public bar of the Abercromby pub on Bootle Street. Paul Fitzgerald's 8ft mural is accessible, is based on contemporary prints, and pulls no punches in its depiction of the chaotic and bloody assault by the Yeomanry. It will form the centre spread of the graphic novel *Peterloo: Witnesses to a Massacre*, due for publication in 2019.

The issue came to another head in 1972, when the Labour council put forward a proposal to rename Peter Street as 'Peterloo Street'. Objections were raised by local business concerns: typical was the reaction of the Midland Hotel, the owners of which disliked the idea of an address associated with a massacre, as well as finding the 'loo' suffix distasteful. The matter went to court and the stipendiary magistrate decided against the council, so Peter Street it remained. In his summing up, the magistrate concluded that Peterloo had been 'an incident about which the city could feel little pride',

Paul Fitzgerald's mural in the Abercromby pub, Bootle Street. (Author's collection)

and with a couple of choice understatements: 'Certainly it appears to have been a dramatic manifestation' and deciding that it had been 'not a very creditable incident'[1] he set the tone for the bland wording of the first plaque which later that year was placed on the outside wall of the Free Trade Hall:

THE SITE OF ST. PETER'S FIELDS
WHERE ON 16TH AUGUST 1819
HENRY HUNT RADICAL ORATOR
ADDRESSED AN ASSEMBLY OF
ABOUT 60,000 PEOPLE
THEIR SUBSEQUENT DISPERSAL
BY THE MILITARY IS
REMEMBERED AS

'PETERLOO'

This blue plaque lasted thirty-five years, before being replaced in 2007 by the current red one:

The former blue commemorative plaque (1972) on what was then the Free Trade Hall. (Author's collection)

The new red plaque, on an outside wall of the Radisson Hotel, Peter Street. (Author's collection)

ST. PETER'S FIELDS
THE PETERLOO MASSACRE
On 16th August 1819 a peaceful rally
of 60,000 pro-democracy reformers,
men, women and children,
was attacked by armed cavalry
resulting in 15 deaths and
over 600 injuries.

The twenty-first century has seen no quietening of the debate. In 2012 the council proposed the idea of a commemorative design incorporated into the gates which were to close off Library Walk, the passage between the renovated Central Library and the Town Hall annex. The idea was vehemently rejected by the Memorial Campaign group, partly because of the lack of consultation with them, but principally because it was felt that the prohibitive symbolism of barriers would send out the wrong signals.

Instead, when the library was reopened in 2015, Library Walk became the site of a tasteful, if understated, memorial. The floor of the covered area now contains the design of the cotton flowers which also feature on the Town Hall floor. A number of the ruby-red centres of the flowers show a subdued light when a passer-by pauses above them, illuminating the names of the

Cotton flower design on the floor of the Library Walk, commemorating Martha Partington. (Author's collection)

Peterloo fallen. Installed by architects SimpsonHaugh, the idea is effective, but one feels that a nearby indicatory and explanatory notice is needed. Most people I asked were not even aware of the existence of the installations, which are closed to public viewing overnight when the outer doors to the passage are locked.

In recent years the increasing awareness of Peterloo has prompted a need for a more conspicuous memorial.

The pedestrian approach to the Great Northern Square off Peter Street is to be aligned with stone blocks which will feature selected stanzas from 'The Masque of Anarchy' in handcrafted script. The terrace walkway, parallel with Deansgate, will be illuminated at night. Comparing this statement with the relatively obscure cotton flowers, there is a higher profile and a greater public accessibility.

The planned 2019 monument, to be designed by Turner Prize winner Jeremy Deller, will take the process one stage further (see Appendix 17).

On 20 August 2017 – the most recent memorial gathering prior to the publication of this book – proceedings were removed to Albert Square, between the Town Hall entrance and the statue of Prince Albert: an anachronism, but the site served the purpose well. Actor Christopher Eccleston, acting the role of near namesake the Reverend Ethelston, leaned out of a second floor Town Hall window and read out the Riot Act. Getting into the spirit of things, a gentleman in the crowd responded to the 'disperse

Part of the crowd at the August 2015 memorial gathering. In 1819 the foreground would have been the site of the Windmill Street knoll. (Peterloo Memorial Campaign collection)

themselves, and peaceably depart to their habitations' directive with a curt Mancunian 'Bugger off!'

From the statue steps, a list of the Peterloo dead and extracts from 'The Masque of Anarchy' were read out by Maxine Peake, John Henshaw, Paul Fitzgerald, Robert Poole, Martin Gittins, cultural historian C.P. Lee, Lord Mayor Eddy Newman, and others. Maxine Peake also read out a message from film director Mike Leigh, part of which is given at the end of this section.

Three days later, at the Working Class Movement Library, Colin Smith gave a convincingly costumed and acted one-person Living History Performance of Peterloo. His assumed voices included a shouting and bigoted gentleman of privilege, a mill owner, a coachman, and a washerwoman who had been witness to the slaughter. Hopefully we will see more of this deeply researched and gripping production.

For August 2018 an enlarged event will involve the whole of the Greater Manchester area, and 2019 will see the culmination of a consortium of efforts to put into place a three-month long commemoration of the incident.

Some commentators have discerned shades of Peterloo and its brain-scrambling aftermath in the legal and factual fog that gathered around Orgreave and Hillsborough.[2] Such a comparative study is beyond the scope of this book; but the modern-day question of fake news and manipulated language issuing from some spheres of officialdom and the media – often working in tandem – remains a threat to our hard-won and fragile democracy. Film director Mike Leigh has defined the St Peter's Field atrocity and its aftermath as 'the event that becomes more relevant with every new episode of our crazy times'.

We forget the lessons of Peterloo at our peril.

Appendices

APPENDIX 1

Handbill produced by the Manchester Police Office, 21 July 1819:

The Magistrates and Local Authorities of this district having declared that the peace and safety of these Towns and the immediate Neighbourhood are threatened with great and imminent danger from the attempts of seditious men to overturn the Constitution and to involve us in the miseries of a Revolution, – the loyal and well-disposed Inhabitants of these Towns are called upon to enroll themselves in an ARMED ASSOCIATION, *for the Preservation of Public Peace.*

It is not intended to interfere with the time and occupations of those who enroll themselves, more than is absolutely necessary; or to incur any unnecessary expense; and the general plan of the Association will be sufficiently intelligible from the two following Resolutions of the Committee for strengthening the Civil Power:

1st That this Committee do not conceive that any uniform will be necessary for such Armed Association;

2nd That it is on every account desirable that the least possible sacrifice of time should be required in drilling; as it is considered only necessary that the most simple parts of military discipline should be acquired by such Association.[1]

APPENDIX 2

Text of Mary Fildes's speech intended to be given on the Peterloo Hustings:

Sir –

Permit the Female Reformers of Manchester, in presenting you with this flag, to state, that they are actuated by no motives of petty vanity. As wives, mothers, daughters, in their social, domestic, moral capacities, they have come forward in support of the sacred cause of liberty – a cause in which their husbands, their fathers, and their sons, have embarked the last hope of suffering humanity. Neither ashamed nor afraid of thus aiding you in the glorious struggle for recovering your lost privileges – privileges upon which so much of their own happiness depends; they trust that this tribute to freedom will animate you to a steady perseverance in obtaining the object of our common solicitude – a radical reform in the Commons House of Parliament. In discharging what they felt an imperative duty, they hope they have not 'overstepped the modesty of nature' and they shall now retire to the bosoms of their families with the cheering and consolatory reflection, that your efforts are on the eve of being crowned with complete success.

May our flag never be unfurled but in the cause of peace and reform! And then may a female's curse pursue the coward who deserts the standard![2]

APPENDIX 3

Ann Fildes's affidavit, sworn before a magistrate:

Ann Fildes the wife of Charles Fildes, of Manchester, upon her oath, saith, that having an errand to go near St. Peter's Church, on Monday the 16th of August, she took her child, an infant of two years old, in her arms. Several of her neighbours were with her at the time; it was, as near as she can recollect, half-past one – that seeing the immense number of people assembled at the meeting on St. Peter's Field and the military, examinant and her neighbours returned towards their own houses in Kennedy-street; that on turning back along Cooper-street, she saw the Manchester Yeomanry Cavalry coming up. Examinant, after seeing the whole pass, as she thought, crossed the street, from the house occupied by Dr. Bancks to Mr. Slater's, and when in the act of doing so, one of the Yeomanry, who, being behind the rest, was coming up the street at a gallop, came against her, she was thrown down, and her infant fell from her arms to a distance of about two yards and a half, and afterwards died from the effect. Examinant can state nothing further, as she was stunned by the fall.[3]

APPENDIX 4

Earliest known official communication from St Peter's Field to London on the day:

Manchester August 16 1819

Gents,

The meeting took place at 1 o'clock Hunt in the chair with 16 flags and 7 caps of liberty hoisted up amongst upwards of 60,000 people the cavalry has just broke in upon them the flags are taken Hunt and his party secured. Several lives are lost and a number wounded. The cavalry are now scouring the streets in all directions.

½ past 2 o'clock

Yours H. Allen[4]

APPENDIX 5(A)

Hunt's account of his arrest:

While we were passing to the house, amidst the screams of the flying, and the piercing cries and groans of the dying people, two ruffian Yeomen made several attempts to cut me down, but each time I guarded myself, by placing Nadin between myself and them as they renewed their charge upon me. Nadin endeavoured to escape, and to leave me to their mercy, but, with the aid of providence, I held him fast, and used him as a shield to ward off the blows of these blood-thirsty cowards. Nadin was so alarmed that he at length yielded like a child to the direction of my arm, and quietly suffered himself to be placed before me as they came up, hallowing lustily for them to desist, and using his staff for his protection. They, however, charged, and cut at me several times, and I received three cuts from them, a slight one on the back of my hand, and two others in my head, which cuts penetrated through my hat. As I entered into Buxton's house, pinioned between two constables, Nadin and another, a ruffian came behind me and levelled a blow at my head with a heavy bludgeon, which would have felled me to the earth, had I not been supported by the constables, who had hold of my arms. One fellow very deliberately took off my hat, that the other coward might have a fairer blow at me, which he instantly repeated, and had I not at the moment fortunately slipped my head on one side, my skull must have been fractured. Nadin cried shame at this, and replaced the hat upon my head, saying it was too bad![6]

APPENDIX 5(B)

Extracts from Hunt's deposition at his trial, as recorded by the *Manchester Observer*:

[The deponent said under oath that he was:]

...dragged on to the house where the Magistrates were assembled, and he was repeatedly assaulted with the bludgeons of several constables; and while in this situation, pinioned by the said constables; he...received a severe blow upon the head, inflicted from behind...

After this, [he] got into the house where the Magistrates were, and in passing through the passage, he received more violent blows from both sides of a double row of constables.[6]

APPENDIX 6

Letter from the Reverend W.R. Hay to Lord Sidmouth, written later that evening:

Manchester, 16th August, 1819.
Quarter past Nine.

My Lord,

MR. NORRIS being very much fatigued by the harassing duty of this day, it becomes mine now to inform your Lordship of the proceedings which have been had in consequence of the proposal put forward for a meeting. The Special Committee have been in constant attendance for the last three days, and contented themselves till they saw what the complexion of the meeting might be, or what circumstances might arise, with coming to this determination only, which they adopted in concurrence with some of the most intelligent gentlemen of the town, not to stop the numerous columns which were from various roads expected to pour in, but to allow them to reach the place of their destination.

The assistance of the military was of course required, and arrangements in consequence made with them, of such description as might be applicable to various circumstances.

About eleven o'clock the Magistrates, who were very numerous, repaired to a house, where they might see the whole of the proceedings of the meeting. A body of special constables took their ground, about two hundred in number, close to the hustings; from them there was a line of communication to the house where we were. Mr. Trafford Trafford was so good as to take the situation of attending Colonel L'Estrange, the commanding officer.

From eleven till one o'clock, the various columns arrived, attended by flags, each by two or three flags; and there were four, if not more, caps of liberty. The ensigns were of the same description as those displayed on similar occasions, with this addition, that one had a bloody pike represented on it; another 'Equal representation or death.' There was no appearance of arms or pikes, but great plenty of sticks and staves, and every column marched in regular files of three or four deep, attended with conductors, music, &c. The most powerful accession was in the last instance, when Hunt and his party came in. But, long before this, the Magistrates had felt a decided conviction that the whole bore the appearance of insurrection; that the array was such as to terrify all the king's subjects, and was such as no legitimate purpose could justify. In addition to their own sense of the meeting, they had very numerous depositions from the inhabitants, as to their fears for the public safety; and at length a man deposed as to the parties who were approaching, attended by the heaviest column. On a barouche-box was a woman in white, who I believe was a Mrs. Gant [sic], from Stockport, and who, it is believed, had a cap of liberty. In the barouche were Hunt, Johnson, Knight, and Moorhouse of Stockport: as soon as these four parties were ascertained, a warrant issued to apprehend them. The troops were mustered, and Nadin, preceding the Manchester Yeomanry Cavalry, executed it. While the Cavalry was forming, a most marked defiance of them was acted by the reforming part of the mob; however, they so far executed their purpose, as to apprehend Hunt and Johnson on the hustings: Knight and Moorhouse in the moment escaped. They also took on the hustings, Saxton, and Sykes [sic] who is the writer to the Manchester Observer, and which Saxton had before been addressing the mob. The parties thus apprehended, were brought to the house where the magistrates were. In the mean time the Riot Act was read, and the mob was completely dispersed, but not without very serious and lamentable effects. Hunt, &c. were brought down to the New Bailey; two magistrates and myself, having promised them protection, preceded them; we were attended by special constables and some cavalry. The parties were lodged in the New Bailey; and since that have been added to them, Knight and Moorhouse. On inquiry, it appeared that many had suffered from various instances; one of the Manchester Yeomanry, Mr. Hulme, was, after the parties were taken, struck by a brick-bat; he lost his power over his horse, and is supposed to have fractured his skull by a fall from his horse. I am afraid that he is since dead; if not, there are no hopes of his recovery. A special constable of the name of Ashworth has been killed – cause unknown; and four women appear to have lost their lives by being pressed by the crowd; these, I believe, are the fatal effects of the meeting. A variety of instances of sabre wounds occurred, but I hope none mortal; several pistols were fired by the mob, but as to their effect, save in one instance deposed before Colonel Fletcher, we have no account. We cannot but deeply regret all this serious attendant on this transaction; but we have the *satisfaction of witnessing the very grateful and cheering countenances of the whole town; in fact, they consider themselves as saved by our exertions. All the shops were shut, and for the most part, continued so all the evening. The capture of Hunt took place before two o'clock, and I forgot to mention, that all their colours, drums, &c. were taken or destroyed: since that I have been to the Infirmary, and found myself justified in making the report I have; but Mr. Norris now tells me, that one or two more than I have mentioned may have lost their lives. The parties apprehended will have their cases proceeded on tomorrow; but it appears there may arise difficulties as to the nature of some of their crimes, on which it may be necessary to consult Government.*

The whole Committee of Magistrates will assemble tomorrow as usual. During the afternoon, and part of the evening, parts of the town have been in a very disturbed state, and numerous applications made for military. These have been supplied, but in some cases have, in the Irish part of the town, been obliged to fire, I trust without any bad effect as to life, in any instance. At present, every thing seems quiet; the reports agree with that, and I hope that we shall have a quiet night. I have omitted to mention, that the active part of the meeting may be said to have come in wholly from the country, and that it did not consist of less than 20,000 men, &c. The flag on which was 'Equal representation or death', was a black one; and in addition, on the same side, had 'No boroughmongering – unite, and be free', at the bottom, 'Saddleworth, Lees, and Morley [sic] Union,' on the reverse, 'No Corn Laws: - Taxation without representation is unjust and tyrannical'. On the Middleton flag was, 'Let us die like men, and not be sold as slaves'; reverse, 'liberty is the birthright of man'.

I close my letter at a quarter before eleven; every thing remains quiet – many of the troops have returned to the barracks, with the consent of the Magistrates. I have to apologise to your Lordship for the haste in which this is written, but I trust that the haste will naturally be accounted for.

I have the honour to be, my Lord,

With sincere respect,

Your Lordship's faithful and obedient humble servant,

W. R. Hay[7]

APPENDIX 7

Letter from Lord Sidmouth to the Earl of Derby (Lord Lieutenant of Lancaster):

Whitehall, 21st August 1819

My Lord,

Having laid before the Prince Regent the accounts transmitted to me from Manchester of the Proceedings at that Place on Monday last, – I have been commanded by his Royal Highness to request that you will express to the Magistrates of the County Palatine of Lancaster, who attended on that day, the great satisfaction derived by his Royal Highness from their prompt, decisive and efficient measures for the preservation of the public tranquillity: and likewise that your Lordship will signify to Major Trafford, his Royal Highness's high approbation of the support and assistance to the Civil power afforded upon that occasion by himself, and the Officers, Non-Commissioned Officers and Privates, of the Corps serving under his command.

I have the honour to be,

My Lord,

Your Lordship's most obedient humble Servant
SIDMOUTH[8]

APPENDIX 8

List of those taken into custody in the New Bailey prison on 16 August 1819:

Remanded till Friday: – Henry Hunt, Robert Jones, Joseph Johnson, Geo. Swift, John Thacker Saxton, Robt. Wild [*sic*], Thos. Taylor, Sarah Hargreaves, Elizabeth Gaunt, Valentine Faulkner, James Johnson, William Bolton, Thos. Keough, James Moorhouse, John Knight, Isaac Murray, Abraham Whittaker, Thos. Johnson, John Wild, John Unsworth, Ann Coates, James Lang, John Edwards, Joseph Kershaw, James Swindles, John Bell, William Barnes, John Mills, Isaac Howe, Thomas Hallmark, William Chantler, Samuel Stockwell,

Peter Barlow, Thomas Fidlin, and Robert Stott.

Committed: – Wm. Billinge, Thomas Ashton, Thomas Worthington, Moses O'Hara, James Makin, Thomas Hollis, Jonathan Smith, Henry Clarke, John Fielding, Wm. Mason, James Langley, John Davies, James Green, William Finn, George Whittle, Arthur O'Neil, James Higgins, Thomas Bancroft, Thomas Mellor, James Taylor, John Selton, Thomas Worsley, George Ashcroft, John Wild, and Samuel Stringer.

Discharged: – Mary Waterworth, Edward Perrins, William Ashworth, John Hindley, John Senior, Thomas Crabtree, Cornelius Shaw, Daniel Shaw, John Haslam, Thomas Dawson, William Renshaw, Dennis Burns, George Bell, Martha Canroy, Thomas Standing, Peter Siddall, Thomas Shyrock, William Middleton, Thomas Armstrong, William Hampson, Thomas Wane, James Leech, Tomms Thomas [*sic*], Joseph Chator, David Chator, James Williamson, James Thompson, Daniel Richardson, add [*sic*] John Wilkinson.[9]

APPENDIX 9

Hunt's letter to the Manchester Magistrates, 18 August 1819:

New Bailey Prison, Wednesday Noon, Aug. 18, 1819

Gentlemen, –

As I was informed by the Magistrates, before whom I was taken yesterday, that a Coroner's inquest would sit tomorrow (Thursday) on those persons who lost their lives on Monday last, in consequence of the dreadful attack of the military, upon an unarmed and peaceable multitude, and as I was present, and saw the commencement of this illegal and unconstitutional act of violence and can identify some of those who first committed a breach of the peace; I demand, as an act of common justice, that I may be permitted to be present at such an inquest, in order that the Coroner, if he thinks proper, may interrogate me, before the Jury; also, I beg to suggest the propriety of the gentleman, who is the reporter to the Times London newspaper, being also present at the said inquest, as he was an eye-witness of the whole; and being altogether unconnected with those who called the meeting, or meant to take any part in the proceedings of the day, will be a peculiarly important because a disinterested evidence.

And as I have seen quite enough already to convince me that the real murderers are endeavouring to wipe the bloody stain from their remorseless, guilty souls, by casting imputations and suspicions upon others that they know had no hand, directly or *indirectly, in the foul and cowardly deed, I am bold to say, that such inquest will be esteemed in the eye of God and man, <u>worse than suspicious</u>, unless all the parties who are imprisoned, or said to be instrumental in the act, be permitted to be present, and interrogated before the Jury by the Coroner. You will recollect, Gentlemen, that you have no common case in hand, and that the eye of the whole country will shortly be fixed with a scrutinizing penetration upon every step you take in this bloody affair.*

I am, Gentlemen,

Your Prisoner,

HENRY HUNT[10]

APPENDIX 10

Extract from the Special Constables' Account Book (August–November 1819):

Police Office Manchester 27th Augt 1819
A numerous and highly respectable meeting of the loyal inhabitants of Manchester, Salford and the neighbourhood held here this day.
John Moore Jnr. Esq. in the Chair.
It was resolved unanimously
1st that a subscription be immediately entered into for the relief of the Special Constables who have suffered or who may suffer in the discharge of their Official Duty during the disturbed state of affairs of these towns and the neighbourhood which relief may in extraordinary circumstances be applied to the families of the suffering parties...

Each of the following gave five guineas to the cause: Hugh Hornby Birley and his brother Joseph, the Boroughreeve Edward Clayton, Chief Constables John Moore and Jonathan Andrew, and factory owner Francis Phillips. Two entries, of £2 and 2 guineas respectively, are given as from 'A. Friend'. Around £300 had been collected from 114 contributors by November 1819, when entries in the account book cease.[11]

A page from the Special Constables' Account Book. (Chetham's Library)

APPENDIX 11

Evidence given under Oath by William Pollard, Special Constable, tailor and draper, 11 Oldham Street, 2 November 1819:

Informant saw the Manchester Yeomanry come on the ground and draw up in front of the house where the Magistrates were. On seeing them the Mob shouted Hurrah three times which was done as Informant believes by way of defiance. They then advanced to the Hustings on a gentle trot. As they advanced they waved their swords over their heads, and Informant did not see the least attempt to injure the people. Informant waited until they were in the act of surrounding the Hustings, & then the confusion was so great that Informant got away at some distance as well as he could. In about 5 minutes the area was so far cleared of the Mob as to admit his return. His object of such return was to assist any persons that might have been hurt. Informant saw a heap of people lying that appeared to be hurt – one person apparently dead. He immediately examined them one by one to ascertain how they were hurt. In every case of injury which he saw Informant is confident proceeded from having been trampled upon. Some of their faces were much bruised but not one of them had any sabre cut or wound, not so much as the scratch of a pin…[12]

APPENDIX 12

Extracts from James Moorhouse's narrative of Peterloo, given at Hunt's trial, April 1820:

I went into Deansgate to get a little refreshment, where I had not been long before Mr. Hunt was announced; and upon going into the street, near the Dog Tavern, on the carriage passing where I stood, Mr. Hunt perceived me in the crowd; he cried out to me, saying, 'Moorhouse, will you get into the carriage? We will make room for you.' In an instant the door was opened; I was seized by the arm by John Collier, and instantly shoved into the carriage, but before I had time to take away my hand, the door was hastily shut, and three of my fingers were caught and most severely trapped, so as to give me very great pain, and immediately on the carriage arriving at the hustings I got out, and went to the public-house [The Windmill] to get some brandy to allay the pain; I remained in the public-house until the dispersion had in a great measure taken place… and I left the house in search of my wife, who was at that time six months advanced in her pregnancy. It was near two hours before I met with her, during which I was several times informed she was thrown in a cellar-hole, and crushed to death; but, thank God, it was not so; we met at the Flying Horse, and while drinking a glass of wine and water, and returning God thanks for delivering her from the perilous situation which she was in, (being betwixt the constables and the carriage at the time the cavalry surrounded the hustings), two police officers, Platt and another, came into the room, and told me I was their prisoner. I demanded their authority; they produced their staves. I observed, that is no authority; you must produce a warrant, and I will go with you; to which Platt replied, if I did not choose to go without a warrant, he would fetch some soldiers, who would not be trifled with; I then rose up and went along with them to prison.[13]

APPENDIX 13

Ann Scott's deposition, given in October 1819. Ann was arrested on the evening of 16 August and taken to the New Bailey prison. She is quite possibly the 'uncontrollable woman, whose tongue no human effort could check' mentioned in the report in *Wheeler's* of 21 August. If so, the deposition creates an impression far removed from the foul-mouthed harridan suggested in the press report:

I, Ann Scott, wife of William Scott, boat-builder, of Liverpool-road, Manchester, declare, that on the 16th of August last, about seven o'clock in the evening, I was violently laid hold of in Deansgate, by Mr. Charles Ashworth, said to be a Special Constable, who dragged me to the Police-office, where I remained for about twenty minutes, with several other persons, with whom I was conveyed, under a guard of soldiers, to the New Bailey; here I was committed to what is called 'the Lock-ups', which is the room that forms a receptacle for all prisoners taken up during the night, for paupers, and for common thieves. In this room, and in such company, I was detained from Monday evening until the following Friday, without being permitted to go into the open air; during which time I had no bed to lie upon, nor anything on which to repose, except a common form, although the floor was floating with water and filth produced by the paupers, etc., and their children; nor were either they nor I, nor any other prisoner in the room, permitted to leave it for the performance of the common offices of nature. The smell was consequently so very offensive as to materially affect my health. On the Friday after my arrest, I was taken into the New Bailey Courtroom, where Ashworth the constable charged me before the Rev. Mr. Ethelstone with endeavouring to excite the People to commit an assault – a crime of which I solemnly declare I am perfectly innocent. The Magistrate ordered that I should procure bail; which, at that time, I was unable to obtain. I was therefore recommitted to prison, where I was confined with other women, and allowed occasionally to take the air in a small yard; but, in consequence of my sufferings in the Lock-up Room, for the want of air and repose, together with the excessive moisture and bad smell, which I was doomed to endure, I became so very unwell, that I was unable to leave my bed, and where I became so ill, that I informed the Turnkey (Jackson) of my situation, and requested him to let me see the Doctor; but he took no notice of my application, and, locking the cell-door upon me every day, prevented me from communicating with my fellow prisoners. I think I should have died from extreme thirst, had it not been for the humanity of the 'Constable Woman' (as she is called), who attends the female prisoners, by whom I was occasionally supplied with tea, and toast and water. I repeated my complaints daily but in vain, to Jackson; and at length, about six days after, I was *confined to my bed. The Doctor then visited me, who immediately ordered my removal to the Hospital, where I was carried by the woman constable and another female. In the Hospital, the disease with which I was afflicted, according to the statement of the Doctor, was an inflammation of the liver, accompanied by a high fever.*

… During the nine weeks that I have been in prison, I was never permitted to see my husband, but the twice that I have stated, although I frequently solicited the Turnkey to let him in. Throughout my confinement, I had only the common gaol allowance, excepting a little tea and sugar, which the keeper said my husband sent me. To this statement I am ready to depose on oath.[14]

APPENDIX 14

A view of Maxine Peake performing *The Masque of Anarchy*, Manchester, 12 July 2012:

All standing. Dark and hot because it was lovely summer night. Candles all over stage and surrounding area. Albert Hall – a fantastic venue, beautiful, atmospheric, old, previously unused and unknown.

Maxine Peake in plain white dress, no fuss, but held our attention with amazing, strong reading of poem. One of best performances I've ever seen. Line still rings out for me: 'Ye are many, they are few.'

Mikaela Sitford-Howarth

APPENDIX 15

Peterloo has been commemorated many times in music. Popular songs were composed and sung from almost immediately afterwards, but the best known modern folk song narrating the incident is Harvey Kershaw's standard from 1971 which he wrote for the Oldham Tinkers, with the famous chorus:

> *Salute once more these men of yore*
> *Who were to conscience true*
> *And gave their blood for the common good*
> *On the fields of Peterloo.*[15]

In 1968 Malcolm Arnold – prolific composer who wrote the theme music for many British films in the 1950s and '60s – was commissioned by the TUC to create a *Peterloo Overture*. It is a dramatic, accessible piece, in which the pastoral innocence of the opening sequence is drowned in a crescendo of drums and braying horns. But eventually 'after a lament for the killed and injured, it ends in triumph, in the firm belief that all those who have suffered and died in the cause of unity amongst mankind will not have done so in vain' (Arnold's introduction to the score).

A similar musical idea is used by folk group Steeleye Span in their track 'Peterloo the Day' (2006): the initial a cappella harmonies followed by Maddy Prior's ethereal voice are progressively dominated by the thumping percussion and strident electric guitar.

The seven-minute organ solo 'Peterloo 1819' composed by Jonathan Scott – a distant relative of Sam Bamford – follows a similar pattern, in that the simple nobility of the earlier phrases shifts with frightening abruptness into a thunderous avalanche of sound.

Ted Edwards, the multi-tasking folk singer from Oldham, composed the musical *Peterloo* in 2009. On each 16 August it is broadcast in its entirety on Oldham Community Radio. The rendition is historically precise, and the weightier matters are occasionally seasoned by some black and bleak humour: a tongue-in-cheek hymn to rickets, for example.

Probably the most sophisticated musical interpretation is currently Geoff Higginbottom's *Soldiers on the Rampage*. The roadshow with Geoff, Martin Gittins and Bob Ashworth – The Free Radicals – which includes a suite of songs (some traditional, most written by Geoff) and readings from contemporary records is well worth catching. Favoured venues are those with historical relevance, such as the Bull's Head pub in Stockport, where Hunt once gave a political speech.

APPENDIX 16

Peterloo

I beg you will endeavour to preserve the most
perfect silence. Put your hand to the ground and
take its pulse.
The time of the martyr is at your feet. A climate
of angels lying low in a buried world, fragment
seeds of liberty,
sixpences of bone spent for us. This is the archaeology
of the heart, be meticulous with it and know that
their ballad is in your blood.
Their cries still rent the air outside the room
where the Sex Pistols played, outside the rooms
chasing Michelin stars,
where borough mongers and their abettors from
an umbilical distance away severed the contract
of the heart.
As hussars' sabres cut the seams of heaven
and bled down on to the field a holy alliance,
not to be petitioned by prayer.
A flock that had drawn from the four corners of the
North West, a forest of men, women, children and liberty
cut down, made to buckle in its bloom.
The ball in their right breast a Tory sphere
that still orbits the poor today as they rust in a
half-life harbour
eclipses the truth on bedroom tax suicides and
blots out the sun on the homeless wards. All evidence
must be received, we are all the body of John Lees.
Look up two hundred years and we see time like
a mirage, the ghosts of us, hold their dreams aloft
like something new born.
And let us sit beside poverty, have a word in its ear.
Say, listen 'We are here.'

Oliver Lomax

APPENDIX 17

THE MANCHESTER PETERLOO MEMORIAL
RESPECTFUL, INFORMATIVE, AND PERMANENT

The Peterloo Memorial Campaign is dedicated to ensuring that a fitting memorial is in place for the 200th Anniversary of the Peterloo Massacre in 2019.

Peterloo is a landmark event in the history of British and international democracy. We believe that the people of Greater Manchester deserve a democratic say in the design, location and construction of the memorial, with extensive public consultation and input from inception to completion.

A fitting memorial should be Respectful, Informative, and Permanent.

RESPECTFUL

The memorial location must be both prominent and public, on a site of historical significance for the massacre.

It should be of comparable size and quality of materials to other major city centre monuments, with a respectful space around it for people to gather in contemplation or commemoration.

The memorial needs to be an object of civic pride which resonates with the people of Manchester and which expresses the spirit of democracy, economic justice and human rights.

INFORMATIVE

The memorial should communicate the events of 16 August 1819 on St. Peter's Field in Manchester in an easily comprehensible and unflinching way.

We believe the connection of the design to Peterloo should be straightforward and easy to understand, particularly in light of the fact that many people have only a limited awareness of the massacre.

The memorial needs to both inform and inspire, and should be accompanied by a descriptive plaque, with wording about the massacre similar to the red plaque on the side of the former Free Trade Hall.

PERMANENT

The memorial should be a permanent and durable object, one that will still be there in 2219, in a fixed location (as described above) to which the public have access at all times. The memorial could require some form of public interaction to make it complete at each anniversary, as is appropriate for a monument to the ideals of citizenship and democracy, as long as the substantial and meaningful part of it is permanently in place.[16]

Comments on the Notes

Two sources have been used for the Redford vs. Birley etc. civil action. The abridged version written mostly in indirect speech (65 pp.) is designated **Red–Bir**. The full transcript in book form (632 pp.) is designated **Redford vs. Birley**.

The **HO** references, with identifying numbers, are from the Home Office archives. The 'f.' refers to the folio number. The **TS** references, also with identifying numbers, are from the Treasury Solicitor's archives. The full text of many of the **HO** and **TS** items may be viewed on the website www. peterloowitness1819.weebly.com. **PRO** is an item from the Public Record Office.

JRL indicates a source from the John Rylands Library English Manuscripts 1197 (1–89).

Wroe refers to the series of pamphlets produced by James Wroe, published in book form under the generic title of P*eterloo Massacre, containing a faithful Narrative of the Events…* (*Manchester Observer* 1819).

MCC refers to the *Report of the Metropolitan and Central Committee Appointed for the relief of the Manchester Sufferers* (London 1820). The pages in the Report naming the sources
wounded and deceased are not numbered, but page references given herein are easy to track down, as the list is mostly in alphabetical order.

Thompson, Making is a reference to E.P. Thompson's *The Making of the English Working Class*.

The page numbers given for **Hunt's *Memoirs*** are taken from the text supplied on the website www.fulltextarchive.com in pdf format.

All other entries are self-explanatory, or are easily interpreted by reference to the Bibliography and Sources section.

Endnotes

1   *Manchester Observer* 14 August 1819. The handbill had been posted in the Manchester streets Wednesday 11 August

2   Bamford, *Passages*, Vol. 1, p. 222. For the significance of the man without a hat, see below, 'A Gallery of Pictures', note 12

3   Dowling, p. 139

4   Hansard, 15 May 1821. John Cam Hobhouse was Chairman of the Relief Committee for the wounded and bereaved of Peterloo. No relation to Henry Hobhouse of the Home Office, Secretary to Lord Sidmouth

Introduction

5   Details collated from Bush, *Casualties of Peterloo*, p. 45, Wroe, pp. 119–214, and the 1820 report of the Manchester and Central Committee. See bibliography. William Bradshaw and Sarah Jones are in Hunt's list of those killed, which is based on Wroe's information. William Evans was 'in a dying state' according to the Peterloo Relief List, and 'not expected to recover' according to the report in *Wheeler's*.

The exact number of fatalities has long been disputed. The extreme right-wing assertion of two dead, expressed on a number of occasions soon after Peterloo, may be dismissed out of hand. In 1883 Revd Canon F. R. Raines maintained that just 'four or five people were pressed to death' (Raines, p. 290). Bruton in *Three Accounts* (p. 81) quotes from the 1906 *Political History of England* 'the loss of life did not exceed five or six', before concluding that the actual number was higher. In 1958 T.H.G. Stevens put the total at eight (Stevens, p. 96). None of these authors named names or gave any primary source. Also in 1958 Read made a case for eleven dead. Current thinking seems to have settled on 'at least fifteen'. Some historians maintain that William and Edmund Dawson were one and the same person, even though respective details of time, place and manner of death appear to differ. (See Bush, *Casualties*, pp. 45, 88, 89) Bush (p. 45) also states that the death of Margaret Downes, Sarah Jones and William Evans is 'disputable'. No firm evidence has since emerged that any of them died.

6   Wroe, p. 3

7   Bruton, *Three Accounts*, p. 9: 'A space comparatively vacant; partially occupied by stragglers, the mob condensing near the hustings for the purposes of seeing and hearing.'

PART ONE: FOREWARNINGS

1: The Janus Country

1 See Kettle, *Guardian*, 18 June 2015. Seeking refuge in England seems to have been Napoleon's ace in the hole. In a flattering letter to the Prince Regent on 13 July he wrote: '*Je viens comme Themistocles m'asseoir sur le foyer du peuple Britannique*'. The Prince, perhaps aware of Themistocles' duplicitous strategy *vis-à-vis* the Persians, ignored the request.

2 An examination of the professions of the recorded casualties at Peterloo suggests very strongly that weavers made up the vast majority of those present. (Bush, *Casualties*, p. 25; Bee and Bee, 'Casualties', p. 46)

3 Bamford, *Early Days*, pp. 118–140

4 Reid, p. 19

5 From Hunt's speech at St. Peter's Field on 18 January 1819; quoted in *Wheeler's Manchester Chronicle*, 30 January 1819

6 See Prentice, p. 52, however, for an account of a food riot, caused by the overpricing of potatoes, in Shudehill Market, Manchester, in April 1812. The poorer classes were unconcerned by, or were unaware of, the snobbery and bigotry expressed by certain of the more affluent commentators when considering the traditionally Irish staple. See Hobson, pp. 36–9.

7 The MCC Report of January 1820 recorded a weekly wage of six shillings (72 old pence = 30p) at most (MCC, p. 21). Weavers in Rochdale around 1810 were on a rate of a penny an hour, working a fourteen-hour day (Robertson, p. 304). Also see Farrar and Brownhill, p. 309.

8 *Manchester Gazette*, 28 May 1808

9 Thompson, *Making*, p. 307

10 MCC, p. 20

11 *Oldham Chronicle* 20 February 1885

12 J. Smith, *Memoirs of Wool* (1747); quoted Thompson, *Making*, p. 306

13 Contemporary (1818) magistrate's view; quoted Thompson, *Making*, p. 306. This degree of affluence was not claimed even by Bamford!

14 *Cowdroy's Manchester Gazette*, 25 April 1812

15 Thompson, *Making*, p. 339

16 Southey, *Letters from England*, pp. 81–97

17 *Black Dwarf* 30 September 1818. The outspoken radical publication *Black Dwarf*, edited by Thomas Wooler and partly financed by Major John Cartwright, existed from 1817 until 1824.

18 *Factories Inquiry Commission*, Manchester 1833, Section D3, pp. 17–18; Simmons, *Carlile*, p. 24

19 Engels, *The Condition of the Working Class*, pp. 87, 89

20 Ibid., p. 83

21 Ibid., p. 100

22 Kay, p. 28

23 Thompson, *Making*, p. 362

24 *Report on the Sanitary Condition of the Labouring Classes* (1842), p. 153; quoted in Thompson, *Making*, p. 365

25 See Thompson, *Making*, pp. 359 *et seq.*; Engels, pp. 173–6, 179–182

26 *Oldham Chronicle* 'A Night with Peterloo Veterans', 29 November 1884. Further essentials that were taxed included: salt, candles, sugar, paper, window light, leather, tobacco, and tea. See Hobson, p. 19

27 Prentice, p. 146. Population of Manchester in 1819 was around 125,000; that of Salford, around 25,000 (Axon, p. 165). By 1830 Manchester would have 180,000 inhabitants

28 Dunning, *A History of Somerset*

2: Law and Order

1 Redford vs. Birley, p. 355. The group typically included church dignitaries. An indication of the alliance between the civic and church powers in the town may be inferred from the detail observed at Peterloo by an eyewitness in one of the Mount Street houses overlooking the field. The arrests of the radicals had just been made, and the brutal dispersal of the crowd had begun, when: 'The Rev. Mr. Hay then stood on the steps of the house and addressed the constables. I could not hear what he said, but he was cheered when he concluded'. (John Benjamin Smith; Bruton, *Three Accounts*, p. 69)

2 Bamford, *Passages*, Vol.2, p. 74(n)

3 Ballad written a short time after Peterloo – *Ballads and Songs of Lancashire*, p. 262

4 Bamford, *Passages*, Vol.2, p. 75

5 Hewitt, *A History of Policing in Manchester*, p. 23

6 Thompson, *Making*, p. 633; and see Hansard 13 February 1818, pp. 399–405, 412–3, for examples of Nadin's brutal and intimidatory style. The letter accusing Nadin appeared in the *Manchester Observer*, 4 April 1818

7 Bamford, *Passages*, p. 77

8 *Manchester Observer* 7 March 1818. The report described the bridle as 'an iron instrument from the iron-hearted age of ignorance'

9 Prentice, p. 160

10 HO 42/138. Nadin received £300 expenses from the Treasury following this letter

11 Dowling, p. 471

12 *Lancaster Gazette*, 20 June 1812

13 Bamford, *Passages*, Vol. 2, p. 76

14 *Oldham Weekly Chronicle*, 16 April 1960. He was described as 'a stout man, weighing 18 stone [114kg]'. (Wilson, *Vicars*, p. 60)

15 Thomis, p. 123; HO 40/1

16 A newsroom, library and meeting-place for the local elite, the Portico had been

launched in 1806 by a consortium of Manchester businessmen.

17 Axon, pp. 129, 132

18 HO 40/1; Taylor, pp. 21, 38–9, 40–4, 47–50, 53, 61

19 www.manchesterorange.co.uk

20 HO 40/1/1, and see below for the attack on Westhoughton Mill.

21 Dowling, p. 511

22 MCC, p. 47

23 Letter from James Cardwell 26 November 1819 to Birley's sister. But see Samuel Davenport's testimony in Dowling, p. 147, and Redford vs. Birley, p. 177: John Leigh claimed that Birley cut him with his sabre.

24 HO 79/3 f.440. Typical of the Home Office advice to Byng and others of similar position: '…avail yourself of all the Force conceded to you'. (July 1819)

25 Thompson, *Making*, p. 534

26 Peel, p. 291

27 Hansard, 3 March 1818

28 *Leeds Mercury*, 13 June 1817

3: Of Machines and Mammon

1 *Wheeler's Manchester Chronicle* of 25 April 1812 claims there were several such warning shots fired over the heads of the demonstrators 'for at least ten minutes'.

2 The *Lancaster Gazette* of 20 June 1812 gives 200, but *Wheeler's* of the same day says that the number had grown

3 *Cowdroy's Manchester Gazette*, 25 April 1812

4 *Leeds Mercury*, 25 April 1812

5 The number of power looms in the UK: 1813: 2,400; 1820: 14,000; 1829: 55,000. (Farrer and Brownhill, p. 384)

6 Thomis, pp. 129–30

7 Taylor, p. 151

8 HO 40/1/1 f.333. In the same letter Fletcher requested Home Office authority to intercept suspicious mail at the Post Office.

9 Taylor, p. 199

10 *Lancaster Gazette*, 6 June 1812; HO 40/1/1

11 Prentice, pp. 48–9

12 *Aston's Exchange Herald* 14 April 1812

13 *Wheeler's Manchester Chronicle* 11 April 1812

14 Prentice, p. 51

15 Taylor, p. 205

16 www.ludditebicentenary.co.uk

4: Voices of Dissent

1 Belchem, p. 108

2 Bamford, *Passages*, Vol. 2, p. 33

3 Ibid., p. 20

4 Dolby, p. 166

5 JRL MSS 1197 (39)

6 *Manchester Mercury*, 27 July 1819

7 Woodward, p. 21(n)

8 See Bamford, *Passages*, Vol. 2, pp. 199–200: '[Hunt's] self-love, for which his whole heart seemed to beat'; and editor Henry Dunckley was of the opinion that Bamford considered that '[Hunt was] willing to sell his soul for the cheers of the mob'. (*Passages*, Vol. 1, p. 15)

9 *Manchester Observer*, 21 August 1819

10 Bulkeley, p 131

11 Bamford, *Passages*, Vol. 2, p. 19. It is interesting to compare Bamford's view with the messianic impression suggested by this passage in *The Manchester Man*: '...a man of gentlemanlike bearing and attire, agreeable features, mobile in expression, and dull grey eyes which lit like fiery stars when in the fervour of his speech his soul shone out of them.' (Banks, p. 183)

12 Hunt's letter to Brave Reformers of Lancashire; Wroe, p. 75

13 *Manchester Observer*, 11 March 1820

14 www.pixnet.co.uk/Oldham Historical Research Group

15 Bamford, *Passages*, Vol. 2, pp. 53–6

16 Hunt, *Memoirs*, Vol. 3, p. 506

17 www.archiver.rootsweb.ancestry.com/FILDES

18 Swift, p. 12. Baines was a reporter from the *Leeds Mercury*

19 Butterworth, p. 172

20 Dolby, p. 38

21 www.davidcsutton.com; 'The Spa Fields Riots of 1816'. It was at this rally that Bamford and Hunt met up for the first time

22 *The Times*, 3 December 1816

23 Hansard, 28 January 1817

24 Hunt, *Memoirs*, Vol. 3, p. 357

25 Bamford, *Passages*, Vol. 2, pp. 31–5

26 Prentice, pp. 92–4. Josiah Gatley from Salford claimed that between 150 and 200 made it to Ashbourne, and around twenty reached Derby, where they were intercepted by local Yeomanry at the Royal Oak inn. At 11.30 at night they were forced to turn back, and were escorted to a point two miles north of the town, where they were threatened with imprisonment if they were to return. (*Manchester Times*, 11 March 1848)

27 *Manchester Mercury* 11 March 1817. Bruton has this to say about the Cheshire Yeomanry's intervention: '...the farmers and country squires who rode in its yeomanry had a special interest in preserving intact the Corn Law, which the Reformers were out to repeal'. (Bruton, *The Story of Peterloo*, p. 13)

28 *Manchester Mercury*, 18 March 1817

29 Ibid.

30 Ibid., 20 July 1819

31 Bamford, *Passages*,Vol. 2, pp. 73–114; Prentice, pp. 96–7
32 Prentice, p. 96
33 HO 42/162 f. 329
34 St Peter's Church, built in 1788, was demolished in 1907. The old church cross remains on top of the monument in the middle of the tramlines close by the Metrolink stop.
35 *Wheeler's Manchester Chronicle*, 23 January 1819
36 Ibid., 30 January, 1819; *Annals of Manchester*, p. 156
37 Prentice, pp. 147–50, in which he quotes extensively from Bamford's account
38 Letter from John Lloyd to Henry Hobhouse, 16 February 1819 (Stockport Local Heritage Library)
39 Bamford, *Homely Rhymes Poems.* Chief Constable William Birch, incidentally, was shot whilst arresting a radical three weeks before Peterloo. He survived, and the bullet was found embedded in his rib after his death from old age!
40 Prentice, p. 151
41 *Wheeler's Manchester Chronicle* 26 June 1819
42 HO 41/1/1; Taylor, pp. 1–3
43 *Manchester Observer* 24 July 1819
44 Ibid., 31 July 1819
45 *Wheeler's Manchester Chronicle* 17 July 1819

5: 'Make Way for the Female Reformers!'

1 Redford vs. Birley, p. 437
2 *Oldham Express*, 15 February 1883; William Hulton (although facetiously), quoted by Prentice, *Manchester Times*, 24 December 1831
3 Campbell, p. 23
4 Innes (printer), handbill 17 August 1819 (Working Class Movement Library, Salford). The many errors reveal the haste with which this broadsheet was produced. Also, it is worth noting that at this time not even the reformers – with one or two notable exceptions such as Carlile – seriously considered extending 'universal suffrage' to women.
5 *Wheeler's Manchester Chronicle*, 17 July 1819
6 Manchester Archives and Local Studies, Broadsides Collection, GB 127
7 *Aston's Exchange Herald*, 17 September 1822. There is more of this clodhopping verse below in Part Three: 'A Gallery of Pictures'
8 Thompson, *Making*, p. 456
9 Dowling, pp. 86–7
10 Taylor, p. 35
11 Ibid., pp. 37–8; the only identification given of the writer is (G)
12 There is a copy of this publication – reputed to be the only surviving one – in Chetham's Library. See the chapter 'A Gallery of Pictures' below for more on this fascinating work.
13 Belchem, p. 86

14 Fairburn, p. 32

15 www.liberator.net

16 Hunt, *Memoirs*,Vol. 3, p. 495

17 *Manchester Observer*, 17 July 1819

18 Ibid., 10 July 1819

19 Ibid., 17 July 1819

20 Ibid., 31 July 1819

21 'Let woman share the rights and she will emulate the virtues of man; for she must grow more perfect when emancipated…It is time to effect a revolution in female manners – time to restore them to their lost dignity – and make them, as a part of the human species, labour by reforming themselves to reform the world.' *A Vindication of the Rights of Woman*, chapters 3, 13.

22 *Manchester Observer*, 31 July 1819

6: Manoeuvres

1 HO 41/4 p. 434

2 HO 79/3 f. 356; Hobhouse to William Chippendale, the Oldham adjutant

3 HO 79/3 f. 396; Hobhouse to Norris

4 HO 79/3 f. 440; Hobhouse to General Sir John Byng, Commander of the Northern District. I am indebted to the research of Robert Poole for the compilation of these Home Office Records. See bibliography: 'By the Law or the Sword: Peterloo Revisited'.

5 HO 42/188

6 *Manchester Observer*, 24 July 1819

7 *British Volunteer*, 3 August 1819

8 Hunt, *Memoirs*,Vol.3, p. 494

9 Ibid., p. 492

10 Ibid., p. 495

11 *Manchester Observer*, 14 August 1819

12 Bamford, *Passages*,Vol. 2, pp. 144–6

13 Hunt, *Memoirs*,Vol. 3, p. 497

14 Bruton, *The Story of Peterloo*, p. 15

15 Dolby, p. 180; *Oldham Chronicle*, 'A Night with Peterloo Veterans', 29 November 1884

16 Bamford, *Passages*,Vol. 2, p. 143

17 Dolby, pp. 46–7; given Murray's returning home the very next day, the Magistrates' assertion that he had been 'left in an almost lifeless state' would appear to be an exaggeration. (HO 40/15 f.284)

18 *Manchester Observer*, 21 August 1819

19 Redford vs. Birley, p. 286

20 HO 42/191; Taylor, p. 21

21 Taylor, p. 66 (n); *The Times*, 27 September 1819

22 JRL English MSS 1197 (23); Hunt's letter to *The Observer* 12 August 1819

23 Swift, p. 9; Hunt, *Memoirs*, Vol. 3, p. 498

24 Hay's letter to Lord Sidmouth, 7 October 1819

25 HO 42/191; Taylor, p. 53

Part Two: FLASHPOINT (16 August 1819)

1: On the Roads to Manchester

1 Redford vs. Birley, p. 466

2 Dowling, p. 566; one such 'large printed placard' was produced at the John Lees inquest. An example of the original may be seen at the John Rylands Library: English MSS 1197 (24)

3 Prentice, p. 159

4 The Stalybridge band which had arrived by stagecoach – but never got as far as the field – also included a serpent, an ancestor of the tuba which looked like a misshapen and bravado piece of plumbing. The tale of how the Stalybridge Old Band narrowly escaped having their instruments smashed is one of the few comic episodes of the day: see the website www.ibew.org.uk

5 Bamford, *Passages*, Vol. 2, p. 150; HO 42/192, 198; Glen, p. 312; TS 11/1056; Fairburn, p. 8; *Aston's Exchange Herald*, 17 August 1819

6 Bamford, *Passages*, Vol. 2, p. 153

7 Dowling, p. 448

8 MCC, p. 24; *Wheeler's Manchester Chronicle*, 21 August 1819

9 Wroe, p. 46. For more on the 'bloody dagger' atop the Bury banner, see later in this chapter.

10 Hunt, *Memoirs*, Vol. 3, p. 437. *Liverpool Mercury* reporter recorded his impression of the crowd: 'I saw a great many women and children in the field, and spoke to several of them. They appeared many of them respectable, and clean dressed, as if they came to a holiday feast.' (Dolby, p. 193)

11 Bamford, *Passages*, Vol. 2, pp. 149–60. A replica of the blue and gold banner may be seen in Middleton Local History Library.

12 Bamford, *Passages*, Vol. 2, p. 151; Bruton, *The Story of Peterloo*, p. 20

13 Ibid., p. 166

14 Ibid., p. 151

15 MCC, p. 44

16 Thompson, *Making*, p. 668

17 Cole, p. 11

18 Robertson, pp. 304–6

19 HO 42/198 f. 680–1

20 Carlile wrote: 'At twelve Mr. Hunt, myself, and others entered the barouche…' (Campbell, p. 16); see also *Manchester Observer* 21 August 1819. One account has Knight at the head of the Oldham contingent, but evidence at Hunt's trial contradicts this. (Dolby, p. 289) Also, at Hunt's trial John Hampshire stated that he dined with

John Thacker Saxton at his house between 12 noon and 1 p.m. on the 16 August (Dolby, p. 191), which obviously means that Saxton cannot have been in Hunt's barouche when it left Smedley Cottage.

21 Hunt, *Memoirs*, Vol. 3, p. 498

22 Dolby, p. 100

23 Bamford, *Passages*, Vol. 2, p. 153

24 Wroe, pp. 105, 125

25 Rowbottom, 2 November 1819

26 *The Times* 19 August 1819. Charles Wright wrote the following about the Oldham procession entering the field: 'The Oldham Female Reformers was the most numerous body, and the deputation which came designated *female standard bearers*, by far the most respectable, their banner was made of silk, one of which had an inscription, *Annual Parliaments, Universal Suffrage & Vote by Ballot*'. (TS 11/1056)

27 Red-Bir, p. 7

28 *Oldham Chronicle*, 'A Night with Peterloo Veterans', 29 November 1884. The 'banner of red and green silk' was captured by the Cheshire Yeomanry, according to Bruton. (*The Story of Peterloo*, p. 20)

29 MCC, p. 30

30 Bateson, p. 100

31 Abraham Wrigley's testimony, Red-Bir, p. 8

32 Dolby, p. 226; Bush, 'The Women at Peterloo', p. 212. There are six women from the Ashton area listed as injured, but they appear to have been accompanied by their husband, with one exception. See Bush, *Casualties*, pp. 96, 131, 147, 156, 157–8

33 Dowling, pp. 536–40

34 MCC, pp. 51, 56

35 Giles, p. 226. One source suggests that Elizabeth Gaunt was from Manchester, not Stockport. She was described as 'a tall, thin, pale woman about 45' (*Wheeler's Manchester Chronicle*, 1 August 1819)

36 State Trials, quoted Glen, p. 312

37 Dolby, p. 130

38 Ibid., p. 131–2

39 Philips, p. 21

40 Dolby, p. 256

41 TS 11/1056; the witness is almost certainly the Mr. Wright mentioned in the *Manchester Observer* of 29 January 1820 list of casualties: 'a reporter from London; wounded on the shoulder and on the arm by a sabre'. This tallies with the detail given in his deposition: 'in the scuffle I unfortunately received a sabre wound over the left shoulder'.

42 Bamford, *Passages*, Vol. 2, p. 80

43 *Wheeler's Manchester Chronicle*, 28 August 1819. The MCC Report says 'back much hurt'. (MCC, p. 44) The *Wheeler's* report gives Judith's surname erroneously as 'Killer'!

44 The detail appeared in the *Morning Post*, 19 August 1819 and *Wheeler's Manchester Chronicle* 28 August 1819, but was contradicted by a report in the *Morning Chronicle*

a month later. See Hobson, p. 120.

45 Thomas Rothwell, Dolby, p. 248

46 Dolby, pp. 75, 259. Standard-bearer William Entwisle would sustain a sabre cut on the top of his head, and would be knocked down by a constable's truncheon. (MCC, p. 34)

47 Ibid., p. 248

48 MCC, pp. 40, 45

49 My guess would be a crowd of roughly 3,000, based on the population of Bolton town (30,000) and the number of recorded casualties (18), and comparing these figures to e.g., Bury and Oldham. See Bush, *Casualties*, pp. 11, 22. The other possible meeting place would have been the open ground facing the Commercial Inn, now Victoria Square.

50 *Manchester Observer*, 22 January 1820; Bush, *Casualties*, p. 80

51 Ingham, p. 198

52 Ibid., pp. 229–30

53 Dowling, p. 85

54 Redford vs. Birley, p. 18

55 Ibid., pp. 119, 149, 510

56 Philips, p. 21

57 Fairburn, p. 26. Also see below, 'War of Words and Silence', note 8

58 Reverend Stanley; Bruton, *Three Accounts*, p. 22

59 See Taylor, p. 201: 'The existence of any political knowledge, or fixed political principles, among the poor in this neighbourhood, is of very recent date…' So it would appear that the realistic political clout of the working class was still in a fledgling state, although with enough visible potential to worry the authorities.

60 *Liverpool Mercury*, 27 August 1819

61 Dolby, pp. 205–6

62 Ibid., p. 188

63 Ibid., p. 193

64 Redford vs. Birley, p. 452; Dolby, p. 60

65 Redford vs. Birley, p. 328

66 Ibid., p. 498. Nowadays the Library, having retreated to the top floor, shares its premises with The Bank public house on the corner of Mosley Street and Charlotte Street.

67 Redford vs. Birley, p. 511

68 Red-Bir, p. 35; Dolby, p. 48

69 Red-Bir, p. 37

70 HO 40/16 f. 295

71 Redford vs. Birley, p. 440. Other eyewitnesses, however, stated that a number of shops were left open, with 'business going on as usual'. (Dolby, pp. 229, 250)

72 Red-Bir, p. 27

73 *The Times*, 19 August 1819; Dolby, p. 206; and see Appendix 12

74 Dolby, p. 70

75 Red-Bir, p. 38; Dolby, p. 71

76 Redford vs. Birley, pp. 469–70
77 Lt Jolliffe; Bruton, *Three Accounts*, pp. 50–51

2: Powder Keg

1 Redford vs. Birley, p. 358
2 JRL English MSS 1197 (9) – see Appendix 1. The truncheon illustrated belonged to Special Constable Richard Jones, a pawnbroker.
3 Dolby, p. 221
4 Bush, *Casualties*, pp. 53–4; Bruton, *The Story of Peterloo*, pp. 18–19; Bush, 'The Women at Peterloo', p. 228
5 Horse training information from Clare Hamer, Greater Manchester Police equine trainer and groom team leader
6 Reverend Stanley; Bruton, *Three Accounts*, p. 21
7 *Manchester Guardian*, 26 October 1822; The Peterloo Memorial Facebook pages, 22 June 2017
8 Bruton, *The Story of Peterloo*, p. 14
9 Krantz, p. 21
10 *Manchester Observer*, 17 July 1819
11 Dowling, pp. 161–2
12 Swift, p. 18
13 *Manchester Guardian*, 26 October, 2 November 1822, with additions from various sources; Dowling, pp. 95, 101
14 *Wheeler's Manchester Chronicle*, 21 August 1819
15 Redford vs. Birley, p. 427
16 Ibid., p. 437
17 Reverend Stanley; Bruton, *Three Accounts*, p. 43; Redford vs. Birley, p. 169; Wroe, p. 131
18 John Benjamin Smith; Bruton, *Three Accounts*, p. 66
19 Dowling, pp. 150–1
20 Wroe, p. 25
21 Philips, p. 33
22 Redford vs. Birley, p. 426; JRL English MSS 1197 (67)
23 Redford vs. Birley, p. 438
24 Ibid., p. 495
25 *Aston's Exchange Herald*, 21 August 1819
26 *Leeds Mercury* 21 August 1819. The gist of the *Mercury* reporter's argument that the riot act had not been publicly read at noon (or indeed at any time afterwards) was that (1) he had been on the ground, mostly close to or on the hustings, from 'a quarter of an hour before twelve o'clock' until the arrests, and had not heard the Act read out, nor had the large number of the people he spoke to later; (2) the double line of Special Constables was still in place over an hour after the supposed noon reading, without responding to the order for dispersal explicit in the wording of the Act; (3) it was not Hunt's style to go ahead with a meeting which the reading of the

Riot Act would have designated illegal; (4) the placing of women on and around the hustings was not the action of those who were expecting forcible dispersal; (5) the 'panic and alarm' which would have been caused by the noon reading of the Act were palpably absent in the crowd before the Yeomanry made their appearance. 'Upon this evidence we rest our conclusion, that the Riot Act was not read publicly to the people.'

27 John Benjamin Smith; Bruton, *Three Accounts*, pp. 65–6

28 *Manchester Courier*, 21 August 1819

29 Dolby, p. 212

30 Prentice, p. 159

31 Redford vs. Birley, pp. 116, 124; Red-Bir, p. 19; Wroe, p. 14; Dolby, p. 194; Ibid., p. 253; Dowling, p. 86; Reverend Stanley; Bruton, *Three Accounts*, pp. 21, 29

32 *Leeds Mercury*, 21 August 1819

33 *The Times* 18 August 1819

34 *Wheeler's Manchester Chronicle*, 28 August 1819

35 Dolby, p. 102

36 As E.P. Thompson puts it: '…the fear evoked by the evidence of the translation of the rabble into a disciplined *class*'. (Thompson, *Making*, p. 748) And see below, on the destruction of the banners and flags.

37 Jonathan Andrew, Redford vs. Birley, p. 257

38 Dolby, p. 311

39 *Wheeler's Manchester Chronicle*, 21 August 1819

40 Redford vs. Birley, p. 369

41 Bamford, *Passages*, Vol. 2, pp. 166–7

42 The 'two ranks of men' described by Jemima can only be the double rank of non-uniformed Special Constables, although they are not identified as such in her narrative.

43 Pearson, Harmer and Denison's map of St. Peter's Field, Dowling, frontispiece

44 Swift, p. 11; Dolby, pp. 78–80, 93–4; *The Times*, 19 August 1819

45 Bamford, *Passages*, Vol. 2, p. 155

46 Carlile: 'There were five women upon the hustings.' (Campbell, p. 23) John Tyas: 'Several females also got on the hustings through the barouche.' (Dolby, p. 206) Edward Baines: '…a number of girls, dressed uniformly in white…twelve or fourteen in number…on the hustings to avoid the pressure of the crowd.' (Ibid., p. 217) The women who accompanied Mary Fildes on the platform or in the adjacent barouche probably included Sarah Hargreaves, Mary Waterworth, and Elizabeth Gaunt. Edward Baines was a reporter from the *Leeds Mercury*. According to ex-soldier Nathan Broadhurst's evidence at the John Lees inquest, he was also on or near the hustings at the time of the arrests, before receiving a sabre wound on his leg whilst attempting to hang on to a cap of liberty. (Dowling, p. 179; MCC, p. 29) *Liverpool Mercury* reporter John Smith appears on the hustings according to some accounts, but, although he was certainly close by, at Hunt's trial he denied actually being on the platform. (Dolby, p. 194)

47 See below: 'A Gallery of Pictures'. According to the report in *The Times*: 'Mr. Hunt

desired that some persons on the hustings might be removed, as they were neither speakers nor writers…'. (*The Times* 18 August 1819)

48 Dolby, p. 305

49 Redford vs. Birley, p. 416

50 Hulton's description, Redford vs. Birley, p. 408

51 Wroe, p. 9

52 HO 42/192 f. 390; Wroe, p. 21.

53 Redford vs. Birley, pp. 362, 413, 429

54 Reverend Stanley; Bruton, *Three Accounts*, p. 35; *Sherwin's Weekly Political Register* 18 August 1819

55 JRL English MSS 1197 (26)

56 Wroe, p. 166

57 Ibid., p. 165

58 *The Manchester Man*, p. 187. Hunt was to refer to 'straggling drunken soldiers' and 'drunken, infuriated Yeomanry' at his trial (Dolby, pp. 68, 154) and to 'drunken Yeomanry' during his August 1830 speech at St. Peter's Field (*The Manchester Times* 14 August 1830). Also see Marlow, p. 127, although, unusually in such a well-documented work, not one of the 'countless witnesses in public houses' is brought forward in evidence. Francis Philips gave the opposite impression of the Yeomanry: 'I am convinced they were sober. I spoke to some, and they evinced not the slightest inebriety'. (Dolby, p. 68)

59 Hansard, 15 May 1821

60 Dowling, p. 75. 'Fuddled' was contemporary working-class slang for 'worse for drink'. The later nuance of 'confused' was not current. There was a popular song at the time: 'Molly, I'll Fuddle No More', in which the singer promises his sweetheart he will lay off the booze.

61 Dowling, pp. 169–70

62 Red-Bir, p. 16

63 *8 Days' Diary of a Member of the Yeomanry Cavalry*, p. 12

64 Dowling, pp. 93, 169; Barrett, Greater Manchester Archives, quoted in *Return to Peterloo*, p. 135

65 MCC pp. 24, 35; *Leeds Mercury*, 21 August 1819; Ann Fildes's affidavit, quoted in the *Durham County Advertiser*, 18 December 1819 (see Appendix 3)

66 *Bell's Weekly Messenger*, 29 August 1819, p. 1. In an attempt to minimise the blundering violence of the incident, one R. H. Wilson gave the following version: '…the soldier himself did not touch the Woman or Child, their fall was accidental, and solely occasioned by her crossing the street so suddenly in face of the Horse…no blame could attach to the Rider, as it was impossible to draw up in time to prevent his going up against the woman.' (JRL English MSS 1197 (82)

67 Redford vs. Birley, p. 443. Taylor gives 'kept quiet' rather than 'kept secure', as does the report in the *Times*. (Taylor, p. 178; *The Times*, 19 August 1819)

68 Redford vs. Birley, pp. 393, 453

69 Edward Owen the attorney says he heard the name Cartwright mentioned in the crowd at that moment. (Dowling, p. 448)

70 Dowling, p. 135

71 *Liverpool Mercury*, 20 August 1819; Dowling, p. 81; Redford vs. Birley, p. 385. Charles Wright maintained that Hunt's words were: 'This is a treat!' (TS 11/1056)

72 Wroe, p. 3; *The Times*, 18 August 1819

73 Dolby, p. 186

74 Redford vs. Birley, p. 501

75 Robert Hughes: 'five or six deep' (Redford vs. Birley, p. 457); Sergeant Hullock: 'seven or eight rows deep around the hustings' (Red-Bir, p. 28); Magistrates' narrative: 'ten or twelve deep, linked together' (JRL English MSS 1197 (67)

76 Dolby, p. 219

77 *Leeds Mercury*, 21 August 1819

78 Philips, p. 24

79 Reverend Stanley; Bruton, *Three Accounts*, p. 15

3: 'That Horrid Confusion'

1 Redford vs. Birley, p. 237. A curiosity available for perusal at Manchester Central Library is a collection of pamphlets entitled *Political Tracts*. The first entry 'Manchester Represented and Misrepresented' gives a forty-page account of Peterloo, in which the Yeomanry are depicted as disciplined and forbearing lambs to the slaughter, with the unprovoked mob attacking them with 'concealed stone-artillery…large paving-stones, previously provided, brickbats, and bludgeons'. (pp. 34, 36) It claims a death count of just two people. This offensively biased monograph is an anonymous contribution, although the assertion of only two fatalities smacks of Hulton or Birley.

2 Redford vs. Birley, p. 418. At Hunt's trial Hulton seemed to contradict himself on the matter: 'When the yeomanry advanced to the hustings, I saw bricks and stones flying…I have not stated that they were levelled at the yeomanry, nor can I swear it.' (Dolby, p. 108)

3 Redford vs. Birley, pp. 145–7

4 Red-Bir, p. 11

5 Redford vs. Birley, p. 381

6 Ibid., p. 102. The major reason for Garnett's defection from *Wheeler's Chronicle* was that his original report was significantly doctored by the newspaper before publication, as a result of his showing the radicals and the people in too sympathetic a light. Garnett was to join John Edward Taylor in the launch of the *Manchester Guardian* in 1821.

7 Dolby, p. 193

8 Reverend Stanley; Bruton, *Three Accounts*, p. 29

9 Dolby, p. 264. A good number of other witnesses at Hunt's trial said much the same thing: Ibid., pp. 198, 208, 213, 218, 222, 257, etc.

10 Redford vs. Birley, p. 466

11 HO 40/16 f. 305

12 Bruton, *The Story of Peterloo*, p. 32. Also see above, note 2.

13 Redford vs. Birley, p. 465

14 Dolby, p. 222; and see Taylor, p. 181

15 Taylor, pp. 167–8; and see Dolby, Preface p. vii. Merchant's agent Robert Britton claimed he saw people emptying their pockets of 'stones a pound and a half or two pounds of weight' as they fled, and asserted that after the dispersal he collected thirty or forty 'very large stones as thick as his wrist' and placed them in Buxton's house. (HO 40/16 f.305) Dubious details elsewhere in Britton's statement, however – such as the Yeomanry being assaulted by dense volleys of stones as they made their way to the hustings – make one doubt the complete veracity of his evidence, given to James Norris the following June.

16 Quoted in Lawson 1989, p. 42

17 The closest we get to this detail is the observation by Francis Philips, in which he names four Special Constables who were 'forced to the ground by the Cavalry'. (Philips, p. 37) And another policeman, Samuel John Smith, was to recall: 'I was obliged to use great care, in order to keep my legs'. (Redford vs. Birley, p. 509) The report in the right-wing *Wheeler's Manchester Chronicle* the following Saturday mentions Major-General Clay, John Moore, 'Mr. Charles Rider of Collyhurst, Mr. Thos Sharp, &c. &c. &c., were all forced to the ground by the Cavalry'. There is still no mention of about 100 policemen being on the ground. Also, under cross-examination at the John Lees inquest Mutrie retracted his assertion that the people were armed. (Dowling, p. 440)

18 Reverend Stanley; Bruton, *Three Accounts*, pp. 15–16; Bruton, *The Story of Peterloo*, p. 28; *Liverpool Mercury*, 20 August 1819

19 *Manchester Region History Review* Vol. 3 1989, 'The Casualties of Peterloo', p. 45

20 Bush, *Casualties*, p. 31

21 Bruton, *The Story of Peterloo*, p. 32. Bruton quotes from Birley's speech at the King's birthday celebrations in Manchester on 24 April 1820. The *Manchester Mercury* of 2 May 1820 quotes Birley's claim that '*only one person*, hurt on the 16th August, died of a sabre wound'. And the report in *Wheeler's Manchester Chronicle* of 21 August 1819, amidst several paragraphs praising the Yeomanry for their 'forbearance' and 'humanity', stated that 'no death has been occasioned by any sabre wound'.

22 *The Times*, 23 August 1819. A widely reported detail reflects the vindictive ferocity of the attack: as the Yeomanry hacked and slashed, each blow was accompanied by a curse – 'the most horrible and disgusting imprecations, every blow being attended by an oath!' See also Dowling, pp. 57, 70, 72, 76.   Among the infuriated shouts from the Yeomanry as they set about their business was: 'Damn your bloody eyes, I'll break your back!', and 'I'll let you know I am a soldier, today!' (Nathan Broadhurst's testimony, Dowling, p. 179) 'Damn your soul, what do you want here?' (William Norris Buckley's testimony, Dowling, p. 95)

23 *The Times*, 23 August 1819. This attack was later denied by Yeoman Samuel Street (TS 11/1056)

24 *Liverpool Mercury*, 20 August 1819. From other reports of the same incident, the woman appears to be Mary Fildes

25 Dowling, p. 46

26 George Swift in his letter to his brother corroborates this:'The inside of this circle [of men] we had filled with women from the Union Schools.' (Swift, p. 14)

27 See below, the inquest on Martha Partington; and Bush,'The Women at Peterloo', pp. 219–20

28 *Manchester Observer*, 22 January 1820;The *Northern Star*, 15 March 1845; *Henry Hunt's Addresses to Radical Reformers* No. 12, p. 87; Bush, *Casualties*, p. 90; for specific details of the women killed or badly injured, see Bush,'The Women at Peterloo', pp. 226–30

29 Lt Jolliffe; Bruton, *Three Accounts*, p. 52

30 Dolby, p. 103; Magistrates' narrative (JRL English MSS 1197 (67))

31 Bamford, *Passages*,Vol. 2, p. 156.

32 Francis Philips: Philips, p. 24; Lt-Col L'Estrange: Redford vs. Birley, p. 470; John Benjamin Smith: Bruton, *Three Accounts*, p. 68; Reverend Stanley: Bruton, *Three Accounts*, p. 17

33 Bamford, *Passages*,Vol. 2, p. 156; also see Reverend Stanley; Bruton, *Three Accounts*, p. 15.The cries of 'Have mercy!','Murder!' and 'Save us!' from the people were recalled by witnesses at the John Lees inquest. (Dowling, pp. 75, 90). Prentice added the detail: '…the yeomanry…some with pale faces and firmly-closed eyes, striking with their sabres as if they were insane'. (Prentice, p. 161)

34 Bush, *Casualties*, p. 3 gives well over 250 injured by sabre cut – i.e., with the blade, and not with the flat of the sword.

35 Magistrates' narrative (JRL English MSS 1197 (67)); Reverend Stanley; Bruton, *Three Accounts*, pp. 19–20:'a quarter of an hour at most'.

36 Dowling, pp. 40, 46 and 180;Taylor, p. 121

37 MCC, p. 25

38 Redford vs. Birley, pp. 73–4. Mary Dowlan was a former worker at Birley's factory, and she recognised the trumpeter Meagher by sight.

39 Riding, p. 17

40 Bamford, *Passages*,Vol. 2, pp. 167–8.The woman whom Jemima assumed was dead was possibly the unconscious Ellen Brindle who was carried into the Windmill Street house; see above,'On the Roads to Manchester', note 29.

41 Witnessed by John Hobson, Red-Bir, p. 20

4: Gauntlet

1 Bamford, *Passages*,Vol.2, p. 158

2 Ibid., p. 160

3 Redford vs. Birley, pp. 60, 67

4 Dowling, p. 95

5 JRL English MSS 1197 (172)

6 HO 40/16 f. 295 – Edward Owen

7 Dowling, pp. 109–16.The Mount Street barrier – the 'strong bar-gate' – was 'forced down by the pressure of the crowd escaping' (ibid., note to frontispiece map).

8 Philips, pp. 35–6

9 Lt Jolliffe; Bruton, *Three Accounts*, p. 54

10 Dowling, p. 176;Wroe, p. 168

11 Bush, *Casualties*, p. 53. Jolliffe was of the opinion that 'nine out of ten of the sabre-wounds were caused by the Hussars', and that 'The Hussars on the left pursued down the various streets which led from the place; those on the right met with something more of resistance'. (Lt. Jolliffe; Bruton, *Three Accounts*, p. 53)

12 Dowling, p. 173

13 Philips, p. 36.

14 Wroe, p. 140; Railton (JRL English MSS 1197 (100))

15 Redford vs. Birley, pp. 516, 524.

16 Brockbank, p. 26; also see Dowling, p.97

17 *The Examiner*, 12 September 1819, Issue 611; Fairburn, p. 13(n)

18 Wroe, p. 151

19 Redford vs. Birley, p. 39

20 Wroe, p. 178

21 Ibid.

22 Dowling, p. 57. It was John Lees, a Waterloo veteran, who told a friend that he felt more in danger at Peterloo, since 'at Waterloo it was man to man, but at Manchester it was downright murder'. (Dowling, p. 74)

23 Dowling, pp. 71, 78, 511

24 Redford vs. Birley, p. 41

25 MCC, pp. 24, 33, 42

26 Ibid., pp. 24, 38, 50; and see below, note on 'Eliza Grant'/Elizabeth Gaunt

27 MCC, p. 34; Bush, *Casualties*, pp. 45, 92; see above: Introduction, n. 5

28 MCC, pp. 45, 52. The MCC report gives the following information: 'Eleven non-demonstrators were also injured, including eight constables (one killed), a newspaper reporter and Captain Birley's coachman. Five of these non-demonstrators received sabre wounds and others were trampled. Injuries to soldiers were not listed, but were reported as sixty-seven men struck by stones and sticks, with twenty horses injured.' (MCC, p. 17) For a full list of injuries to horses and soldiers, see JRL English MSS 1197 (25/26).

29 Red-Bir, p. 16

30 MCC, pp. 20, 29, 34, 51

31 Red-Bir, pp. 11, 36

32 Wroe, p. 85

33 Dowling, p. 183. It is noteworthy that in the professional cavalry the trumpeter, immediately recognisable in his red uniform and on his grey horse, was deemed a non-combatant

34 Ibid., pp. 95, 97

35 MCC, p. 35, Dowling, p. 177

36 HO 40/16 f.313

37 Wroe, p. 85; JRL English MSS 1197 (58)

38 Dowling, pp. 184–5; JRL English MSS 1197 (45)

39 Red-Bir, p. 36

40 Bush, *Casualties*, p. 47; MCC, pp. 35, 39, 42, 52, 57; Bush, 'Women at Peterloo', p. 231

41 Wroe, p. 210; *Wheeler's Manchester Chronicle* 21 August 1819 (which asserts 'killed... by pressure of the mob'); MCC, pp. 24, 50. One of the contributory factors which

forced a number of people into cellars as the crowds fled was the narrowness of the pavements on most of the Manchester streets at the time: 18 inches (45 cm) according to Bruton. (*The Story of Peterloo*, p. 23)

42 Wroe, p. 29

43 Dowling, p. 186

44 Wroe, p. 133. According to one depiction of Peterloo (see p .116) the Yeomanry were carrying rifles. However, this detail has no corroboration in any visual or written material, so would appear to be a confusion with the hussars and their carbines.

45 *Wheeler's Manchester Chronicle* 21 August 1819

46 L'Estrange's letter to Sir John Byng, 16 August 1819; Taylor, p. 63

47 Taylor, p. 59(n)

48 Reverend Stanley; Bruton, *Three Accounts*, p. 19; Robert Keymer, Red-Bir, p. 36; William Carroll, Redford vs. Birley, p. 525; Robert Hughes, Redford vs. Birley, p. 457; Dowling, p. 315. To add to the confusion, carrier John Thompson, in the yard of the Quakers' Meeting House during the early stages of the dispersal, 'heard a report which he thought louder than a pistol, he could not see the direction…he heard a female twice call out that one of the Cavalry had shot another. Deponent looked away and saw one of the Manchester Yeomanry lying upon his face'. (HO 40/16 f.289)

49 Dowling, pp. 526, 529

50 Bruton, *The Story of Peterloo*, pp. 31–2

51 Reverend Stanley; Bruton, *Three Accounts*, p. 20; John Benjamin Smith, *Three Accounts*, pp. 68–9. Smith saw Hunt roughly handled by the Constables: 'When [the prisoners] reached the Magistrates' house [Hunt] was surrounded by constables, some pulling him by the collar, others by the coat'. (Ibid., p. 69)

52 Wroe, pp. 98–9

53 Address to Radical Reformers No. 12; Hunt also mentioned in a letter written in the New Bailey prison on 26 August: 'I was wounded in my head by a sabre, & suffered from bruises on my head by Constables' staves, as well as from a blow I received from the *Gallant* half pay officer [i.e., General Clay, on the steps of the house].' (JRL English MSS 1197 (36)) Also see Appendix 5

54 Swift, p. 18

55 JRL English MSS 1197 (34, 36). Hunt was escorted to the New Bailey by Lt-Col L'Estrange and a detachment of the 15th Hussars. 'The staffs of two of Hunt's banners were carried in mock procession before him.' (*Times* 19 August 1819)

56 *Oldham Chronicle*, 20 February 1885

57 Wroe, p. 185

58 Reverend Stanley; Bruton, *Three Accounts*, p. 20

59 JRL English MSS 1197 (36)

60 Bruton, *The Story of Peterloo*, p. 31

61 MCC, p. 35

62 This was the badly injured Elizabeth Gaunt, who was possibly mistaken for fugitive Mary Fildes. Elizabeth, 'severely beaten on the head and back by constables' (MCC, p. 36) had been placed in Hunt's carriage 'for safety' in all the confusion. Hunt would maintain that she was pregnant. (Wroe, pp. 41–2, 99; Fairburn, p. 36)

63 *Liverpool Mercury*, 20 August 1819; see Appendix 8 for the full list given by *Wheeler's Manchester Chronicle*

64 Bamford, *Passages*, Vol.2, pp. 156–7. The detail of unmoving piles of bodies – a number of whom were presumably dead – appears to be corroborated by the report in *Wheeler's*: '…in many places they lay in masses, piled body upon body'. (21 August 1819) However, given the number of known fatalities, this detail would appear to be an exaggeration.

65 Lt Jolliffe; Bruton, *Three Accounts*, p. 55

66 Reverend Stanley; Bruton, *Three Accounts*, p. 19

67 Barrett, Greater Manchester Archives, quoted in *Return to Peterloo*, p. 136

68 Taylor, p. 176

69 Bamford, *Passages*, Vol.2, p. 158

70 Ibid., p. 169

71 Dowling, pp. 76, 79, 172, 179–80, 471, 541

72 Bamford, *Passages*, Vol. 2, p. 159

73 Prentice, p. 160

74 *Oldham Express*, 15 February 1883

75 JRL English MSS 1197 (100)

76 *Oldham Chronicle*, 'A Night with Peterloo Veterans', 29 November 1884

77 *Wheeler's Manchester Chronicle*, 21 August 1819

78 Dolby, pp. 238, 257

5: Nightfall

1 Campbell, p. 16

2 Ibid., pp. 16–17. It was possibly this mail coach which bore the accounts of Peterloo written by Prentice and John Edward Taylor to London.

3 Lt Jolliffe; Bruton, *Three Accounts*, pp. 56–7; John Moore: 'On my arrival, I found a very large body of men standing in front of the new cross with a great quantity of paving stones standing before them…the constables and soldiers had been so pelted with stones, that they had determined to separate the solid mass of people…and were then engaged in clearing the streets.' (HO 42/199 f. 41)

4 MCC, pp. 24, 37, 42

5 *Wheeler's Manchester Chronicle* 21 August 1819

6 Wroe, p. 27. For an indicator of the indiscriminate nature of that night's suppression and arrests, see Ann Scott's deposition (Appendix 13).

7 Quoted in Lawson 1989, p. 42. According to the *Manchester Star* of 18 August: 'A deathlike stillness pervades the town'

8 TS 11/1056. Some transcripts give 'amused' instead of 'assured' – the word is unclear in the surviving (copied) manuscript. The letter was timed 'Monday 4 o'clock'.

9 Handbill, Innes (Printers); (Working Class Movement Library, Salford)

10 *Manchester Observer* 28 August 1819

11 Letter from Home Office to magistrate James Norris, 25 August 1819

Part Three: AFTERMATH

1: War of Words and Silence

1 Bamford, *Passages*, Vol. 2, p. 80

2 Jones, pp. 61–2; also see Appendix 13

3 Fairburn, p. 28; Dolby, p. 167. The *Leeds Mercury* of 21 August reported that initially Hunt was refused even a drink of water by the constable on duty, until a magistrate intervened and allowed him one.

4 JRL English MSS 1197 (34, 36)

5 Bamford, *Passages*, Vol.2, p. 83

6 *Sherwin's Weekly Political Register*, 18 August 1819

7 Wroe, pp. 27–8

8 *Oldham Express*, 15 February 1883. Perhaps adding to the sense of alarm, the frequent mention of 'long pikes' may have rekindled the memory of Cromwell's foot soldiers in his New Model Army, whose victory in the Civil War had paved the way to social upheaval and a regicide a century and a half before.

9 *The Times* 20 August 1819

10 Prentice, p. 169

11 Taylor, p. 189(n)

12 *Wheeler's Manchester Chronicle*, 21 August 1819

13 Bamford, *Passages*, Vol. 2, p. 160

14 *Wheeler's Manchester Chronicle*, 21 August 1819

15 Taylor, p. 185

16 *Wheeler's Manchester Chronicle*, 21 August 1819; *Aston's Exchange Herald* of 24 August gave the same impression of tranquillity in the Manchester streets. Both newspapers were emphatically right-wing

17 *Wheeler's Manchester Chronicle*, 21 August 1819

18 *Manchester Mercury*, 24 August 1819

19 *Wheeler's Manchester Chronicle*, 21 August, 18 September 1819; Taylor, pp. 79–80

20 Taylor, pp. 90–91; letters from W. Rae and John Dunlop to Sidmouth 14–15 September 1819

21 Navickas pp. 88–9; *Manchester Observer*, 9 October 1819

22 www.british-history.ac.uk; Byng wrote to Sidmouth on 18 November, adding to the list of venues of recent reformers' meetings: Carlisle, Barnsley, Newcastle-under-Lyme, Nottingham, Blackburn, and Coventry. (Taylor, p. 134) He could have added the 11 October political rally on the open ground by the Commercial Inn, Bolton, and the ones in Sheffield (25 October) and Hull (27 October). All of these assemblies were conducted peaceably enough.

23 www.magdalengreen.blogspot.co.uk

24 HO 42/199 ff.305-9

25 *Manchester Observer*, 20 November 1819; Taylor, pp. 131–3

26 *Manchester Observer*, 13 November 1819

27 Ibid.,

28 Wroe, p. 47

29 *The Times*, 24 August 1819; Redford vs. Birley, pp. 306–8

30 Taylor, p. 77; letter from Chief Constables Moore and Andrew to Lord Sidmouth, 16 September 1819

31 HO 42/198 f.679. James Whittaker in Blackley asserted that he was told by certain of the returning crowd: 'We shall come back again and give you some *cold steel*. We will not come naked as we have done this time, we shall come armed, we have plenty of arms at home and we will fetch them'. This spoken threat adds to the evidence that the crowd at Peterloo was unarmed. (HO 42/198 f.680)

32 *The Republican*, 27 August 1819

33 Bamford, *Passages*, Vol. 2, p. 163

34 Ibid., pp. 164–5

35 Taylor, pp. 125, 129. Even an offered reward of £500 for evidence leading to the arrest of the alleged perpetrators of the attempted assassination of Nadin bore no fruit. The broadsheet advertising this mentioned two assailants, one 'about 5 feet 2 or 3 inches high, pale complexion, long visage, in-mouthed, and his nose and chin rather long'. The other was observed to have been 'about five feet nine inches high, slenderly formed, and his clothes were all of a dark cast'. (Manchester Central Library Archives+)

36 John Benjamin Smith; Bruton, *Three Accounts*, p. 70

37 Prentice, pp. 163–6; see Appendix 7

38 Aldred, pp. 77–8

39 Fairburn, pp. 24–5

40 Bamford, *Passages*, Vol. 2, pp. 170–2

41 Wroe, p. 4; MCC, p. 40. Healey, although escaping arrest at Peterloo, had been apprehended at his home in Saddleworth the following Saturday. (*The Times* 26 August 1819)

42 Wroe, pp. 35–6. At Hunt's trial the following year many of these questions, or ones similar, put by Hunt to Cowper were allowed by Justice Bayley.

43 Ibid., pp. 30–31

44 Ibid., p. 44

45 Ibid., p. 41

46 Ibid., p. 30

47 Ibid., pp. 71–3. Bamford received a popular accolade similar to that of Hunt when returning home from Lancaster on bail. Waving a cap of liberty, he was carried through Blackley on the shoulders of cheering supporters. (Seen by James Whittaker outside the White Lion pub – HO 42/198 f.681)

48 *The Times*, 10 September 1819

49 Belchem, p. 115

2: Inquests

1 *Manchester Observer*, 9, 23 October 1819; *Wheeler's Manchester Chronicle* 13 November 1819

2 HO 40/16 f.309

3 *Wheeler's Manchester Chronicle*, 18 September 1819

4 JRL English MSS 1197 (82); MCC, p. 52. See above for the inquests on Martha Partington and the infant William Fildes.

5 JRL English MSS 1197 (75)

6 Ibid.

7 Dowling, pp. 12, 27, 29–30, 42, 44–5, 76, 261

8 Ibid., pp. 99–100, 548

9 Ibid., p. 537

10 Ibid., p. 183; Alice's surname is given as Kenyon in *The Times* of 3 September 1819

11 Dowling, p. 147

12 Ibid., p. 540

13 Ibid., p. 187

14 Dowling, p. 177

15 Wroe, pp. 188–9

16 *Manchester Observer*, 8 January 1820; Fairburn, p. 48

17 Wroe, p. 177

18 MCC, pp. 24, 25, 41, 45, 55, 58; Prentice, p. 167. According to Prentice, Thomas Blinstone was more upset about his broken spectacles!

19 Author's interview with Mary Ward's descendant Debbie Rose, 14 August 2016. Although the building now housing the Sir Ralph Abercromby pub on Bootle Street existed in 1819, there is no record of it being a pub at the time. The stories of the wounded being tended in this building are unsubstantiated.

3: For King and Constitution

1 *Manchester Observer*, 13 November 1819

2 Belchem, p. 113(n)

3 *Wheeler's Manchester Chronicle*, 6 May 1820

4 Dolby, p. 288; closing remarks of James Scarlett, for the prosecution. The judge, however, gave an opposing view in his summing-up (pp. 296–7)

5 JRL English MSS 1197 (88). The Seizure of Arms and Seditious Meetings Acts were repealed in the near future: the former after two years, the latter after four. The longest lasting was the Training Prevention or Unlawful Drilling Act, which survived in various forms until 2008.

6 Dolby, Preface, p.(i)

7 Ibid., p. 154

8 HO 40/11 f.173

9 Bamford, *Passages*, Vol. 2, pp. 221–2

10 Dolby, Preface

11 Ibid., pp. 5, 153

12 Bamford, *Passages*, Vol.2, p. 252; Dolby, p. 145

13 Dolby, pp. 76, 171

14 Ibid., pp. 67, 301, 304

15 Ibid., pp. 100–111

16 Ibid., pp. 118, 144, 268, 280

17 Ibid., pp. 294, 303

18 Ibid., p. 282

19 Ibid., p. 308

20 Bamford, *Passages*, Vol. 2, p. 251

21 Prentice, p. 196; www.pixnet.co.uk

22 Dolby, p. 309

23 MCC, p. 7. Quite separate from these contributions were the subscriptions levied for the relief of the Special Constables injured in the fray: see Appendix 10.

24 Thompson, *Making*, p. 761

25 *Manchester Mercury*, 2 May 1820

26 *Manchester Observer*, 19 August 1820

27 *Manchester Mercury*, 22 August 1820

28 Redford vs. Birley, p. 1

29 Ibid., p. 418

30 Ibid., pp. 489, 491

31 Ibid., pp. 495, 501

4: A Gallery of Pictures

1 *Manchester Observer*, 28 August 1819. Those commentators who have found it absurd to compare the killing of a handful of civilians to a major battle in which 50,000 lost their life are missing the point. 'Peter-Loo' was originally coined as an ironic indicator, decrying the excessive and lethal deployment of force better suited to a battlefield than to the dispersal of a peaceful rally which included women and children.

2 *Manchester Observer*, 21 August 1819

3 *8 Days' Diary of a Member of the Yeomanry Cavalry*, p. 3

4 'A Slap at Slop', p. 1 (British Library). For an in-depth appraisal of Hone's contributions to the radical cause, the reader is referred to 'William Hone and Peterloo' by John Gardner in *Return to Peterloo* pp. 79–92, and Ben Wilson's *The Laughter of Triumph*, esp. pp. 285–29: see bibliography.

5 *The Observer*, 11 November 1822; Belchem, p. 162

6 *Manchester Comet*, 30 October 1822. For an example of right-wing satirical exaggeration that lurches into sick and insensitive attempts at humour, see the London *Morning Post* of 9 November 1819. (Quoted in Hobson, p. 117) Almost as gross was George Buxton's *The Political Quixote of Don Blackibo Dwarfino and his Squire Seditiono*. (See Hobson, p. 119)

7 Manchester Archives and Local Studies, Broadsides Collection, GB 127; and see above, Part One, Ch. 5

8 *Aston's Exchange Herald*, 17 September 1822; extract from 'A Metrical History of Manchester'

9 This second image has been determined as 'probably by Cruikshank'. (Donald, p. 25) This is either George Cruikshank or his brother Isaac Robert.

10 See Part Two, Ch. 4 above, and Wroe, p. 178

11 The best-preserved example is held at the Platt Hall Gallery of Costume, view by appointment. The 50cm x 60cm artefact was possibly a headscarf, and not a handkerchief. (Leach, p. 186)

12 At the time there were precise conventions governing men's wearing of hats outdoors. For a man to be seen outdoors without a hat was considered a serious breach of propriety: see Carlile's involved efforts to replace his. There were a few exceptions, such as an orator when speaking, which explains why Hunt is carrying his white top hat in most of the visual representations of Peterloo.

13 Donald, p. 21. The Whaite drawing cost a relatively expensive 3s 6d (17½p). There is a copy in the Manchester City Art Gallery.

14 Ibid., p. 27

15 Donald's opinion is that the artist is 'probably Cruikshank'. (Donald, p. 24) The original is in the Manchester City Art Gallery.

16 'The Masque of Anarchy', stanzas XXXVIII, XCI

17 Ibid., stanzas LXXIX, LXXXIV, LXXXV

18 Ibid., stanza LV

19 Ibid., stanza VI

20 *Black Dwarf*, 22 September 1819; quoted in *Return to Peterloo*, pp. 174–5

21 'Don Juan Canto the Third', stanza LXVII

22 Poem by Allen Davenport, *The Theological and Political Comet* 6 November 1819

23 *Manchester Observer*, 26 February 1820. The deleted names are obviously Meagher and Hay. Bamford toned down the poem considerably for the later (1846) version. Future Prime Minister George Canning was President of the Board of Trade and a supporter of the Magistrates' actions at Peterloo; Lord Castlereagh – also an object of Shelley's censure in 'The Masque of Anarchy' – was Leader of the House of Commons and proposer of the Six Acts. Hay was also the recipient, post-Peterloo, of a number of disparaging and threatening letters, some of them anonymous. (Raines, pp. 300–10; Marlow, pp. 169–170) Chetham's Library has a large collection of correspondence with Hay, including the unflattering communications, which Hay meticulously preserved

24 See *Return to Peterloo*, pp. 183–94 for the full text of the Dickens narrative

25 Emmeline Pankhurst's grandfather had been one of the demonstrators at Peterloo

5: Reflections

1 Dr Cooke Taylor, *Life and Times of Sir Robert Peel*, quoted in Prentice, p. 154

2 Taylor, p. 169

3 Prentice, p. 158

4 *Manchester Observer*, 28 August 1819

5 Ibid.; Chetham's Library pamphlets 4.C.26 (3). The *Observer* published a retraction of the story the following week, albeit in somewhat opaque prose.

6 Sheffield Archives; WWM/F52/50

7 Chetham's Library pamphlets 4.C.6.26 (3)

8 Taylor, p. 180

9 See John Railton's letter (JRL English MSS 1197 (100): '…there was coming down Cooper Street, and closely upon us, a body of infantry from the King Street barracks, but their approach was so quiet that we were not sooner aware of them. We followed them to the corner of Dickinson Street, where they took post round the corner and formed there, but they were not seen by the orators, and their business was proceeding very quietly.' Bruton defines the deployment of these troops as waiting 'in ambush'. (*The Story of Peterloo*, p. 19)

10 This list is based on the one compiled by Brian S. Foster – see bibliography – and the Petition to Parliament of November 1819 (Salford Local History Archives)

11 Walmsley, *Case Reopened*, p. 233

12 Challinor, p. 35

13 Handbill 21 March 1831; *Bolton Chronicle*, 26 March 1831

14 Thompson on Peterloo', p. 75; *Manchester Times*, 24 December 1831

15 *Manchester Mercury*, 13 June 1820

16 *Bolton Free Press*, 2 July 1836

17 www.rochdaleparishchurches.org.uk; Wilson, *Vicars*, p.60: 'He took little interest in parish work'. Also Raines, p. 329: 'the long absenteeism of Dr. Hay…had well-nigh crushed out the religious life of the church in the parish'.

18 Axon, p. 161; Prentice, *Manchester Times*, 10 July 1830. The Birley family had set up a factory on Cambridge Street in 1828, in association with Charles Macintosh, for the manufacture of waterproof material. Nearly a century later, in 1925, the enterprise was taken over by Dunlop's. (France and Woodall, p. 187)

19 Albrecht, pp. 197–8. Hugh Hornby Birley died in 1845, and with an oblique reference to the past, was buried in the crypt of St Peter's Church.

20 www.manchesterorange.co.uk; the quotation is from the engraving on one of the gold cups.

21 Belchem, pp. 168–171

22 *Manchester Times*, 1 September 1832. The Act banning large gatherings and martial music had been repealed eight years before.

23 *Manchester Guardian*, 26 March 1842

24 Ibid. 3 October 1888

25 Pimlott, pp. 46–7, 54–5

26 www.pixnet.co.uk/Oldham Historical Research Group/Jeremy Sutcliffe

27 *Cobbett's Weekly Political Register*, 29 December 1819

28 www.archiver.rootsweb.ancestry.com/FILDES

29 Gibbins, p. 377, n.1, quoted in Terry Wyke's essay 'Remembering the Manchester Massacre', *Return to Peterloo*, p. 118; Read, Preface, p. (vii). Many commentators have chosen to distance themselves from the word by packaging it in inverted commas. Typical was L. S. Wood, writing in 1927 in the quixotically titled *The Romance of the Cotton Industry in England*: '… an event that was not a 'massacre' as it has been called (at the most eleven persons, some of them special constables, were killed or died afterwards of injuries).' The accuracy of Wood's narrative is then further compromised by his conclusion: 'The riot had the unfortunate effect of checkmating the efforts…of the master manufacturers…to secure a minimum

wage.' (Wood, pp. 154–5) Walmsley made his position on the matter abundantly clear with a section heading – a handwritten addition to the typed manuscript – 'THE MASSACRE THAT WASN'T!' in his monograph 'The Peterloo Reopener and his Critics' (p. 45).

30 See Thompson, *Makings*, p. 752 ('It really was a massacre'), and Poole, 'By the Law or the Sword', p. 263 ('…it was not a battle but a massacre – limited and inefficient by historical standards perhaps, but most decidedly a massacre in spirit.') Also consider the fact that over the past forty years or so mass killings of fewer than twenty people have frequently been termed 'massacres' in the media and subsequent literature.

The cynics might claim that the headline use of the word sells newspapers, and since Peterloo, Manchester itself has experienced numerically more devastating carnage in both war and peace; but despite the persuasive, albeit sometimes convoluted, arguments of Walmsley and others, one has to conclude that, certainly employing as a descriptive yardstick the modern usage of the word, calling Peterloo a massacre is no misnomer.

Epilogue

1 *Manchester Evening News*, 7 September 1972

2 A more fundamental parallel with Orgreave has been proposed: 'The sight of blundering, overbearing, unreasoning authority reacting with violence to peaceful demonstrators would recur…at the battle of Orgreave during the miners' strike in 1984.' (Stephen Bates, *Guardian* 4 January 2018)

Appendices

1 JRL English MSS 1197 (9)

2 Wroe, p. 21

3 Durham County Advertiser 18 December 1819

4 HO 42/192 f.206-7. H. Allen is Haigh Allen, a Huddersfield magistrate acting as liaison between the North and Lord Sidmouth. The missive was delivered by a London coachmaster to the Home Office at 7.30 p.m. the following day.

5 Hunt, *Memoirs*, Vol. 3, pp. 502–3

6 *Manchester Observer*, 27 May 1820

7 HO 42/192 f.174

8 *Manchester Observer* 28 August 1819. There was another reason for the government's support of the magistrates: censure would have risked their resignation and the loss of services which they had so far provided free of charge.

9 *Wheeler's Manchester Chronicle*, 21 August 1819. Arthur O'Neil later died from his injuries, and Elizabeth Gaunt was imprisoned for twelve days despite her serious physical condition. She was discharged on the 27 August. 'Robt. Wild' is Robert Wylde, who appeared with Hunt, Bamford, etc., in the dock at York. John Tyas, reporter for *The Times*, although arrested is not mentioned.

10 *Manchester Observer*, 28 August 1819
11 Chetham's Library Archives
12 HO 42/198 f.671
13 Dolby, pp. 131–2
14 *Manchester Chronicle*, 16 October 1819
15 ©Harvey Kershaw/Oldham Tinkers. Used by permission.
16 Peterloo Memorial Campaign August 2017

Bilbliography and Sources

Several of the earlier sources are available online. If the reader wishes to consult them, before investing time and money, it may be worthwhile conducting a web search.

Adkins, Roy and Lesley, *Eavesdropping on Jane Austen's England* (Abacus 2013)

Aldred, Guy A., *Richard Carlile, Agitator: His Life and Times* (Pioneer Press 1923)

Arnold, Malcolm, *Peterloo: Overture for Orchestra – Opus 97* (Faber Music Ltd. 1979)

Axon, William E.A., *Annals of Manchester* (J. Heywood, Deansgate and Ridgefield 1886)

Ball, Dennis, *The Story of Failsworth* (Oldham Cultural and Information Services 1973)

Bamford, Samuel, *Early Days* (London 1893)

Bamford, Samuel, *Homely Rhymes and Poems* (London and Manchester 1864)

Bamford, Samuel, *Passages in the Life of a Radical* (2 vols) (London 1893/Frank Cass 1967)

Bancks's Manchester and Salford Directory 1800 (Neil Richardson 1997)

Banks, Mrs G.L., *The Manchester Man* (Abel Heywood 1874/Northen Grove 2012)

Bantock, Granville (ed.), *One Hundred Songs of England* (Oliver Ditson, New York 1914)

Bastow, Don, *A Bastow Family by Way of Peterloo* (Westmorland Books 1992)

Bateson, Hartley, *A History of Oldham* (pp. 99–103) (Evans and Langley Associates 1974)

Bee, Malcolm, *Industrial Revolution and Social Reform in the Manchester Region* (Neil Richardson 1997)

Belchem, John, *'Orator Hunt': Henry Hunt and English Working Class Radicalism* (Clarendon Press 1985, Breviary Stuff Publications 2012)

Bradshaw, L.D. (ed.), *Visitors to Manchester: A Selection of British and Foreign Visitors' Descriptions of Manchester from c1538 to 1865* (Neil Richardson 1987)

Brierley, Benjamin, *Home Memories: The Autobiography of a Handloom Weaver* (Manchester 1886)

Briggs, Asa (ed.), *Chartist Studies* (Macmillan 1959)

Brimelow, W., *Political and Parliamentary History of Bolton* (Bolton 1882)

Brockbank, William, *The Early History of Manchester Preparative Meeting of Friends* (Handwritten manuscript 1856 – Society of Friends, Mount Street, Manchester)

Brooks, Ann, and Haworth, Bryan, *Boomtown in Manchester 1800–1850: The Portico Connection* (The Portico Library Manchester 1993)

Bruton, F.A., *The Story of Peterloo* (Manchester Univ. Press 1919)

Bruton, F.A., *Three Accounts of Peterloo by Eyewitnesses* (Manchester Univ. Press 1921)

Bulkeley, E.W., *A Quarterly Journal of Matters Past and Present Connected with the County Palatine of Chester* (London 1888)

Bush, Michael, *The Casualties of Peterloo* (Carnegie 2005)

Butterworth, Edwin, *Historical Sketches of Oldham* (pp. 167–74) (Oldham 1856; reprinted E.J. Morten 1981)

Campbell, Theophila Carlile, *The Battle of the Press* (pp. 21–6: Chapter III 'The Manchester Massacre') (London 1899)

Cannadine, David, *Victorious Century: The United Kingdom, 1800–1906* (pp. 130–2, 136–8) (Allen Lane 2017)

Challinor, Raymond, *The Lancashire and Cheshire Miners* (pp. 35–6) (Frank Graham 1972)

Cole, John, *Conflict and Cooperation: Rochdale and the Pioneering Spirit 1790–1844* (George Kelsall Littleborough 1994)

Cotton, N., *Popular Movements in Ashton-under-Lyne and Stalybridge before 1832* (M. Litt. Thesis, Birmingham University 1977)

Crane, David, *Went the Day Well?: Witnessing Waterloo* (William Collins 2015)

Dolby, T., *The Trial of Henry Hunt, Esq.* (London 1820)

Dowling, Joseph Augustus (ed.), *The Whole Proceedings Before the Coroner's Inquest on the Body of John Lees* (William Howe 1820)

Dunning, Robert, *A History of Somerset* (Phillimore 1983)

Engels, Friedrich, *The Condition of the Working Class in England* (Penguin 2009)

Fairburn, John, *Manchester Massacre!! An Authentic Narrative of the Magisterial and Yeomanry Massacre…* (Fairburn, Ludgate Hill 1819)

Farrer, William and Brownhill, J., (eds) *A History of the County of Lancashire* (Constable and Co. 1908)

France, E., and Woodall, T.F., *A New History of Didsbury* (pp. 187–8) (E.J. Morten 1976)

Frow, Ruth and Edmund, *Political Women 1800–1850* (Pluto Press 1989)

Garratt, Morris, *Samuel Bamford: Portrait of a Radical* (George Kelsall 1992)

Giles, Phyllis M., *The Economic and Social Development of Stockport 1815–1836* (Manchester University 1950)

Glen, Robert Allan, *The Working Classes of Stockport during the Industrial Revolution* (University of California 1978)

Goffin, Magdalen (ed.), *The Diaries of Absalom Watkin, a Manchester Man 1787–1861* (pp. 38–43) (Alan Sutton 1993)

Griffin, Emma, *Liberty's Dawn: A People's History of the Industrial Revolution* (Yale University Press 2014)

Harland, John, *Ballads and Songs of Lancashire* (EP Publishing 1976)

Heginbotham, H., *Stockport: Ancient and Modern* (London 1882)

Herbert, Michael, *Up Then, Brave Women: Manchester's Radical Women 1819–1918* (North West Labour History Society 2012)

Herbert, Michael, *The Wearing of the Green: A Political History of the Irish in Manchester* (pp. 29–31) (British Irish in Britain Representation Group 2001)

Herbert, Michael, *Women's Role at Peterloo Revisited* (Text from Anniversary Walk 15 August 2012)

Hewitt, Eric J., *Capital of Discontent: Protest and Crime in Manchester's Industrial Revolution* (The History Press 2014)

Hewitt, Eric J., *A History of Policing in Manchester* (E.J. Morten 1979)

Hobson, James, *Dark Days of Georgian Britain: Rethinking the Regency* (Pen & Sword History 2017)

Hone, William, *The Political House That Jack Built* (London 1819)

Hunt, Henry, *Memoirs* (London 1822)

Hylton, Stuart, *A History of Manchester* (pp. 94–100) (Phillimore 2010)

Ingham, Alfred, *Altrincham and Bowdon* (London/Manchester 1896)

Jones, Steve, *Manchester…The Sinister Side* (pp. 61–7) (Wicked Publications 1997)

Kay, James Phillips, *The Moral and Physical Condition of the Working Classes Employed in the Cotton Manufacture in Manchester* (London 1832)

Kirby, Dean, *Angel Meadow: Victorian Britain's Most Savage Slum* (pp 19–24) (Pen & Sword Books 2016)

Knight, John, *A Correct Report of the Proceedings on the Trial of thirty-eight Men on a Charge of Administering an Unlawful Oath* (England 1812)

Krantz, Mark, *Rise Like Lions: The History and Lessons of the Peterloo Massacre* (Bookmarks Publications 2011)

McKeiver, Philip, *Peterloo Massacre 1819* (Advance Press 2009)

Marlow, Joyce, *The Peterloo Massacre* (Rapp and Whiting 1969)

Marshall, L.S., *Development of Public Opinion in Manchester* (Syracuse University Press 1946)

Navickas, Katrina, *Protest and the Politics of Space and Place 1789–1848* (Manchester University Press 2016)

Peel, Frank, *The Risings of the Luddites* (Heckmondwike Herald 1880/Frank Cass 1968)

Philips, Francis, *An Exposure of the Calumnies Circulated by the Enemies of Social Order and Reiterated by their Abettors against the Magistrates and Yeomanry Cavalry of Manchester and Salford* (London 1819)

Phythian, Graham, *South Manchester Remembered* (The History Press 2012)

Pigot and Dean's Trade and Street Directory of Manchester 1817/1820 (Manchester 1824)

Pimlott, Joe, *The Life and Times of Sam Bamford* (Neil Richardson 1991)

Poole, Robert (ed.), *Return to Peterloo* (Manchester Centre for Regional History 2014)

Potts, Bob, *The Old Pubs of Rochdale Road and Neighbourhood, Manchester* (Neil Richardson 1985)

Prentice, Archibald, *Historical Sketches and Personal Recollections of Manchester* (Gilpin and Parkes 1851/British Library 2011)

Procter, Richard Wright, *Memorials of Manchester Streets* (Thomas Sutcliffe, 1874)

Raines, Revd Canon Francis Robert, *The Vicars of Rochdale* (pp. 284–325, 329) (Chetham Society 1883)

Read, Donald, *Peterloo: The 'Massacre' and its Background* (Manchester University Press 1958)

Redford, Arthur, and Russell, Ina, *The History of Local Government in Manchester* (Longmans, Green & Co., 1939)

Reid, Robert, *The Peterloo Massacre* (Heinemann 1989)

Ridings, Elijah, *The Village Muse* (Macclesfield 1850)

Robertson, William, *History of Rochdale Past and Present* (Schofield and Hoblyn 1876)

Rowbottom, William, (Handloom Weaver, Burnley Lane, Oldham) *Diaries* (*Oldham Standard* 1887–1889)

Shercliff, W.H., *A Short History of Peterloo* (City of Manchester Publicity Office 1969)

Simmons, James R., and Carlisle, Janice (eds) *Factory Lives: Four Nineteenth Century Working-Class Autobiographies* (Ontario 2007)

Slater, Ruth, *Bury Folk at Peterloo* (Bury Local History Society Journals 2005)

Southey, Robert, *Letters from England* (London 1808)

Stevens, T.H.G., *Manchester of Yesterday* (John Sherratt & Son) 1958

Sutton, C.W. (ed.), *Handbook and Guide to Manchester* (Sherratt and Hughes 1907)

Taylor, Jonathan Edward, *Notes and Observations, Critical and Explanatory, on the Papers Relative to the Internal State of the Country* (London 1820) (a reply to Philips – see above)

Thomis, Malcolm I., *The Luddites: Machine-Breaking in Regency England* (David & Charles/Archon Books 1970)

Thomis, Malcolm I. and Grimmett, Jennifer, *Women in Protest 1800–1850* (Croom Helm 1982)

Thompson, E.P., *The Making of the English Working Class* (Victor Gollancz 1963/ Penguin Modern Classics 2013)

Tonge, Thomas, *Reminiscences by his Father-in-Law James Fellows, of Ashton-on-Mersey* (*Manchester Examiner* 1883)

Walmsley, Robert, *Peterloo: The Case Re-opened* (Manchester University Press 1969)

Wheeler, James, *Manchester: Its Political, Social and Commercial History* (London 1836)

Wilson, Ben, *The Laughter of Triumph: William Hone and the Fight for the Free Press* (Faber and Faber Ltd 2005)

Wilson, Revd J.M., *The Vicars of Rochdale, in Connection with the History of their Times* (pp. 59–62) (Rochdale 1905)

Wollstonecraft, Mary, *A Vindication of the Rights of Woman* (Boston 1792)

Wood, L.S., *The Romance of the Cotton Industry in England* (OUP 1927)

Woodward, Llewellyn, *The Age of Reform: England 1815–1870* (OUP 1992)

Wroe, James, *Peterloo Massacre, containing A Faithful Narrative of the Events which preceded, accompanied and followed the fatal Sixteenth of August, 1819, on the area near St. Peter's Church, Manchester* (Manchester Observer 1819 – originally produced as a series of weekly pamphlets)

Documents, Letters and Newspapers

Allen, Haigh, letter to Home Office 16 August 1819 (HO 42/192 ff. 206-7)

Barrett, Joseph, Account of Peterloo (Greater Manchester Archives; reproduced in *Return to Peterloo* pp. 135–7)

Britton, Robert, statement recorded 17 June 1820 (HO 40/16 f. 305)

Burdett, Sir Francis, Address to the Electors of Westminster, 22 August 1819 (Fairburn, pp. 24–5)

Burrington, Revd G., of Chudleigh, Devon, letter to Sidmouth 25 November 1819 (HO 42/199 ff. 305-9)

Cardwell, James, letter to his sister-in-law Eliza (née) Birley, 26 November 1819 (*Transactions of Lancashire and Cheshire Antiquarian Society* 1922–3, pp. 195–6)

Carlile, Richard, A Letter to Lord Sidmouth on the Conduct of the Magisterial and Yeomanry Assassins of Manchester on the 16th August 1819 (*Sherwin's Weekly Political Register*, 21 August 1819)

Chadwick, Thomas, letter to his brother, 17 August 1819 (Touchstones Rochdale)

Factories Inquiry Commission, Manchester 1833

Five Lancashire Magistrates, letter to Lord Sidmouth, 1 July 1819

Fletcher, Col. Ralph, letters to Home Office, 6 April, 22 April 1812

Hansard, 13 February, 5 March 1818, 15 May 1821

Hanson, Colonel Joseph, letter to *Manchester Gazette*, 28 May 1808

Hay, Revd William Robert, letter to Major-General Sir John Byng, 23 January 1819

Hay, Revd William Robert, Report on the Proceedings in Manchester 16 Aug 1819 (written the same evening – see Appendix 5) (HO 42/192 f.174)

Hay, Revd William Robert, letter to Lord Sidmouth, 7 October 1819

Hay, Revd William Robert, comment on indictment of soldiers, 26 October 1819 (JRL MSS 1197 (75))

Home Office to James Norris, 25 August 1819

Hunt, Henry, Address to Radical Reformers No. 12 (1831)

Hunt, Henry, letter to Lord Sidmouth, 17 August 1819 (HO 42/192 f. 390)

Hunt, Henry, letter to Brave Reformers of Lancashire, 10 September 1819 (Wroe, p. 75)

Hunt's letters in John Rylands Library English Manuscripts 1197 (14, 23, 34, 36, 39, 40, 42)

Innes, George (Printer, Manchester): *An Account of the Manchester Meeting, which took place on the 16th of Aug., 1819* (Working Class Museum Library, Salford)

L'Estrange, Col. George, letter to Major-General Sir John Byng, 16 August 1819

Lord Sidmouth, letter to Earl of Derby, 21 August 1819 (see Appendix 6)

Lloyd, John, letter to Henry Hobhouse, 16 February 1819 (Stockport Local heritage Library)

Magistrates' Narrative on Peterloo, sent to Lord Sidmouth 7 October 1819 (JRL English MSS 1197 (67))

Magistrates' Statement (HO 40/15 ff. 284–293)

Manchester and Salford Yeomanry Official Narrative on Peterloo (JRL English MSS 1197 (26))

Manchester Comet: or a Rap at Radicals (1822; Chetham's Library)

Manchester Infirmary Weekly Board minutes, 6 September 1819 (Sheffield Archives WWM/F52/50)

Moore, John and Andrew, Jonathan, letter to Lord Sidmouth 16 September 1819

Mutrie, Robert, letter to Archibald Moore, 9 September 1819

Nadin, Joseph, Last Will and Testament, 4 December 1847, 20 October 1848 (codicil) (Cheshire Archives)

Nadin, Joseph, letters to the Home Office, 11 October 1812, 26 March 1814 (HO 40/2/2, 42/138)

Newy, Mary Anne, statement recorded 23 November 1819 (HO 40/16 f. 313)

Norris, Clayton, Moore, and Green, letters to Lord Sidmouth 18–19 November 1819 (HO 42/199 ff.41-8)

Norris, James, letter to Lord Sidmouth 20 February 1819 (PRO No. 49)

Ogden, Samuel, statement recorded 9 November 1819 (HO 42/198 f. 679)

Owen, Edward, statement recorded 6 November 1819 (HO 40/16 f. 295)

Pearson, Charles, letter to Major Cartwright and S. Brookes, Esq., 5 September, 1819

Petition to Parliament November 1819 (Salford Local History Archives)

Peterloo Relief Fund Account Book (JRL Eng MSS 172)

Police Office handbill 21 July 1819 (JRL Eng MSS 1197 (9))

Pollard, William, statement recorded 2 November 1819 (see Appendix 11) (HO 42/198 f. 671)

Railton, John, letter to his wife (JRL Eng MSS 1197 (100); published in *Manchester Guardian* 18 August 1919)

Report of the Metropolitan and Central Committee Appointed for the Relief of the Manchester Sufferers (London 1820) (Manchester Pamphlets, Central Library Special Collections 942.730731/P.88)

Report on the Proceedings of the Trial Redford v. Birley, Oliver, Withington, and Meagher (Wheeler & Son, London 1822) (635 pp)

Smith, John, letter to Right Hon. Earl of Derby, 18 August, 1819

'Squib', 8 Days' Diary of a Member of the Yeomanry Cavalry, during Permanent
   Duty (Chetham's Library Pamphlets)
Subscriptions for Special Constables (Chetham's Library)
Swift, George, 'The Swift Narrative', August 1819 (Manchester Central Library)
Thompson, John, statement recorded 2 November 1819 (HO 40/16 f. 289)
The Trial, Redford against Birley and Others for an Assault on the Sixteenth of
   August 1819 (Manchester 1822/Cornell Law Collections) (65pp)
Warrant for the arrest of Hunt, Johnson, Knight and Moorhouse, issued at 1–15 p.m.
   16 August 1819 (HO 42/192 f.390)
Whittaker, John, statement recorded 9 November 1819 (HO 42/198 ff. 680-1)
Wright, Charles, statement (TS 11/1056)

A Collection of Four Historic Maps of Manchester 1807–1876 (Mapseeker Archive
   Publishing 2014)
Aston's Exchange Herald, 14 April, 16 June 1812; 17 August, 24 August 1819; 17
   September 1822
Black Dwarf, 30 September 1818; 22 September, 29 September 1819
The Bolton Free Press, 2 July 1836
The British Volunteer, 3 August 1819
Cobbett's Weekly Political Register, 29 December 1819
Cowdroy's Manchester Gazette, 28 May, 4 June 1808; 25 April 1812; 21 August 1819
Durham County Advertiser, 18 December 1819
The Examiner, 12 September 1819
The Guardian (and see *Manchester Guardian*), 18 June 2015, 4 January 2018
Lancaster Gazette, 13 June, 20 June 1812
Leeds Mercury, 13 June 1812, 21 August 1819
Liverpool Mercury, 20 August, 27 August 1819
Manchester City News, 16 August 1919
Manchester Courier, 21 August 1819
Manchester Gazette, 28 May 1808
Manchester Guardian, 26 October, 2 November 1822, 26 March 1842, 3 October
   1888, 18 August 1919
Manchester Mercury, 24 August 1819, 22 August 1820
Manchester Evening News, 7 September 1972, 29 February 1988
Manchester Observer, 7 March, 18 April 1818; 10 July, 17 July, 24 July, 31 July, 14
   August, 21 August, 28 August, 9 October, 23 October 1819; 8 January, 29 January,
   11 March, 19 August 1820
Manchester Star, 18 August 1819
Manchester Times, 14 August 1830, 24 December 1831, March–April 1848
The Morning Chronicle, 21 October 1819
The Morning Post (London), 25 August, 9 November 1819
The Northern Star, 15 March 1845
The Observer, 16 August 1819, 11 November 1822, 27 March 1842

Oldham Chronicle, 29 November 1884, 20 February 1885, 16 April 1960

Oldham Express, 15 February 1883

The Republican, 27 August, 3 September 1819

Sunday Telegraph, 6 March 1988

The Theological and Political Comet 6 November 1819

The Times, 18 August, 23 August, 24 August, 26 August, 3 September 1819

Weekly Dispatch, London 5 September 1819

Wheeler's Manchester Chronicle 28 May 1808; 11 April, 25 April, 13 June, 20 June 1812; 23 January, 30 January, 26 June, 17 July, 21 August, 28 August, 4 September, 18 September, 13 November 1819; 6 May 1820

Articles

Albrecht, J.R.M., 'Major Hugh Hornby Birley' (*Transactions of Lancashire and Cheshire Antiquarian Society* 1922–3 pp. 194–8)

Anonymous, 'Manchester Represented and Misrepresented', (1820), *Political Tracts* (Manchester Central Library Special Collections 942.730731/P.968)

Bates, Stephen, 'The Bloody Clash that Changed Britain' (*Guardian* 4 January 2018)

Bee, Malcolm, and Bee, Walter, 'The Casualties of Peterloo' (*Manchester Region History Review* Vol. 3 1989 pp. 43–50)

Belchem, John, 'Henry Hunt and the Evolution of the Mass Platform' (*English Historical Review* 93 (1978), pp. 739–73)

Bush, M.L., 'Dear Sisters of the Earth: The Public Voice of Manchester Women at the Time of Peterloo' (*North West Labour History Journal* No. 28, 2003, pp. 14–21)

Bush, M.L., 'The Women at Peterloo: The Impact of Female Reform on the Manchester Meeting of 16 August 1819' (*The Journal of the Historical Association* Vol. 89 April 2004 pp. 209–32)

Clayson, Jim, 'The Poetry of Peterloo' (*Manchester Region History Review* Vol. 3 1989 pp. 31–7)

Custer, Paul A., 'Refiguring Jemima: Gender, Work and Politics in Lancashire 1770–1820' (*Past and Present* No. 195 May 2007 pp. 127–58)

Donald, Diana, 'The Power of Print: Graphic Images of Peterloo' (*Manchester Region History Review* Vol. 3 1989 pp. 21–9)

Duffy, Michael, 'Peterloo – Fact or Ballyhoo?' (*Manchester Evening News* 29 February 1988)

Foster, Brian S., 'To What Extent was Peterloo the Outcome of Class Hatred?' (MA thesis, Manchester University 1996)

Glasgow. G.H.H., 'The John Lees Inquest of 1819 and the Peterloo Massacre' (*Transactions of the Historic Society of Lancashire and Cheshire* Vol. 148 (1998) pp. 95–118)

Haines, Ronald, 'Council Meets its Own Peterloo' (*Manchester Evening News* 7 September 1972)

Harvey, Harry, 'Priest had Link with Peterloo' (*Oldham Weekly Chronicle* 16 April 1960)

Herbert, Michael, 'Women's Role at Peterloo Revisited' (Anniversary Walk 15 August 2012)

Kettle, Martin, 'Napoleon's Dream Dies at Waterloo – and so did that of British Democrats' (*The Guardian*, 18 June 2015)

Lawson, Philip, 'Peterloo: A Constable's Eye-View Re-Assessed' (*Manchester Region History Review* Vol. 3 1989 pp. 39–42)

Lawson, Philip, 'Reassessing Peterloo' (*History Today* March 1988 pp. 24–9)

Leach, Helen, 'Protesting Peterloo: the 'Fanciful' and the 'Domestic'' (www.open. conted.ox.ac.uk)

Marlow, Joyce, 'The Day of Peterloo' (*Manchester Region History Review* Vol. 3 1989 pp. 3–7)

Poole, Robert, 'By Law or by the Sword: Peterloo Revisited' (*History* 91, pp. 254–76)

Poole, Robert, 'The March to Peterloo: Politics and Festivity in Late Georgian England' (*Past and Present* No. 192, August 2006)

Porter, Robert, 'Eye-witness letter 'rewrites history' of Peterloo battle' (*Sunday Telegraph*, 6 March 1988)

Thompson, E.P., 'God and King and Law' (*The New Reasoner* Winter 1957/58 No. 3 pp. 69–86)

Thompson, E.P., 'Thompson on Peterloo' (*Manchester Region History Review* Vol. 3 1989 pp. 67–75)

Tomlinson, V.I., 'Postscript to Peterloo' (*Manchester Region History Review* Vol. 3 1989 pp. 51–9)

Walmsley, Robert, 'The Peterloo Reopener and his Critics' (Manchester Central Library 942:733073)

Weeden, Len, 'John Moore (1774–1857) and the Peterloo Massacre' (*Ashton and Sale History Society Newsletter* June 2009, pp. 9–13)

Websites

www.peterloowitness1819.weebly.com

www.nationalarchives.gov.uk

www.peterloomassacre.org

www.british-history.ac/commons

www.historyofparliamentonline.org

www.link4life.org [Search: Peterloo]

www.ludditebicentenary.blogspot.co.uk

www.pixnet.co.uk [Search: Oldham Historical Research Group]

www.ibew.org.uk [Search: Stalybridge Old Band]

www.fulltextarchive.com

www.hansard.millbanksystems.com/commons

www.davidcsutton.com

www.archiver.rootsweb.ancestry.com/FILDES

Index

Page numbers in bold refer to illustrations